The Real McCoy

"Bill" McCoy.

Books by Frederic F. Van de Water

Grey Riders
The Social Ladder (co-author)
Horsemen of the Law
The Eye of Lucifer
The Family Flivvers to Frisco
Elmer 'n Edwina
Hurrying Feet
Still Waters
Alibi
Havoc
The Real McCoy
Plunder
Thunder Shield
Glory-Hunter
Hidden Ways
Death in the Dark
A Home in The Country
Rudyard Kipling's Vermont Feud
We're Still in The Country
Father's Are Funny
The Circling Year
The Reluctant Republic
Members of the Family
Mrs. Applegate's Affair
Fool's Errand
The Sooner to Sleep
Lake Champlain and Lake George
Reluctant Rebel
Catch a Falling Star
In Defense of Worms
Rebel's Progress
The Captain Called It Mutiny
Wings of the Morning
This Day's Madness
Day of Battle
Tempest

FLAT HAMMOCK PRESS

Flat Hammock Press
5 Church Street
Mystic, CT 06355
(860) 572-2722
www.flathammockpress.com

Printed in the United States of America

10 9 8 7 6 5 4 3 2 1

Library of Congress Cataloging-in-Publication Data

Van de Water, Frederic Franklyn, 1890-1968.
The real McCoy / by Frederic F. Van de Water; publisher's afterword.
p. cm.
Originally published: Garden City : Doubleday, Doran & Company, Inc., 1931.
ISBN 0-9718303-2-0
1. McCoy, William, b. 1877. 2. Prohibition—United States. 3. Liquor industry—United States. 4. Smuggling—United States. 5. Searches and seizures—United States. I. Title.
HV5089.V3 2004
364.1'33—dc22
[B]

2003015337

ISBN-10: 0-9718303-2-0
ISBN-13: 978-0-9718303-2-5

The Real McCoy

Frederic F. Van de Water

Publisher's Foreword
by Stephen Jones

Flat Hammock Press
Mystic, Connecticut

William Frederick McCoy (1877-1948)
(Courtesy of The Mariners' Museum, Newport News, VA.)

PUBLISHER'S FOREWORD

For a long time newspapers featured operations of Rum Row. Ships with valuable cargoes of choice liquors hovered or lurked beyond coastal waters, to supply bootleggers who could run the blockades along our shores. The most notorious Rum Rows were off the coasts of New Jersey and Florida. Cities along the eastern seaboard received practically their entire supply of foreign liquor from such sources. At one time it was quite apparent that no real effort was being made to put an end to such open defiance of our laws.

—Mabel Walker Willebrandt
Assistant Attorney General
in Charge of Prohibition Enforcement, 1922-1929
The Inside of Prohibition, 1929

He was really somebody to meet, this gentleman, whom I shall call Captain Bill McCoy. He was a composite of Errol Flynn, Howard Hughes, and Captain Bligh. He was good-looking, courteous, soft-spoken, had a charming and ever-ready sense of humor; and he loved money, good boats, and good living. And he had a sense of honor...

—Ellery Thompson
Draggerman's Haul, 1958

I'D OFTEN HEARD OF WILLIAM MCCOY (1877-1948), the rum running schooner captain from the Roaring Twenties with whom my father's own exploits had been sometimes confused, at least in our family. Many of these stories were hints and scraps that my father'd run whiskey from Canada, made beer in the cellar and had a tired old schooner that had had its foremast shot off by the Coast Guard. Even into the 1940s he kept the culture of the period very much alive in our house. The furniture of Prohibition was constantly in the air in these stories, the notorious Liberty airplane engines bought by the rum-runners from World War surplus; gaff schooners, the rig of choice for the mother ships on Rum Row; musty bottles in the cellar in which he'd brewed "Ed's Pansy Beer;" the roadster that he drove... even the very bathtub in which I'd bathed and which my mother made gin. Most of all was the jazz. He recreated his speakeasy moments when with the old Conn trumpet and battered Harmon mute he'd played taking over the obligatory "Melancholy Baby" for a weary Red Nicholas, and opened "Bugle Call Rag" with the Dorsey Brothers in their early group The California Ramblers. Most memorably, I recall being snugged up in a brackish backwater of the Connecticut River in an old William Atkin gaff centerboarder when in the middle of the night I awoke to the throbbing of engines. "Liberties," whispered my father and then to my alarm, climbed on deck to take the lines from the dark boat.

When I began playing the trumpet around ten years old and most students were playing scales and "Westminster Chimes," my father wrote out for me "Melancholy Baby." For me Prohibition was as much about the smell of brackish river water and that old trumpet case, the musty green felt and the sweet pungency of valve oil, as it was about juniper berries and alcohol. We went to see all the old speakeasy trumpeters: Muggsy Spanier, Jimmy McPartland, Wild Bill Davison, Hot Lips Page, Bobby Hackett and, of course, Louie.

To fulfill my military obligation I'd joined the Coast Guard and after playing bugle in boot camp and one of my billets was aboard the last of the 125-foot class, the very vessels that had been designed a generation before to challenge McCoy out on Rum Row. But it wasn't until I met Ellery Thompson that I first had a sense of what the legend really meant outside the family.

It was in the early 1960s. I'd recently been discharged and was attempting to earn a living as a lobsterman. I was standing with my crewman outside the back door to Grossman's Fish Market with a peach basket of rejected lobsters. Grossman's was, as it yet is, a shack on the Mystic-Noank Road, which connects these two fishing villages on the edge of an estuary halfway between Boston and New York on the eastern approach to Long Island Sound.

It had been a rough morning off the reefs and I'd been too busy trying to handle the boat to check my young sternman who had been doing the best he could to insert the gauge on the eye-socket of our squirming catch. Grossman's had a big, plate glass window upon which is soaped the daily specials. In those days it was the marketing ploy of the owner Earl Bradshaw to misspell words like *Sord Fish* and *Blu fish*. "It gets the educated summer folks to stop," he liked to say. He had not been so expansive in appreciating our efforts and had asked us to leave before we got him in trouble with the marine police.

The screen door had just slammed behind me when on cue appeared an ancient man in a slouch hat so battered by life that his posture almost formed a question mark. "You boys wanna off load those shorts?" He favored us with a hard twinkle which somehow escaped sidewise out from under his slouch hat. You find eyes like that in winter when they fall out of the bait fish and roll around the cockpit like marbles. "I'll make you a good deal."

I'd seen this fellow lurching about town near the edges of buildings. The man who ran the store where I bought my bottom paint and seam compound had pointed him out to be Captain Ellery Thompson (1899-1986). This forlorn figure was once the famous dragger captain who'd been portrayed by the *New Yorker*'s Joseph Mitchell and gone on upon the wings of that fame to cause his own autobiography to appear under the aegis of no less than the Viking Press. He had been courted by Hollywood and the rumor was that Gary Cooper was to play his part, but that negotiations had bogged down. Now Ellery's beloved vessel *Eleanor* lay in the mud up river and he was eking out a living by painting portraits of her over and over again on masonite employing boat paint from our shopkeeper friend and what was charitably described as a "primitive" technique. I'm afraid I was a bit slow to rise to his bait to conspire in compounding my crime. He sensed my reluctance.

"You know," he said stepping closer, but yet managing only the side-wise glance. "I used to work with Bill McCoy."

He waited for the effect to seep in.

"You know…" he shot a glance as best he could manage over his off shoulder: "The Real McCoy."

Of course I did know exactly what he meant. And I must confess I felt—ludicrous as the comparison was—the excitement of somehow continuing in the great tradition of furtive maritime endeavor. This was a tradition that in New England at least, reached way back to the days when the Revenue Cutter Service became the nation's first floating military branch. I must have mentioned something about my father and how the foremast of his schooner had been shot off by the Coast Guard. Ellery countered with his version of McCoy. We got into a bit of a verbal scuffle over who had title to the most vicarious glory in the shadow of this famous outlaw. I decided in any case that after thirty years, the residue of McCoy did not retain quit enough aura—at least at the back door of Grossman's, to umbrella an illegal transaction. Captain Ellery and I did, however, become friends through the years. I visited him in his apartment up over the local paint store and I dutifully read *Draggerman's Haul* and a subsequent book Ellery published through the Pequot Press, *Come Aboard the Draggers.*

In both of Ellery Thompson's accounts of his life in commercial fishing he devotes a chapter to McCoy. You get the idea that his connection with the icon of Rum Row is what, when all else fails, not only lends his life distinction, but stands, in some back-door way, as the wink and a nod to all the other less grandiose shenanigans that locals knew Ellery to have been up to in his "naughty boy" phase. The historical gist is that when Thompson was a young man fishing out of New London some of the older, respectable citizens recruited him to run McCoy out to his schooner. Thompson makes it seem that this vessel is the beloved *Arethusa*, which was jogging just outside the twelve mile limit off Montauk Point "with six thousand cases of the finest whiskey."

Thompson's account is about as close a wide-eyed first-hand encounter with McCoy as I've come across:

> The story begins in a seaport sporting club to which I had come by request. The place was crowded with businessmen

> and hazy with cigar smoke. There were deep leather chairs, and heavy glass ash trays, and the walls were hung with oil paintings which ranged in subject from a beautiful nude to President Harding. Being a young fisherman, I felt out of place. But not for long; the atmosphere was too sociable. After an hour spent in meeting the boys, I was taken aside and introduced to Captain Bill McCoy. We talked of boats and other things, and the evening passed swiftly... I had been asked as a favor, having refused flatly to be hired, to smuggle a load of whiskey for private consumption from Rum Row, and by men who were the most respected in the community.
>
> And then the next night, before I realized that I decided and answered them, we were in Block Island Sound and heading seaward in my dragger. There were three of us—my mate (whom I shall not name), and Captain Bill McCoy and I.

Thompson goes on to say how McCoy stood by him at the wheel and "spoke lovingly of his Gloucester schooner, *Arethusa*" which was loaded with whiskey and waiting for him twelve miles off Montauk point (some thirty two miles from the pier in New London where Ellery kept his boat). McCoy fills the young fisherman with grandiose plans for making a quarter of a million on the East Coast, moving his vessel to the West Coast and doing the same and then retiring to "get some real fun out of my life with my family and with fine boats."

Thompson runs into "a dirty fog" off Fort Pond Bay just inside Montauk and takes his vessel into the harbor where they spend three days, during which time McCoy goes ashore. On the third night the fog clears and McCoy returns with "two presents for his schooner captain—a Colt .45 and a box of fifty-cent cigars. He tells Thompson that, "Both are useful in smoking out the worries a man may have out where there a various kinds of sharks."

When they are "far off Montauk" a "heavily laden black hulled Gloucester type fishing schooner looms up ahead. His description evokes a vivid picture of what the McCoy operation might look like to an outsider: (The "hams" were indeed one of McCoy's innovations.)

> Near [the schooner] were a dozen small boats lying-to, waiting. We had priority, for we had the boss. We went alongside and in a minute were tied up with bumpers overside. To say that she was loaded hardly described it; cases of whiskey overflowed her hatches from bow to stern. Burlap-covered "hams" (six quarts) were piled on the cabin aft. The dropped mainsail was serving as an awning for the schooner's captain. McCoy passed a list to the mate with instructions to load us. He then went aft to chat with his captain, a three-hundred-pounder who might have been Rex Stout's prototype for Nero Wolfe.
>
> The rough, unsmiling crew began to unload them, a job made more difficult by the long ground swell rolling in all the way from Spain. The "nautical fat man aft never moves from his chair." As the loading draws to a conclusion, McCoy steps to the rail of his schooner and wishes Thompson "happy landings."

At last free of his burden, Thompson heads for home and decides, "never again." Thus would seem to be the end of McCoy's local impact.

In 1965, however, I came across an autographed copy of *The Real McCoy* for the then stiff price of $75. There on the inside of the cover was boldly written in ink:

Howard M. Friend
Compliments of "Bill" McCoy

Just looking at the actual handwriting of McCoy gave me goose bumps. In reading the text I found at least partial confirmation of some of the stories I'd heard from Ellery and my father.

While we now think of Prohibition as an unpopular law that had been somehow thrust upon the majority of the people by a cranky, but well-organized minority, support for it had been building for several generations. Indeed there were states that had been dry since deep in the 19th Century. Riding on an unlikely wave of xenophobia, fundamentalism, reactionary politics, patriotism and feminism, the Prohibition movement reached its apogee with the First World War when its proponents we able to link abstinence with patriotism (ironically, those Liberty engines). Despite a veto by President Woodrow Wilson, Congress passed the National Prohibition Act, enforcing the 18th Amendment, to become effective January 16, 1920.

Prior to turning temporary smuggler McCoy had been a professional mariner for twenty years. He had graduated first in his class from a top training ship program, gone on to run the large yachts of wealthy men such as transportation tycoon Henry Plant. With his older brother Ben and sister Violet, he opened an intra-coastal transportation line across Florida to the West Coast. On Florida's Halifax River just north of Daytona, they built boats for the likes of Andrew Carnegie and department store king, John Wanamaker. Carnegie loved to visit the McCoy's boatyard on Florida's Halifax River and sit next to McCoy's father, a veteran of Civil War blockades. Bill remarked that seeing the two old Scots sitting side by each on a saw horse, you could not tell the one from the other. After Prohibition the McCoys went back to boatbuilding and following the Second World War were meeting with yachting maven L. Francis Herreshoff with whom Ben continued a warm correspondence after Bill's death.

Just how McCoy got into the rum running business is a bit fuzzy. In his cavalier book composed with writer Frederic F. Van de Water after his prison time, but before Repeal, McCoy would have us believe his new career was a spur of the moment thing. In the early 1920s, the McCoy family found their maritime market depressed. A chance encounter with a ne'er do well local wanna-be rum-runner sporting a new car seems to have provided the impetus. Bill, like the rest of his family, was a Methodist teetotaler. He seemed inspired, or perhaps more accurately, given his nature, provoked, to go the automotive rum-runner one better and try the transshipment of alcohol by boat. There also seems to have been some strife in McCoy's short marriage to a woman barely out of her teens, and this might may or may not have helped cut him loose.

Aside from the importing business, however, McCoy stayed close to convention. When not on the road, he continued to live in the ample house his father built, where he shared not only quarters but work with his older brother and younger sister and her husband. The sister kept the boatyard books and under the name of Valma Clark wrote gothic thrillers for *Weird Tales* magazine and novels of family history, at least one of which was reviewed in the *New York Times*. Her husband ran the McCoy's bus line which by then had replaced the brothers' inland waterway company. Ben stayed home, or at least ashore, and seems to have handled some of the land-side of the rum business. It is interesting to speculate as to whether the sister also did the books for the booze operation. Her daughter, in any case, grew up to be a music professor specializing in organ composition. After the matriarch died, the McCoy brothers donated $10,000 in her name to provide bells for the local Methodist Church. Perhaps most significantly, when *Arethusa* eventually wrecked under the ownership of a Newfoundland fishing operation, McCoy traveled a thousand miles to retrieve the part of the main beam upon which was carved her documentation number.

Because of the rampant hypocrisy and corruption that came to mark Prohibition, many came to see McCoy as a Robin Hood figure smuggling under the noses of the corrupt government to supply the traditional needs of the common folk. Others saw him as a Horatio Alger type, but this ignores the fact that the McCoys were a hard-working family in the building trade. They had never been in rags and managed to hang onto the quarters on the Halifax River through two generations. As for the riches, thanks to lawyers and gangsters, the McCoys never really arrived at what any self-respecting modern entrepreneur would call wealth. What McCoy did have were his boats, especially the iconic "Queen of the Gloucester Fishing Fleet:"

> Her name was *Arethusa*, and I was standing on a Gloucester pierhead when I first saw her. It was toward sunset, and the air was light so that she seemed a ghost into the harbor's mouth under full sail. She was an aristocrat, a thoroughbred from her keel to her trucks. The late sun turned her spread of canvas golden, and my throat was tight and stiff as she came walking up the harbor like a great lady entering a room. Her long, low black hull told the mariner

of speed and grace. . . [she] sailed in through the harbor of Gloucester that night and straight into my heart.

McCoy often did talk expansively to people like the young Ellery Thompson of his post-rum running plans of escaping to the South Seas. Decades after Prohibition he and brother Ben were building a motor yacht called the *Blue Lagoon* and giving interviews to starry-eyed journalists about the same South Sea dream. Bill even died aboard the *Blue Lagoon* in 1948, age 71, when she was yet in her backwater Florida slip.

As for Prohibition, when it came down to it, McCoy seemed to enjoy nothing more than sailing his beloved *Arethusa* up what he called "the broad blue highway" of the Atlantic Gulf Stream. As an added kick, he loaded her near to the gunwale with his clandestine cargo with the prospect of outfoxing the hypocritical authorities. More important than the money, however, was the integrity of his operation. While etymologists have haggled for years over the origin of the phrase "the real McCoy," it is clear that in the 1920s William F. McCoy put the power into that phrase in a way by which we, in our precarious moral age, could certainly profit. A few years before the G-men came up with the "most-wanted" designation, McCoy clearly had become that man. As one outside the law, McCoy, unlike those other outlaw icons of the era, the psychotics Capone, Dillinger, Bonnie and Clyde, and Baby Face Nelson, McCoy never killed anybody or even wounded anyone. The guns he carried were only to protect him from the gangsters. He was at worst a sometime sociopath of the prankster variety and one could make the claim it was his cockiness that lost him his schooner the afternoon of November 23, 1923 off Sea Bright, New Jersey.

All agree, however, McCoy had a code of honor unique in an era when America was looking for mythic heroes. McCoy was there with Wyatt Earp whose biography came out the same year as *The Real McCoy* and it was perhaps with the heroes of the Far West that his story seems most at home. McCoy's writer, Frederic Van de Water, said, "One might as well ignore Wild Bill Hickok in an account of the early days of Dodge City as to write of Nassau in its mad, bad prime and omit McCoy." More than that, however, it has become clear to me that to know McCoy is to know America—its dreams and its disillusionments, its sense of the free spirit and the souring when the wind shifts. The furniture may be different today, but many of the key issues persist under different banners. James Butler "Wild Bill" Hickok of Deadwood and his horses became more than a mere border legend but a way into the Heartland. In the same way, McCoy and his schooners becomes a vehicle for understanding the complexities of contemporary America.

McCoy himself, of course, had no such grand notions of his place in history. More in exasperation than pride he tells us mid-way through his book:

> After death… my ghost might keep right on, a new variety of *Flying Dutchman* to warn sinners into obedience to the laws of Volstead.

Stephen Jones
Schooner Wharf
Mystic, Connecticut

Bill McCoy's schooner *Arethusa*.
(Courtesy of The Mariners' Museum, Newport News, VA.)

FOREWORD

FRAGMENTS OF BILL MCCOY'S HISTORY are embodied in the records of the Department of Justice and the log books of sundry revenue cutters. These comments on the most daring and successful of rum-runners are pardonably acid and prejudiced. Nothing is more offensive to officialdom than a reiterant, light-hearted disregard. Nothing is more maddening to the agents of constituted authority than derision.

For four lively years, while he mocked the increasingly portentous blockading fleet the Volstead Act mobilized on the Atlantic seaboard, McCoy was a thorn in the twitching flesh of the United States government, a rankling and most persistent thorn. He was the founder of Rum Row off New York and the trade's most daring and successful exponent. Time and again his ships were located, triumphantly captured. Subsequent relief always was brief. He evaded those who had caught him and almost immediately was prodding elsewhere.

He landed the first sea-borne rum shipments in New England. He opened up St. Pierre et Miquelon as a rum base. He drove cutter captains to the brink of apoplexy. He enraged prohibition agents, distracted the Department of Justice, and troubled the Olympian calm of the State Department itself, which eventually entered into a special agreement with the British government whereby he finally was laid by the heels.

In the abstract, the slippery, irreverent, swaggeringly resourceful McCoy was a scourge, a menace, a continual threat against the peace and dignity of the United States, and a jeering foe of that swelling army which strove to make the nation dry. In the flesh, even his bitterest foes admitted, he was the most genial and endearingly candid of law breakers.

Other, less caustic, records of McCoy's past may be gleaned in the Bahama group, those white scraps of firmament carelessly brushed from the Creator's trestleboard into the blue glare of the

Spanish Main. Nassau, that sun-steeped haunt successively of buccaneers, blockade runners, and rum-runners, is filled with yarns of his achievements. Here you will find none of the hard, brief animus of the government reports. In Bahamian reminiscences, Bill McCoy already is trailing clouds of legendary glory.

Of all that hard, wild, unrestrained crew of rascals who infested Nassau in the early, disorganized era of the rum trade, McCoy was the most personable, the most trustworthy. In a day when a man's word was worth no more than the breath that bore it, when contracts were enforced by lynx-like vigilance backed by firearms; when theft, double-crossing, piracy, even murder were frequent and usually unpunished. McCoy strode his boyishly grinning, zestful way, respected and honored by the underworld rabble through which he went, ruefully admired even by the United States Consul, Lorin A. Lathrop, a veteran of the service who in official moments was his firm antagonist and, after hours, his friend.

The liquor McCoy's ships carried to Rum Row was always the best. Debts he incurred, whether oral or written, were paid on time and in full. Friends whom he made, he kept. Persistently he struck at the law of his country, but he held to his own not inconsiderable moral code.

To Nassauvians, who profited greatly during his rum running years, he has become a glamorous Robin Hood of the Main. His erstwhile associates have epitomized his square crookedness in a phrase that has become a part of the nation's slang: "The real McCoy"—signifying all that is best and most genuine. Eventually dictionaries may pick it up, a verbal monument to one who played a hazardous game daringly and, after his lights, fairly and honestly.

I knew the slang long before I met the man. Several times in a stretch of years our trails crossed. In December of 1923 I went, at the behest of a magazine editor, to Nassau to write of rum running and rum piracy. The editor, I have since suspected, was prone to dramatize matters, as all good editors must. He dwelt at length on the hazards of the enterprise, counseling me to go as a tourist and to reveal to no one the purpose of my mission. So stoutly did I attempt to portray the role he had imposed that within twenty-four hours of my landing at Nassau the entire island had leaped to the conclusion that I was a secret-service man. It took much time and considerable liquor to eradicate that unfortunate first impression.

McCoy and his cherished schooner, born *Arethusa* and rechristened *Tomoka*, at this time was North on Rum Row, serving the

Christmas trade. From the American Consul, the late Lorin A. Lathrop, a gracious and cultured gentleman who wrote under the pseudonym "Kenyon Gambier" much worthwhile fiction; from rum-runners, from schooner captains, from liquor dealers, I heard of the "King of Rum Row." So he was called. Even in that day legend was solidifying about him. One might as well ignore Wild Bill Hickok in an account of the early days of Dodge City as to write of Nassau in its mad, bad prime and omit McCoy. He figured largely in my articles.

A year or so later Charles R. Patterson, the marine artist, dined at my home.

"Do you," he asked me, "know a person named Bill McCoy?"

"Only indirectly," I answered. "Why?"

"He's under indictment here in New York," Patterson explained. "He's ordered a canvas from me—a picture of his *Tomoka* running away from the revenue cutter *Seneca*. He asked if I knew you and sent his regards."

Since then, McCoy has returned to his home in Florida and resumed his long interrupted trade of boatbuilding. He has been definitely out of the rum running game. No conscientious reformation has turned him from reprehensibility. His reason for retirement has been that the trade has changed and that it no longer is fun. Also, by his own unique yet rigid ethics, it has become too dirty, too wholly crooked.

In this age of consolidation the rum running industry has not been immune. What was once a marine combination of tag and blind-man's buff, with the revenue cutters forever "it" and each individual runner working for himself; what was once a sport as well as a lucrative enterprise has become Big Business with the small independent tradesman absorbed or frozen out. The zestful hazard has been eliminated. It is a sordid bribe-giving, graft-taking racket, coordinated, systematized.

"I don't want any part of it," McCoy says scornfully. I believe him. I know that a few weeks before this was written representatives of a "mob" that handles much of New York's sea-borne liquor approached Bill, urging that he resume his old trade and backing persuasion with financial promises that left a hack writer dazed and a little dizzy.

"Nope," said McCoy. "I'm through. It's a business now, and I'm not that sort of a businessman."

For some years we carried on a desultory correspondence, and one day, while he was in New York, we met.

Six feet two, with shoulders like a cargo hatch, slim waist, a voice like a foghorn, lean tanned face, and steady eyes set in the network of wrinkles that long gazing over glittering water etches, he sat in my suddenly dwarfed living room and talked of the days when liquor was liquor and Rum Row was a marine market running unbroken from Montauk to Atlantic City, when each man worked for himself to outwit revenue cutters and to fend against piracy and hijacking.

He lost himself in his story. Surf boomed through his words, and out of the rush of his speech, now and then, leaped a phrase poetic and vivid, sired by his sheer zest for action and a deep love of the sea and of sail.

He crowds fifty, clean limbed and muscular as he could have been at twenty-five. His outlook upon life is as unscrupulously gleeful, thrill seeking, adventurous as though he were still fifteen. There are moments when you suspect that the essential ego of him is no more than that.

He was, without question, the most successful and notorious of the old-time—as one counts advances and changes in the liquor traffic—rum-runners. He was, literally, the father of Rum Row and the inventor of much rum running technique. When he quit the game, less than five years ago, he had landed or discharged from his schooners into lighters and motor boats for the relief of parched America a total of 175,000 cases of liquor, chiefly Scotch and rye. Practically all of this was cut four times by purchasers—diluted and fortified by grain alcohol—before it was sold. Thus, McCoy actually furnished 700,000 cases to slake America's thirst.

He has been the trusted friend of some of the most outrageous crooks Manhattan harbors. He was a leader in Nassau when that usually placid tropic city was a combination of a cow town on payday and a new gold camp, with additional spectacular and violent features thrown in for good measure. He has known the best of people and the worst, has been indicted over and over, jumped bail, paid fines, been mulcted by lawyers, fired upon by revenue cutters.

Out of all this and more he has emerged, for all that he has done, for all that has happened to him, still with the heart of a mischievous, authority-scorning, rather gallant small boy. He handled millions in cash and today is comparatively poor, but he talks more of the thrills he enjoyed than the money he had.

From that talk with Bill McCoy and many subsequent conversations, this book has grown. It is his book rather than mine. I am not his ghost, but only his more or less unsatisfactory interpreter. Even in print, it remains as closely as possible his story. The hand is the hand of his reporter, but the voice is the voice of William McCoy—the real McCoy.

Frederic F. Van de Water
Yorktown, VA. 1930

CHAPTER I

A HUNDRED MILES OUT TO SEA from the mouth of New York harbor lean four-stackers wallow and slide through the waves. The navy's surplus destroyers have been turned into revenue craft and now form the first line of defense against rum ships.

Thirty to fifty miles out the white orthodox cutters of the service march their sentry beats. Twenty miles from shore the high-power 75-footers, built to break and scatter Rum Row, weave to and fro vigilantly, and between them and the land are the 36-footers, smaller, more plentiful, power boats.

That is not all. There are launches in the lower bay. There are police boats in the harbor itself. The government has thrown out to protect New York against sea-borne liquor a five-ply screen of defense, through which, so I have heard officials boast, no rum-laden craft can penetrate.

Rum Row is no more. The days when the fleet hung offshore from Montauk to Cape May, a rocking line of wholesale liquor stores, and sold its wares to sea skiffs and motorboats that could outfoot the old-style plodding cutters have gone. The wind-jamming skippers who brought their schooners up the blue road of the Gulf Stream from Nassau have vanished. The rust-streaked tramps that came wallowing over from Europe to anchor on the Row go about their lawful or unlawful occasions elsewhere. The seas run clean across the place of their one-time commerce, and the four stackers, the white cutters, the 75-footers, the 36-footers, the harbor craft, march their beats day by day in pious triumph.

Rum, I have been told, no longer comes to America by ocean, save in tiny, smuggled lots. The trade is dead, stifled by the thick blanket of protective craft the government has established offshore. So, I say, I am told.

No rum-runner, I also have been informed, could get through that five-line system of defense.

Nassau, one-time home port of most liquor-carrying craft, must have relapsed into a sleepy town once more, barely kept alive by her sponge and turtle fisheries, her sisal and her tourists. With her liquor trade squashed, there could be no other fate for her. I was in Nassau less than a year ago. My business was real estate, not rum. The little white city never seemed more prosperous. My friends the liquor dealers told me they never had had a better season.

St. Pierre, rum running metropolis of the North, must have gone back to a precarious living from fisheries now that the quintuple protection established by Uncle Sam bars her wares from America. St. Pierre, I happen to know, in one month recently shipped 110,000 cases of liquor into New York alone.

In Bermuda the rum traffic flourishes. In Nova Scotia, as this is written, three big, high-powered craft are being built for the rum running trade: 140 ft. long; 26 ft. wide; draft 8 ft.; power, twin-screw Diesel engine; speed 16 knots; capacity 8,000 cases.

Rum Row is gone. That is fact. The navy mustered offshore by the prohibition enforcement authorities also is fact. The prosperity of the localities that once fed the now supposedly nonexistent Rum Row is fact also. If these facts don't seem to jibe, you can draw your own conclusions. Liquor still comes into America by sea, in large quantities and with fewer seizures than ever before.

How is it accomplished? I shall tell, later, of some of the methods and equipment used by present-day rum-runners. How, in spite of these modern improvements, they bring their cargoes in, past the destroyers and the cutters and the 75-footers and the 36-footers and the harbor craft is a trade secret. I was a pioneer in the old go-as-you-please, every-man-for-himself rum running racket. I quit when adventure went out of the game and Big Business came in. And when I quit, I stay quit.

Down in Florida, my brother Ben and I have gone back to our old trade of shipbuilding, and there we are going to stay. With the little I was able to keep from my rum running profits, plus the income of our shipyard, we are able to get along. There were times, during my years in the game, when I dreamed of buying yachts instead of selling them. A cruise to the South Seas I promised myself never has come off either. Bermuda, Jamaica, Nassau, St. Pierre, and the Newark and New Brunswick and Trenton jails were the farthest I got. As for the cash that was to set me up as king of some far-off Polynesian isle where girls were beautiful and men were scarce, most of it went to make a lot of lawyers richer than, thanks to them, I shall ever be.

I haven't a lot of material profit to show for four years of what was certainly an extra hazardous industry, but I've seen things others haven't and done much that only a few could equal. I've been thrilled and chilled. I've been double-crossed and robbed and shot at and jailed. I've owned and sailed the sweetest schooner that ever carried a bone in her teeth—the *Arethusa*, later the *Tomoka*, still later the *Marie Celeste*. I've made friends I'll remember always, and an enemy or so I'm entirely willing to forget. I've had a lot of fun, even in jail. And if there's anything more than that to life, I don't want it.

Nine months in prison didn't make me quit. If it had been the same old game I might have gone back to it. Rum running, in my time, was a game, played with the sea for a board and cutters and schooners for pieces. It was the sea that kept me at it. Blue water has a lure for me that firewater never can have. And, though my father was a bricklayer by trade, I trace back to him the pull the ocean has for his son.

My old dad served in the Union navy during the Civil War. The ships he sailed on, the *Moccasin*, *Powhatan*, *Gloucester*, and others, were in the blockading fleet that smothered Confederate commerce. His most frequent station was off the mouth of the Wilmington River, on the lookout for blockade runners from Nassau. And from that port, about sixty years later, his own son sailed to dodge another blockade.

I was born in upper New York State and, if we hadn't moved to Philadelphia, I might have been a bricklayer, too. By the time we were settled there I started nosing about the wharves on the Delaware as instinctively as a bird dog ranges a stubble field, and there, one bright, windswept morning, I came face to face with the school ship *Saratoga*. Her masts were lovely against the sky, her yards swarming with cadets, and an officer on the horse block bawled orders through a speaking trumpet. I marched home and told the Old Man he'd have to find another apprentice.

Two happy years I served on the old *Saratoga*, and I was graduated Number One in my class. Herbert Hartley, later to be skipper of the *Leviathan*, was my classmate, and we were taught navigation by a keen young Annapolis man, Ensign Sims, who was destined to become admiral later on.

Business wasn't so brisk in the merchant marine in those days. After years of service on yachts and coast steamers, I had risen to be mate of the *Olivette* on the Key West-Havana run, and my pay was

$75 a month. My family had moved to Florida in 1900. I left the *Olivette* and joined them. There was all the sea I could possibly use right at my doorstep, and my brother Ben and I began to build boats to sail on it. We built craft for the Vanderbilts, John Wanamaker, Maxine Elliott, and Carnegie, among others. Old Andy and my father looked like twins. Let them sit in the end of a pier together, as I often saw them, fish poles in hand, big straw hats on their heads, and you would have a hard time telling which was the steel king and which the retired bricklayer.

Ben and I opened motorboat service by the inside passage from Jacksonville to Palm Beach and from Palm Beach to Fort Myers through the Everglades. This was profitable for a while, and then motor buses came along and killed our business.

The winter of 1919-20 had not been too fortunate for us. Shortly after the season was over I had a visitor at whom I had to look three times before I recognized him.

He drove a shiny roadster only a little smaller than a locomotive. He wore a checked suit that made you blink, and below his bow tie there was a diamond like an arc light pinned in his shirt. The last time I had seen him he had been a scrawny brown fisherman in faded dungarees.

"Hey, Bill," he said out of a corner of his mouth, "want to make some money?"

That was one of my chief aims in life, and I told him so.

"How," he asked, still lower, "would a hundred dollars a day listen to you?"

"You ought to lay off the liquor," I came back. He laughed at that.

"Liquor," he wheezed, "is just what I want to talk to you about."

He took me by the arm and walked me out of earshot before mumbling his proposition. America was dry and begging for a drink. A short sail from the coast was Nassau in the Bahamas, filled with rum and itching to sell it.

My friend had a schooner, the *Dorothy W.*, and a contract to carry a load of rye whisky from Nassau to Atlantic City. He needed a skipper to sail her. Schooner captains were scarce in Florida in those days, and men who could handle the immense profits of rum running and still remain even approximately honest, scarcer still.

"One hundred dollars a day, Bill," the tempter reiterated. I didn't tell him to get behind me. Inwardly I wondered how long this had been going on and where the catch was. Outwardly I asked to see his ship.

I went with him and inspected her. Sailing craft have personalities as definite as those of men. And why shouldn't they have? They are the most nearly animate things ever created by man. They are sensitive to tender or rough treatment. Each of them has its own whims and peculiarities—almost its own soul.

To sailormen, sailing ships are never mechanical contrivances. They are individuals. It isn't by accident that the sailor always speaks of his craft as "she." Women and canvas carriers are similar. Some you like, others you learn to trust, still others you suspect on sight.

I didn't like the *Dorothy W.* She was a shabby, drab little 70-footer that had seen her best days, and these, evidently, had not been too good. I knew we'd never get along together, and I turned down my friend's offer.

But meanwhile I'd learned a good deal. Rum running was in its infancy. There were millions of thirsts to be slaked. There were thousands of cases of liquor in the Bahamas and thousands more being hurried over from Europe. Ships to make the trip to the American coast were few, and shipowners who could guarantee delivery of a cargo and a subsequent return of the proceeds by the skipper were even less plentiful.

I talked the situation over with my brother. I sold my boats and went into the game.

I went into it for the cash. I stayed in it four years for the fun it gave me. Several times I could have quit with money enough to keep me comfortable for the next hundred years, but there was a fascination to it that wouldn't let me let go. I'm not a drinker, but if rum has one tenth the lure of rum running in its heyday, I can understand the souse's viewpoint.

There was money in the game—lots of it, if you could keep it. Beyond that there was all the kick of gambling and the thrill of sport, and, besides these, there were the open sea and the boom of the wind against full sails, dawn coming out of the ocean, and nights under the rocking stars. These caught and held me most of all.

This is explanation, not apology. I have no excuse to make for what the courts of my country decided was a criminal career. If I wished to defend myself, I have precedent right out of American history for my rum running enterprises. Americans, since the beginnings of this nation, have always kicked holes in the laws they resented. The Stamp Act was law, wasn't it? Men who broke it are called "patriots" today. Sometimes I wonder what the rum-runners will be called a century from now. The Boston Tea Party wasn't an exactly legal expedition, either. The Fugitive Slave Act was once as much law of the land as Volstead's legislation. I went to jail for the crime of conspiracy. Well, a lot of our best ancestors conspired to break the Fugitive Slave Law, too, and established the underground railway to get runaway Negroes safely into Canada. I don't know whether any of them were imprisoned for their crime.

There was a man in Massachusetts who might stand as the patron saint of rum-runners. He owned or chartered fast ships, ran liquor up from the West Indies and slipped it ashore when the customs men weren't looking. He smuggled liquor and silk and other things, and he grew richer at his nefarious trade than I did. In the eyes of the law as it stood at that time he was a bigger crook than I, for he resisted the government on other counts as well. He helped overthrow the constituted authority of those days, this original rum-runner. His name was John Hancock, and you can see it still, first of the signatures of patriots to the Declaration of Independence.

From now on I stick to my yarn. In August, 1920, I took the money we had assembled by selling our motorboats and went to Gloucester, Massachusetts, to buy the first of my fleet. She was the *Henry L. Marshall*, a 90-foot fishing schooner, built of white oak by James, of Essex, Massachusetts, with pole masts, a semi-knockabout rig, and twin-screw engines with a speed of 7 knots. She had a capacity of 1,500 cases in wood or 3,000 cases in burlap packages. I paid $16,000 for her, and $4,000 more, refitting.

It was while I was waiting for her to be ready for sea that I fell in love at first sight.

Her name was *Arethusa*, and I was standing on a Gloucester pierhead when I first saw her. It was toward sunset, and the air was light so that she seemed to ghost into the harbor's mouth under full sail. She was an aristocrat, a thoroughbred from her keel to her trucks. The late sun turned her spread of canvas golden, and my throat was tight and stiff as she came walking up the harbor like a great lady entering a room. The lines of her long low black hull told the mariner of speed and grace. The *Arethusa*, fishing schooner of the East Coast Fisheries Company, sailed in through the harbor of Gloucester that night and straight into my heart. I couldn't buy her then. I'd spent almost my last dollar on the *Marshall*. She was a fine schooner, but after I'd seen the *Arethusa* I almost hated her.

The *Marshall* reached Jacksonville in February, 1921. There the

WINTON TOURING CARS AND OLDSMOBILES.

REPRESENT
THE WINTON
MOTOR CARRIAGE CO.
OLDS MOTOR WORKS,
THE BUICK MOTOR CO.

THE Florida MOTOR CO.
AUTOMOBILES & GASOLINE ENGINES.

GLOBE IRON WORKS CO.
THE WHITE
GASOLINE ENGINE.
MARINE,
STATIONARY, PORTABLE.

NAPHTHA LAUNCHES FOR SALE.

Daytona, Fla.

Letterhead from the McCoy Brothers' Florida Motor Co. circa 1908. The brothers raced cars and boats in the early days of Daytona. Bill and Ben sold this operation to focus their efforts on building and chartering motor yachts. (*National Archives)*

McCoy Bros. Marine Construction Co.

EXTREMELY LIGHT DRAUGHT VESSELS AND HOUSE BOATS

MARINE WAYS · FRESH WATER BASIN

Daytona, Florida

Letterhead from the McCoy Bros. Marine Construction Co. circa 1918. (*National Archives)*

CAPTAIN BEN

CAPTAIN BILL

MCCOY BROTHERS

PALM BEACH, FLORIDA

DESIGNERS, BUILDERS AND OPERATORS OF

POWER AND SAIL VESSELS

CONTINUOUS SINCE 1900

Letterhead from the McCoy Brothers, circa 1941. (*National Archives)*

McCOY BROTHERS'

INDIAN RIVER LINE

BETWEEN

St. Augustine and
Palm Beach

Charming Semi-Tropical Scenery
Invigorating Air

EVERGLADE LINE

BETWEEN

Palm Beach, Moorehaven
and Ft. Myers

Fastest Line----Coast to Coast----2 Days

YACHT HOUSE BOATS FOR CHARTER
TO ALL POINTS IN FLORIDA

McCOY BROTHERS

DAYTONA, FLORIDA

PHONE :: 367 :: GREEN

Brochure cover for the McCoy Brothers' Indian River Line and Everglade Line, circa 1918. The brothers closed the Everglade Line due to competition from buses and highways and used the proceeds to purchase the *Henry L. Marshall*. (*National Archives)* crew that had brought her down left her. They had learned what she was to be used for, and in 1921 rum running wasn't yet respectable. They quit. There were moments when, if I could have got my $20,000 back, I might have quit too, but I was in too deep to pull out now. I signed another crew, a Swede whom I shall call Johnson, whom I made mate, and a half dozen seamen, including Murphy, a big Newfoundlander, and Pike, a wild Irishman. None of these men had any objection to trafficking in rum. My only difficulty was to keep them from drinking up the cargo.

We sailed for Nassau, which for four years was to be my home. In the early months of 1921 the little white city was still half asleep. The liquor trade was just beginning to stir; the New York gangs with their rivalries and gunmen had not yet arrived. Beside her peacock-hued harbor Nassau dreamed of her past and did not anticipate her immediate uproarious future.

She has lived, this little old tropic town. Most of her days she has slumbered, but there have been eras when she has stepped out. In her early years the buccaneers nested there, rumming and brawling and wenching between forays into the Main. When they passed, peace descended and prosperity fled. For a century thereafter Nassau dwindled, living upon her slim exports and loans from the mother country. Then the Civil War brought her again a brief blaze of fortune. Blockade running gave her the stimulus piracy once had afforded. Fast black ships, munitions-laden, slid from her harbor, snaked their way through the clutter of little islands that run westward like a long broken jetty, and then, with lights out and boilers throbbing, streaked through the night for the mouth of the Wilmington River dodging the blockading squadron in which my father served.

Once again Nassau momentarily was rich. After Appomattox she relapsed and dreamed away another sixty years. Her next awakening was to be the most violent and lucrative of all.

Perversely, she resented being roused to wealth. When two of her far-sighted younger citizens, the MacPherson brothers, imported the first thousand cases of Scotch for export to the parched United States, there was scandal on the island. There was even talk of arresting the MacPhersons. Then someone pointed out that this incoming shipment would pay a duty of $6 a case. Six thousand dollars put in a lump sum into the colony's treasury caused a sensation and made outraged morality pause and think. The longer the moralists thought, the more convinced they were that importation of liquor was not reprehensible but, as a matter of fact, downright praiseworthy. A lot of them started importation themselves.

In the years that followed, Nassau paid off her debt to the mother country, improved her harbor, dug artesian wells, paved her streets and roads, and still had a surplus remaining in the treasury. And I have learned, although the authorities in America proclaim that rum running is over, that the Bahamas continue to prosper and, strangely enough, largely through the exportation of rum.

Consul Lathrop and I went to the Bahama government and got the contract for American dredges to dig the channel deeper. The colonial secretary said, "We are having a dredge built in England."

I said, "And by that time we rum-runners will go to some deepwater harbor island."

When Pilot Brown steered the *Henry L. Marshall* past the white admonishing finger of the lighthouse and into the blazing pool of emerald, amethyst, and turquoise that is Nassau harbor, the town had not yet fully awakened to the imminence of fortune.

Negroes loafed along Bay Street, carrying immense burdens on their bullet heads or lingering in the shade of the palm and woman's tongue trees. Rickety hacks with flea-bitten racks of bones between the shafts stirred up the dust. Beyond the waterfront, white streets climbed past jalousied houses, and over stone walls bougainvilleas and hibiscus and a dozen other tropic blossoms flared. It was a languorous, lovely town, in which time and labor were worth little. And the *Marshall* was the sole seagoing craft in the harbor.

She was snapped up by a charterer as a kingfisher dives for a minnow. Billy Hain, an old friend of mine, boarded her by the time she was through the harbor mouth. Would I take 1,500 cases of liquor to Savannah at $10 a case? What else was I there for?

We warped the *Marshall* in to a pier, and I planned to go ashore. Before I could land there was a string of donkey-drawn drays, each laden with twenty-five cases of whisky, rumbling down the dock, and black stevedores were swarming over the *Marshall*'s side. I never set foot on land at all. Billy Hain was in a hurry.

From hand to hand the stevedores passed the liquor aboard. At my elbow by the rail stood the tally man, checking the load. "One, two, three, four, tally," he crooned over, and over and at each repetition of "tally" I made a mark in my book. Hain insisted the darkey could count no higher than five. Up to that figure he was quick and accurate.

We were loaded in an amazingly short time. Hain came aboard. "Now," he suggested, "let's get out of here. I'm in a hurry."

"Clearance papers?" I suggested. He tapped his breast pocket. "Got 'em," he replied. "Clear with 1,500 cases of rye to Halifax. Let's go."

It was his game. If he was in such a hurry, all right. My crew, however, put up a terrible roar. We were offending a tradition of the sea. Whoever heard of a ship clearing without its men first roistering ashore and all coming aboard drunk? They were going to run rum, weren't they? For all they knew they might end up in a jail where opportunities for relaxation, sport, and amusement were few. They wanted theirs now. Hain finally acquiesced.

"All right," he snapped. "Come on."

Followed by my men, he raced down the pier, chartered a fleet of hacks, and disappeared in a cloud of white dust toward Grantstown, the happy hunting ground for seamen ashore. An hour later the hack squadron was back on the pier, horses sweating and panting, Billy Hain grinning, and the entire ship's company present and completely drunk. No revel ashore was ever accomplished in a briefer time, but everyone seemed satisfied.

Hain took a seaplane back to America. We managed to make sail. The steady blast of the trade wind heeled the *Marshall* over. I was off on my first rum running enterprise, bound for St. Catherine's Sound, an inlet on the Georgia coast much favored by slave smugglers in the long ago.

First, however, we stopped at West End and obtained duplicate clearance papers from the complacent official there. These proclaimed that we were headed for Savannah "in ballast." This became routine procedure, whereby the West End official profited considerably, until complaints from America put a stop to the practice.

When the revenue cutter *Seneca* captured the *Marshall* off Atlantic City, months later, double clearance papers were aboard her, and the ensuing roar of protest from American authorities killed that game.

Later, on my schooner *Arethusa*, I cleared from Nassau for Halifax. The authorities looked my papers over on my return.

"You never went to Halifax," they accused.

"No," I answered. "I had an opportunity to sell my cargo on the high seas!"

"You can't do that."

"I did do it!"

"But it's not legal!"

"Show me," I demanded, "any law that says a master can't clear for a port, discharge on the high seas, and return to his home port, providing he has touched nowhere else meanwhile."

They tried to find one. There wasn't any.

From then on, my schooner cleared for Halifax and never got there. On her return I made affidavit that she had sold her cargo at sea and had touched at no port. That satisfied the Nassau customs men and became the usual procedure for all rum-runners.

The wind that took us away from West End had grown in strength. By the time we were halfway to the Georgia coast, it was blowing a gale from the northeast. The *Marshall* staggered along over seas that grew continually larger. And then night came, black and howling and starless. We had no idea of our position, only that we were going somewhere with great rapidity. Seas climbed the *Marshall*'s side and ran across her deck. Hurrying along it after one of their invasions I felt grit beneath my feet, stooped, felt, and discovered that the last roller to come aboard had spread sand across the planks.

Lost though we still were, I knew one thing now. We were on the verge of going ashore somewhere. We turned the *Marshall*'s bow to sea, started her engine, and jogged offshore. A cloud-darkened morning revealed the Georgia coast astern. Gale driven and blind, we were not far off our course. We found the mouth of St. Catherine's Sound, but the lighters Hain had promised were not there. Instead a little motorboat came puttering up and down over the rollers, and Billy and a cracker pilot came into the *Marshall*'s lee and clambered aboard.

He dripped sea water, but he was still cheerful and brisk.

"Can't unload her out here," he shouted above the yell of the wind. "Too rough. We'll have to go in."

He pointed to the mouth of the sound. Every cent I had in the world was tied up in the *Marshall.*

"Is it safe?" I said.

"High tide," he replied. "And a pilot. Sure it's safe."

"Tides don't worry me," I persisted. "I'm thinking of the prohibition boats. Is it safe to go on?"

You see, I was still young at the game and ignorant.

"Oh, them?" Hain exclaimed. "Sure. Absolutely."

We went in over the bar, a man in the chains heaving the lead, motor banging, and rollers boosting us along. Inside, the channel was calm, and back from it spread a wide bayou with a tangle of dead yellow cypress trees. It was in their concealment the slave smugglers used to lie and discharge their cargo. We dropped anchor at the channel's edge and waited for the lighters which, Hain had promised, would be along at dusk.

They appeared in due time, and we set to work discharging cargo. It was another black and windy night, and we could hear the seas outside hammering on the bar. Presently, when we were only half unloaded, I saw a red light like a spark burning on the flat curtain of the darkness.

"Hey!" I called and pointed it out to Billy.

"It's the boat," he announced at last. "Better pipe down. I got them fixed, but there's no use rubbing it in."

But he didn't seem too sure he had them fixed. We piped down. On the *Marshall* and on the lighters men stood stock still and waited. The red spark grew in the darkness. A green joined it. She had turned from her course and was heading toward us. I remember wondering whether they could hear my heart pounding aboard the cutter, and the smack of the little waves on the *Marshall*'s side sounded like shell fire.

We could hear the engines, now, pumping louder and louder as she bore down. She loomed before us, was abeam. I blinked at her lights and held my breath for the jingle of her telegraph. She could not help seeing the *Marshall* and the half-filled lighter. I breathed again. The cutter had passed and was throbbing on her way as though we had not been there. Billy and I wiped our sweating faces and resumed the transfer of our cargo.

Long before daylight Hain and his cargo departed. Our hold was cleaned out except for 100 cases I had put aboard as a favor for a small dealer in Nassau. I went to sleep. I had had all the nerve strain I wanted at one sitting. Johnson, the mate, woke me almost, it seemed, before I had got thoroughly asleep.

"On deck," he stammered. "Hurry up."

In the gray dawn the waters of the sound were lead and the crooked cypress limbs like fire-twisted iron. The gale still pushed clouds out of the northeast, and we could hear the sea roaring beyond the bar. It was a gloomy enough prospect without the rest of the spectacle. On the sound, only a short distance off, two great seaplanes swung at their moorings. Government seaplanes.

I only hung onto the rail and stared. After the scare of the night before this was too much.

"If they don't catch us on the water, they jump on us out of the air," Johnson yammered at my elbow.

There was no movement on either craft. Their crews might be asleep, waiting for broad daylight to board us

"All hands on deck," I whispered to Johnson. "Dump the rest of the liquor overboard."

Holding our breaths we formed a line and passed that hundred cases out of the hold and overside into the sound. Pike mourned as though he were watching a friend drown.

"Aw," he wailed, "we're throwin' away the makin's of a pub, Captain."

He produced a soup plate from somewhere, knocked the neck off a bottle and fortified himself with sups while he jettisoned its companions. By the time the last of it had plunged into the sound he was weeping bitterly and presently fell asleep.

My conscience was reasonably calm now. The clearance paper "To Savannah in ballast," was adequate answer to any questions the fliers, or anyone else, might ask. When I looked at the planes now, by the clear light of day and with unterrified eyes, it was easy to see they were deserted. Later that morning their crews reappeared, cast off, and the craft roared skyward. The storm had driven them off their course. They had lighted on the sound and gone ashore to get more gasoline. It was humiliating, after they had scared us into throwing away 100 cases of whisky, to see how incurious they were concerning the *Marshall* and her crew.

The gale continued all that day and the following night. We lay at anchor and took things easy, paying only the scantiest attention when the cutter passed. It was still blowing hard the next morning when Hain boarded us and told us our presence was causing comment and we would have to leave.

"I thought," I said, "you had protection."

"I had," he snapped. "For two nights, not for a ninety-nine-year lease. Get out of here, you damned rum-runner."

So we got out. Seas were breaking like big green walls over the bar, but the *Marshall*, with sail set and engine going full blast, jammed her way through them, shook the water off her back, and slanted, rail under, for Nassau.

Old postcard aerial view of Nassau in the 1920s, looking west to east. The island on the left is Hog Island, since renamed "Paradise Island."

The Bimini Bay Rod and Gun Club, circa. 1922. The three-story, 100-room hotel was destroyed by a hurricane in 1926. (*Courtesy Keyport Historical Society, Keyport, N.J.*)

CHAPTER II

I BANKED $15,000 AT NASSAU, which was not bad pay for about a week's work. My crew swaggered away into Grantstown, taking days to accomplish what Billy Hain had done for them in a single hour. I rambled about the town, hunting shore quarters, and eventually rented the upper floor of the dwelling belonging to Mrs. Kemp. The house was of stone, cool and spotless. It overlooked the town, and from my window, or the balcony outside it, I had a wide view of the incredibly brilliant harbor, of Hog Island with its swaying palms and the brave blue of the Main with great purple cloud shadows marching across it.

Each morning a darkey brought three pails of water to my room, the largest on her woolly head, another in either hand. She would fill my bath and retire. After bathing, I would sit by the window and let the trade wind dry me while my breakfast cooked on my oil stove. Before me lay one of the fairest views in the world. I could watch my schooner, small and clear as the model of a ship, anchored in the harbor. She was mine, and I'd got back three quarters of her purchase price in one short voyage. Life, I decided, was a great invention.

When my crew got over their headaches we watered up and reprovisioned the *Marshall*. Billy Hain's father, a most lovable old scoundrel, arrived by steamer from Florida and chartered the *Marshall* again. A grand walrus was old man Hain, and the most ambidextrous drinker of my acquaintance. I think he used alcohol for fuel.

"Cook," he would shout when aboard my schooner. "Another hocus-pocus," and no sooner had he drained that when he would bawl for another.

Billy Hain followed his parent to Nassau and came overside, in wild haste as usual, waving clearance papers.

"You go to Bimini," he panted, "and we're going with you."

By the time we were ready to sail, one hocus-pocus after another had made old man Hain expansive and valiant. The *Palatino*, Captain Billy Watson's schooner, was getting under way, Bimini bound, also. She was of lighter draft than the *Marshall* and Watson intended to drive her with her engine directly across the Bahama banks to his destination. Our course would be the long way around by the Great Isaacs, but Hain, filled with sporting blood and hocus-pocuses, insisted upon betting one of the *Palatino* crowd that we would beat her to Bimini.

The two ships crossed the bar together. Pilot Brown, before turning the *Marshall* over to me, looked at the sky and shook his head.

"Bill," he warned, "don't carry full mainsail tonight. It's going to blow."

And it did but we didn't take in an inch of canvas all night long. The Bahama conchs, accustomed only to their brittle little sponge schooners, never understood how much a Yankee-built Gloucesterman could stand. There are no better ships in the world than the American fishing schooners. I've proved it.

The wind came up as the sun went down. Old man Hain went down to his cabin and then came up, to hang over the rail like a wet towel and pay penance for his hocus-pocus-infested past. Finally, we carried him to a chair, and he spent the night on deck. We tore up the northwest channel in a whooping half gale, spreading twin furrows of sea fire against the black water and scaring coveys of flying fish who flopped onto the deck and added to old man Hain's misery. But he stuck it out, and he won his bet.

The breeze died away with the dawn. We started our engines and jogged into Bimini. We had been anchored there an hour before the *Palatino* came over the horizon.

The basement of the concrete house of the Bimini Rod and Gun Club was a bonded warehouse packed with American Bourbon and rye. It was from this store that the *Marshall* was to take 1,500 cases North. The liquor was the property of the Vance brothers, for whom the Hains were acting as agents. One brother flew over from Florida to supervise the loading. The other was serving time in Atlanta, an early casualty in the government's war on rum-runners.

Indirectly, the Vances were victims of their own smartness. About a year before, they had bought the liquor entirely legitimately in America, furnishing the government with a certificate that it would be landed on British soil. Their steamer, *Baltimore*, carried it to the Bahamas, but the Vances, on learning they would be obliged to pay $6 a case duty, sheered off, disposed of some of it in the States, and put the rest in bond at Bimini.

Prohibition enforcement agents immediately went into action, quite naturally, though the fashion in which they captured Ralph Vance may be open to question. They took a motorboat to Bimini and lured Ralph aboard it, saying that they wanted to buy liquor and would like him to estimate how much their craft would carry. They then blackjacked and kidnapped him.

On March 12th we began to load "Old Granddad" rye. I have a seaman's dread of sailing on the 13th, so we worked fast. Perhaps if I had stuck more firmly to that superstition, my career would have been smoother and my bank account bigger.

At 11:50 on the night of the 12th, we battened down the hatch, put the rags on her, and went breezing up the warm blue road of the Gulf Stream, Norfolk bound. Off Wilmington, North Carolina, we raised a little fishing schooner. I packed my grip, told Johnson, my mate, to take the *Marshall* to a spot five miles east of Cape Charles lightship and wait me there, and gave the fisherman a case of liquor to land me at Southport.

I took train to Norfolk and there met Billy Hain and his principals, two dark, squat, wise little Wops who were to become leaders in the distributing end of the bootlegging industry. Our liquor, they had learned, was too good and too high priced for Norfolk, and they asked me to take it on to New York. I boarded the *Marshall* off Cape Charles, gave Johnson orders to sail, and on arriving at New York to jog around ten miles southeast of Far Rockaway, and returning to Norfolk, went north by train. Thus the *Marshall* founded Rum Row. She was the first ship to bring New York liquor in large amounts.

When I walked in upon the Italians at the Pennsylvania Hotel, they were holding a lodge of sorrow. They had sold the rye in the *Marshall*, but they had no way of getting it ashore. These were the primitive, unorganized days of early rum running. Prohibition enforcement was still in its early infancy. Most of the bootleggers were getting all the liquor they could handle from government warehouses on forged permits. The idea of bringing in rum from the sea was so novel that no system had been evolved to deal with it, either by the wets or the drys.

I calmed down the Italians, and together we searched for and finally found the man we wanted. His name was Fred. He had two big motorboats, and for $7 a case he guaranteed to land the *Marshall*'s cargo, with full protection.

"Let's go," the Italians babbled, but I wanted my money first. I was learning the first rule of the rum running game which is: "Don't trust anyone." I'd be richer today if I'd learned it more thoroughly. The Italians gave me a draft on their bank. I turned it in for a cashier's check, refusing cash. It's better not to run around with $15,000 in your clothes when you are working with a New York rum mob.

Fred was waiting for us at Tebo's Yacht Basin with two big motor craft. We started down the bay and ran into a northwest storm that drove us back. The following afternoon, the sea was dead calm, and about four o'clock we started again, Fred's two craft and a smaller boat in which I planned to return to shore. I did not intend to ride in on a load of rum, no matter how good the protection was.

The *Marshall* was at her appointed station, jogging about, but as our flotilla bore down on her I saw the blue haze of her engine's exhaust begin to flicker from her side, and she turned away, making sail. Johnson evidently believed that the entire revenue service was attacking him. In the excitement I had forgotten our prearranged signal. When I stood up in the bow, yelled, and waved my black Stetson, the *Marshall* checked her flight, turned, and sailed back toward us.

Dark came down. We drifted four miles off Rockaway, transferring cargo on a sea as level and quiet as a floor. I have never seen the ocean so completely still. One of Fred's boats was of the same height as the *Marshall*'s hull. I picked up a case of "Old Granddad" and balanced it on the two rails. It did not even stir.

Before midnight the *Marshall* was empty. I ordered Johnson to run her twenty-five miles straight out to sea and then take her back to Nassau. I went ashore in my private motorboat, convoying the shipment. Fred was having trouble with the engine of one of his craft and asked me to stand by, and besides, I wanted to see just how good his protection was.

An hour before dawn we drew up alongside a pier in Brooklyn. It was as dark and still as a cemetery until Fred whistled. Then the black shadows seemed to come to life and break apart. Some of them caught the lines and made the boats fast. Others swarmed into the craft and began to pass the cases ashore. At the end of the pier a motor truck coughed and churned.

They had emptied one boat before dawn broke and were about to strip the tarpaulin off the load in the other when a voice hailed us out of the morning mist.

"Hey, Fred," it called, "that's enough for now. Leave the other until tonight. She'll be safe."

The owner of the voice was in blue and brass buttons, and he stood in the pilot house of what Fred said was a police boat. Fred most certainly had protection. I went back to my hotel, and the following day returned to Nassau by way of Florida.

A few weeks before, I had sunk almost my last cent in the *Marshall*. She had cost $20,000. Now, I still had her and $30,000 to boot. I began to wonder whether there would be enough banks in the world to hold the money I was going to make. It was so simple and so safe.

It was, or rather, it had been. From the time my schooner returned to Nassau after her second trip the game grew more strenuous. Trouble doubled and re-doubled. You could say at least one thing for the rum running racket; it never was monotonous. Something always was happening and, usually, it was what you least expected. In time I grew to dread the periods when everything looked rosiest. Experience taught me that it was then something was overdue to blow up right in my face.

I laid the fuse for the first explosion myself. When I got back to Nassau the Italians were awaiting me with a charter to take 1,500 cases of "Blue Grass" Bourbon to Atlantic City. I had business to attend to in Nassau, and I stepped into future trouble way up to my neck. I made Johnson captain of the *Marshall* and appointed a big Down-Easter from Maine mate. They were good men, I thought. And they were, as long as I watched them.

The *Marshall* loaded and sailed with instructions to jog about fifteen miles off Atlantic City until my arrival. The Italians had customers, a Jew and two former olive-oil importers from New York, who were supposed to be ready to take over the cargo at once. When I reached Atlantic City by rail I found the deal had fallen through.

The Jew, a sure-thing specialist, had hired two prohibition agents to protect the cargo. When he introduced them to the olive-oil men, these gentlemen immediately had hysterics and backed out. The thought of branding themselves as bootleggers before representatives of the government was more than they could endure. They went back to New York, wailing as they went, and the Jew did not have enough cash to swing the deal alone.

The Italians thought they had a customer at Charleston and asked me to send the *Marshall* there. That deal also fell through and, at my suggestion, we decided to take the cargo on to New York. My schooner lay off Charleston lightship, and I chartered a tug to take me out to her with the new sailing orders. I loaded the tug with provisions, fresh water, and tobacco, for by then the *Marshall* had been some time at sea.

While we were transferring the stores a dinghy left the lightship and rowed over to my tug, bearing the lightship's captain, who wanted to go ashore. He was a whiskered old man of the sea, and his eyes goggled when he caught sight of a case or so of whisky on the *Marshall*'s deck. At my invitation he poured himself a drink, then several more, so rapidly that they trod on each other's tails going down.

"Cap'n," he said at last, screwing up his sinful old eyes and smacking his lips, "is that stuff for sale?"

I admitted it might be. He came closer and mumbled in my ear.

"I'll buy fifty cases of it off'n ye," he proposed. "Put it on my ship. I can make a pile sellin' it to fishermen."

He was disappointed when I refused. Somehow I didn't believe Uncle Sam would think any more kindly of me for turning one of his lightships into a marine saloon.

The *Marshall* went north again, with orders to wait twenty miles southeast of Montauk Point for two weeks. If I had not appeared by then Johnson was to return to Nassau, discharge the crew, and wait orders there.

I always made it a rule to give each captain of a ship of mine similar instructions every voyage. Many a man did a long stretch in jail for omitting this precaution.

A runner, for example, was arrested in New York. Off the harbor, somewhere, his schooner waited for him and continued to wait, in the absence of any instructions, until water ran low and food gave out. Eventually, to keep from perishing of hunger or thirst, the crew brought the craft into harbor, laying prima facie evidence of the owner's guilt right on the doorstep of the prohibition authorities. Or else, exasperated by endless waiting, the crew would run away with the ship and it would never be heard of again.

When I reached New York, the Italians had sold the *Marshall*'s cargo to a political power in Connecticut. He landed all his pier would hold, but a scant thousand cases filled it up so that it bulged. We handled the remaining cases retail, and they gave us a fine assortment of trouble before we got rid of them.

We were returning to Montauk Point one night with a consignment of 150 cases in two motorboats when a headland just beyond us suddenly was outlined against the blackness and we saw the bright shafts of two searchlights playing upon it. Landing liquor with twin searchlights in the offing comes under the head of neither amusement nor wisdom. We anchored our craft a little way offshore, waded in, and began to scout along the beach.

Beyond the narrow shore the bluffs were perpendicular, and on that strip of sand all the skunks of Long Island—the four-footed variety—were holding convention. There were dozens of them. They smelled like a million. If you want a feeling of absolute helplessness, wander into the heart of a skunk caucus in the dark.

The liquor purchaser said, "Bill—I have a clear right of way except for these skunks. I can bribe a prohibition officer, *but not a skunk.*"

There were too many of them to dodge, and when we threw rocks at them to clear a path, that only made matters worse. Finally, we turned the beach over to them exclusively and waded knee deep to the headland. If we only had had masks we could have landed our liquor through the gas cloud they spread, with absolute safety.

Beyond the headland we found that the searchlights belonged to Merritt Chapman tugs which were hauling a menhaden fishing steamer off a shelving beach on which she had run.

We got rid at last of the remnant of the *Marshall*'s cargo, and the schooner squared away for Nassau. I rode ashore on the last load, which had been bought by the Connecticut politician, discarding my usual practice because I had been assured the protection was perfect. And it was. The rum was guarded by a former Department of Justice man and the chief operative of a big Philadelphia detective agency which specialized in convoying illicit liquor.

The game was growing more strenuous. Individual gunmen and mobs as well were learning that rum-runners were the safest and most profitable people to rob.

We ran into shore openly, on a brilliant summer afternoon. Spic-and-span catboats were slanting and darting around us. Men in flannels were paddling daintily dressed girls about in canoes, and through this bright holiday picture waddled our 65-footer, piled high with cases of rye which were inadequately covered by an old tarpaulin.

That night our politician customer gave a big banquet in celebration of his appointment to the Prohibition Enforcement Bureau. The Italians and I attended.

The next morning the boat and the liquor had vanished. The craft had been anchored, unloaded, with the assurance of the "protection" that it would be quite safe till the next night. But the former Department of Justice man and the agency operative had attended the banquet, and the boat and her crew and cargo had disappeared.

It was none of my business. I had my freight money, but the Italians had been square with me, and they had not been paid, nor would they be, unless they could make delivery. The trouble this liquor load was to cause had just begun.

We hired a sailboat and searched for the missing craft all day long. The boat was owned by a man who looked as though he were half gorilla and who had as his assistant a yellow nigger. They snarled at each other during our entire trip and were still squabbling when they put us ashore at Newport, where we spent the night.

Next day we resumed the search in another, faster boat, but found nothing. We telephoned our politician friend, who told us the liquor craft had not been found but that our gorilla boatman of the day before had returned alone, saying his assistant had fallen overboard and had been drowned. There was talk of an investigation, and the Italians and I lay low for several days. We didn't need any publicity just then.

While we were in hiding we got a telephone from New York announcing that the missing boat had turned up, with cargo intact, at New Rochelle. A gang had gone out to her, the night she lay at Connecticut, and had tried to board her. Without question they were hijackers, and the men we had left with the craft cut her moorings and ran for it. They were safe in New Rochelle now, but the whisky aboard was still brewing trouble. Our politician friend turned it back to the Italians, who sold it to another Italian mob at Bristol, Rhode Island.

When the shipment was landed at Bristol the buyers paid the cash over to my friends, and then, when the liquor had been carted off, held them up and took the money away from them again. Rum running was developing speed and punch.

My own luck still seemed firm and solid. In three months, I had cleared $35,000 net, and the game was just beginning. The forged liquor withdrawal swindle was about at an end. The prohibition enforcement bureau was trying to comb the more flagrant crooks out of its ranks. With domestic sources of whisky drying up, the overseas trade necessarily would become brisker. The rum mobs had money and wanted liquor, but someone had to get it for them. Those supposedly hard-boiled, fearless gunmen and racketeers of New York were even more afraid of salt water than they were of fresh. I saw no reason why in a year or so I shouldn't be a millionaire. There must have been something the matter with my eyesight.

CHAPTER III

ONE OF THE ITALIANS BUMPED INTO ME as I was hurrying through the lobby of the Pennsylvania.

"Whereya off to, Bill?"

"Gangway," I told him. "Nassau bound. My train's leaving."

He grabbed my arm. "Forget it," he said. "There's a million in it if you'll listen."

So I forgot it and let my train go and listened. The longer he talked the better it sounded.

The rum trade, he told me, was just getting under way. What anyone had made out of it so far was chicken feed compared to the gravy that was to come. The Italian mob planned to operate in a big way. As a first step they had just bought 5,000 cases of Hill & Hill at the Kentucky distillery and were shipping it to Nassau.

"You haul for us, Bill," he went on. "Only get yourself a ship that will take it all in one trip. Five thousand cases a load means $50,000 each voyage. How does that sound, guy?"

It sounded better than all right, but I didn't answer right away. I was seeing things. Where the wall of the Pennsylvania lobby ought to be, was Gloucester harbor and a ship coming in like an eager young girl through the long sunset light. I felt like a kid early on Christmas morning.

"I know the schooner I want," I said, "but she may cost more than I've got. You boys may have to give me a lift."

He never batted an eye.

"Go ahead. Write your check and we'll sign it."

The Miami train had gone. I took one to Gloucester instead. I had thought I was lucky before. I had the world by the tail now. Everything was breaking as though I had ordered it that way.

The East Coast Fisheries Company, owners of the *Arethusa*, was in the hands of a receiver, General George W. Goethals & Son, in New York. My beloved schooner herself was laid up at Rockland, Maine. I went on there and looked her over. There was no question now whether I could afford to buy her. I had to have her. She was, I believed—and I still believe—the most beautiful thing of her kind in the world.

She was thoroughbred, every inch of her, the most perfect of all the great sailing craft laid down by those master builders, James & Co. There wasn't an ugly line or a dishonest treenail in her. The lovely turn of her oak hull, the grace of her lofty tapering spars made my throat swell. I hurried back to New York to see the receivers. They could have asked a hundred thousand for her and I would have paid it.

I talked with Colonel Goethals, son of the builder of the Panama Canal. He told me that eventually all property of the bankrupt company would be sold at auction but that I could buy any portion thereof now for one half the appraisal value. My *Arethusa* was appraised at $42,000. I counted out $21,000 in thousand and five-hundred-dollar bills on the Colonel's desk. It cost me $11,000 more to get her ready for sea. I would let nothing but the best go into her.

We brought her down to Gloucester and set to work. The *Mayflower*, proposed defender of the Fisherman's Cup, was outfitting there, but work on her was laid aside to get my ship to sea. We fumigated her from end to end, ripped off her old rigging, made her an entire new suit of sails, restored her beautiful topmasts, added a flying jib to her canvas, and shipped a bowsprit, for till then she had been knockabout rig. We removed her old auxiliary engine, and later I replaced it with a better. In the meantime the space thus saved would take care of an extra thousand cases of whisky, which meant an extra $10,000 per voyage.

I repainted the *Arethusa* a dazzling white, and when, at last, she came off the ways, she rode through the water more like a yacht than a trading craft, but I knew every inch of her was solid and that, laden or light, she could take everything the North Atlantic could give her and come back for more.

All of Gloucester knew what I was outfitting her for. I had made no secret of the fact that she was to go rum running. Everything possible was done to perfect my schooner for sea. Other contracts were laid aside by men like Cooney and Roberts and Masters, craftsmen all, to rush work on the *Arethusa*. One hundred tons of iron ballast, originally intended for the *Mayflower*, went into my ship's hold through the generosity of the *Mayflower*'s skipper, Captain Larkin. Gloucester cheered us when we set out to sea. The

Yankee blood is not as meek or as patient with outrageous legislation as some folk try to make you believe.

There was an amusing aftermath to my Gloucester sojourn, the following fall. Canada had refused to race against the *Mayflower*, terming her, with some justice, a yacht and not a fishing craft. I was in St. Pierre et Miquelon at the time the racing committee met in Gloucester to choose another defender, and I wired them, offering the *Arethusa*.

There was, I have since heard, scandal in the committee room when the telegram was received. It was, some hot-heads insisted, just Bill McCoy's infernal crust. The *Arethusa* was a rum-runner, and that put her out, one man in particular asserted.

"Mebby," one of my friends on the committee remarked "she is and mebby she ain't. You can't prove she is, anyway. I can prove there's several rum-runners, off an' on, in reach of my voice right now."

The subject was dropped like a hot potato.

Captain Albert Gott, a grizzled Down-Easter and a born seaman, was the *Arethusa*'s captain. Her crew were all big, two-fisted men, ideal when there was dangerous work to do, but hell raisers if you let them idle. Gott's sole defect was that he was too easy with his roughnecks. By the time the *Arethusa* reached Nassau there had been one free-for-all on board over the question whether the cook lived up to his title. The cook quit as soon as the anchor chain went on. I read the riot act to the rest of the crew, and peace was restored. Arey, a seaman, signed on as cook. Good sailors were scarce, but jobs as lucrative as those rum running ships offered were scarce, too.

I paid my captains $1,000 per month on voyages they made alone, $500 per month with the privilege of putting $500 more "under the stern"—putting $500 worth of their own liquor aboard—if I accompanied them. My mates got $500 normally, $250 if I were aboard, and $250 additional under the stern. The cook received $150 and could carry $150 worth of his own liquor for sale. Seamen got $100 a month and a bonus of $100 at the end of each trip.

The *Marshall* and the *Arethusa* were in Nassau harbor when I returned. I had determined to get rid of the former. I had the schooner I wanted now, and I had a hunch that sailing her and selling from her was enough of a job for any one man, but the game was just coming into its own. Ships were scarce, and charterers were begging for them. A big Georgian I knew offered me $15,000 for the privilege of sending the *Marshall* north to Atlantic City with a load of rye. I smothered my hunch and turned over the *Marshall* to him, with the understanding that he never was to bring the schooner closer to Jersey than twenty-five miles offshore. I did another thing, so foolish that I deserve most of the later misfortune it caused me. I wrote out specific sailing orders for Captain Johnson and gave them to him. I knew that commandment number two of the successful rum-runner should be "Never put anything in writing," and yet I broke it. I created permanent first-class evidence against myself in my own handwriting.

I placed my new schooner under British registry. We had to change her name, since there was another *Arethusa* on the registry list. We christened her *Tomoka*. Still later she became *Marie Celeste*. I always thought and spoke of her by her original name.

Nassau was beginning to come out of her dream of a prosperous past. She was perking up and appreciating that the future held wealth for her, too. Strangers were arriving by the score each time the Miami boat, the old *Mystery J.*, returned to harbor. There were brisk agents from English and Scotch distilleries that had seen already a new outlet for their liquor. There were sea captains and sailors looking for berths. There were furtively opulent men from the States, gamblers and big shots, with cash to invest, and a scattering of hard-jawed, hard-eyed citizens of no obvious employment on whom the black, gorgeously uniformed police of the colony looked with suspicion and left severely alone.

The first wave of the boom was washing up on Nassau's beaches. Bay Street, usually somnolent, grew active. Liquor dealers enlarged their quarters. Murphy, an American and later my main source of supply, bought a quantity of rye in Baltimore. A United States Shipping Board vessel brought the cargo over and landed it in Nassau. Every case of it thereafter went back to the United States via Rum Row. All Murphy's transactions, however, were entirely within the law. He bought and shipped liquor to Nassau legitimately. He sold it to purchasers equally legally. Where it went thereafter was none of his business.

A big, barrel-chested citizen was Murphy, a one time circus proprietor, and my good friend. If I had listened more carefully to his counsel, I would have kept out of much trouble. He was born in Seneca Falls, New York, and my own family hailed from there. Another Seneca Falls native who later crossed my trail was General Lincoln C. Andrews, director of prohibition.

It was at about this time that the boom rush to Nassau grew so large that a regular seaplane service was started between Miami and the island. Adventurers and businessmen, racketeers and merchants not only came by sea but began to rain down out of the air. The colony was becoming a place of importance once more, and the post of United States Consul stopped being a sinecure and became a job that grew continually more delicate and complicated. Lorin A. Lathrop, a veteran of the service, who had regarded his assignment to Nassau as an easy coast downhill to retirement, discovered to his dismay that it promised to be the most difficult task of his career. As the months marched past, each more violent than its predecessor, he had less and less time to pursue his avocation of novelist.

He was a stocky elderly gentleman with a gray Vandyke beard and quietly humorous eyes. I knew him well. Officially he was my enemy, in private life my friend, but the line of demarcation between those two roles never blurred.

"Bill," he told me more than once, "I don't believe in prohibition, but if my government were to pass a law against hymnbooks I'd uphold it, and every time you send a schooner out of this harbor I'm going to report you to Washington."

And he did. I had the best reason in the world for knowing that. I got a copy of every confidential report he forwarded about me to the State Department. To this day, I don't know who sent them, but they came regularly. I stood in Lathrop's office one day when he was chiding me, half humorously, for my sinful career.

"Save your breath, Consul," I told him. "I know what you think of me." Then I quoted, word for word, a passage from his last communication to Washington. His face was worth watching.

My schooner was in harbor one July 4th. Though she was under British registry, I dressed ship, stringing international code signals on her lines and halyards, but I had no American flag aboard. I marched up to the consulate and asked Lathrop to lend me one.

"Why," he sputtered, "you low-down, nervy rum-runner! You come and ask me, the representative of the government that you're gypping, for a flag? I ought to throw you out of my office."

"If I'm a crook, I'm an American crook, anyway, Consul," I told him. "You won't lend me one?"

"Yes, I will," he snorted. "Certainly I will. Only not officially, Bill."

Stars and Stripes, provided by the United States Consul, flew all that day over my rum running schooner.

If Nassau was waking up to its opportunities, the prohibition authorities at New York and elsewhere were beginning to appreciate the job they had on their hands. The pace of the game was quickening, and its hazards were mounting.

All sorts of rumors were afloat, including one that was forever recurring and frightening rum-runners: the navy was to be used to break up the trade. That kept bobbing up all through my career as a runner and never failed to give us the heebie-jeebies. We knew that if they set the navy on us we were done for.

The revenue cutters were slow. The Department of Justice operatives could not bother me on the sea, and prohibition enforcement agents were few and far between.

Rumors charged me often with bribery. Let me say that never from the time I started in the game until I quit, did I ever give or take a dirty dollar. They pinned enough on me, first and last, but they never even indicted me for bribery, much less made it stick. I played the game clean, according to my lights and, as far as I am concerned, the revenue service, Department of Justice, and prohibition authorities did too. I would have quit before I would have bought "protection," even if it had been offered. Dealings of that sort would have killed the sport of the game for me.

And each month, from now on, rum running became a sportier enterprise. The *Arethusa* loaded 2,000 cases of the Italians' rye and took liquor belonging to the men who had chartered the *Marshall* as the balance of her cargo. Rumors were flying about like mosquitoes when my schooner went north on her first trip. I picked plenty up in Nassau and more when I reached New York by rail. The one about naval intervention was repeated over and over, until I almost believed it myself.

The *Arethusa* hovered off Montauk, and each night we were unloading fast, half expecting cruisers and battleships to sweep down upon us any time. After three nights' steady trade I did not want to press my luck too hard. I ordered the schooner out to sea for several days, with instructions to be at a certain spot off Montauk just before darkness on Wednesday night.

On Tuesday, there was scarcely a breeze, and Wednesday was a day of dead calm. I wasn't so tranquil myself, for my schooner had no power, I had a customer with four boats to be loaded that night and two inquisitive strangers had talked with me on the pier at Fort Pond Bay that morning. They had claimed to be fishermen. I knew they weren't.

Bill McCoy's antagonist by day, friend by night, Lorin Andrews Lathrop was the U.S. Consul in Nassau, Bahamas from 1919 to 1924. He had previously served in Bristol, England from 1882 to 1907, and Cardiff, Wales from 1907 to 1919. Nassau was supposed to be a sleepy posting in which to wind down his long diplomatic career. He was a painter and a fiction writer who wrote under the name Kenyon Gambier—he was born in Gambier, Ohio where his father was a professor at Kenyon College. He also wrote under the name Andrew Loring, a pen name he used to criticize the U.S. government. Lathrop died in Paris, France in 1929. *(Courtesy of Kenyon College, Gambier, OH.)*

Bill McCoy's British-flagged schooner flying the Stars & Stripes.
(Courtesy of The Mariners' Museum, Newport News, VA.)

Arethusa in Nassau, Bahamas, in July 1922.
(Courtesy of The Mariners' Museum, Newport News, VA.)

At dusk, the sea was like glass, but I guided my customer's four boats out toward where I had told the *Arethusa*'s captain to be, on the long chance that she might appear. I had small expectation that she would be there, and when a gray cruiser loomed through the twilight, traveling slowly yet with steam up and smoke pouring from her stacks, I hoped she would not.

"Maybe they've got the navy after you, Bill," my customer said nervously and I thought of the two "fishermen" who had tried to pump me that morning and wondered.

We went pounding along out to sea just the same. All at once I saw my *Arethusa* coming out of the twilight. She had all her canvas set, and she was not drifting. She was sailing in airs that barely cooled a moistened finger held aloft. A ship, a real ship, the *Arethusa*.

In the darkness we saw the warship's blinker working as our boats ran alongside the schooner. My customer grew nervous. He did not want to load, but I sent Captain Gott aloft on the lookout with a pair of powerful night glasses, and we got to work.

Presently, he called down in an uneasy voice.

"Bill, there are blinkers working to seaward."

We loaded the faster. A light east wind was bringing a mist in from the sea. Gott called again a half hour later, still more unhappily.

"Blinkers going to shoreward too."

"They've surrounded us," my customer gasped, but we went on loading. There wasn't anything else to do, and when the last case had been put overside I said:

"You boys stand a better chance if you scatter and take each boat to shore by a different route."

They agreed and slipped away into the black. The clatter of exhausts faded and died. After a little while Gott reported the blinkers had vanished. We had happened to sail into the middle of a squadron working out some night problem. That was all. They weren't at all interested in us, but we certainly were in them. A guilty conscience can do funny things to your mind.

I did not go ashore to Montauk. The "fishermen" were still bothering me. Instead, I had the lad who had brought me out in his motorboat take me to Block Island. The moon came up, and it was a gorgeous sail. I landed late in the evening with a heavy suitcase and six quarts of whisky. A gift of liquor is the best thing in the world to keep people from asking questions, and I thought I might need it.

From the summer hotel, where I registered under another name, I telephoned to the Italians, telling them of my change of base. The next afternoon, from the hotel veranda, I saw a seaplane flop awkwardly into the sea a half mile offshore. The Coast Guard put out their boat and towed her in. I put my glasses on a man who stood in her cockpit and thought I recognized him.

I met him at the dock. It was one of the Italians, and he had evidently nerved himself for the flight by getting excessively drunk. At the hotel desk he weaved back and forth, still in oilskins and sou'wester, and looking, with his dark face and heavy brows, like a pirate.

"What's your name?" he asked with drunken gravity.

"Frank Kent," I told him. He roared with laughter.

"Hell," he guffawed. "I know you. You're Bill McCoy, the well known rum-runner."

He had advertised me thoroughly. I managed to get him upstairs and to bed. Thereafter everyone in the hotel kept watching me and whispering. I felt it was time to move, packed and paid my bill, but the Italian, who had sobered up meanwhile, urged me to stay, saying he had an order for 500 cases that had to be filled.

We walked to the telegraph office together. There was a crowd about the door on which bulletins were pinned. Over their heads I read:

> "New York: *Henry L. Marshall*, McCoy mystery ship, seized off Atlantic City with 1,500 cases of whisky. Government searching for *Arethusa*, rum-runner, seen off Montauk."

We left Block Island after that, but we landed our 500 cases that night. I told Gott to take my schooner to sea for two weeks and then to wait for me twenty miles southeast of Gay Head, off the tiny island called Nomans Land. Then, worried to death, I took a train to New York. I got no additional cheer out of the morning paper which announced that the big Georgian who had chartered the *Marshall*, and Ben and Bill McCoy had been indicted by the grand jury and that the crew of the schooner was in jail, held without bail.

Ben had gone north to Atlantic City to superintend operations of the *Marshall* for me. He never had a chance. The Georgian who chartered her had contracted to sell her load to a political group in New Jersey for $40 a case. When my schooner reached her station off Atlantic City the Georgian had found another dealer who would buy the cargo at $60. He broke his original agreement and, incidentally, ruined himself, for the political group turned him in to the authorities as a rum-runner. Even then, my schooner would have been clear, if Johnson had obeyed my instructions. He and his mate, instead of remaining aboard and keeping the *Marshall* a strict twenty-five miles offshore, went in to Atlantic City, were picked up noisily drunk on the Boardwalk, and my schooner, with no one in authority and all hands drunk on board except Weatherly, the supercargo, a youngster who knew nothing of the sea, drifted about till the *Seneca* towed her in. My written sailing orders in Johnson's cabin implicated me, and the *Marshall*'s double clearance papers made matters worse.

This was the mess I faced when I reached New York. The big Georgian, usually a noisy swaggerer, was stiff with fright. Weatherly, his nephew, a nice lad but with little backbone, turned from his uncle to me for help. Ben was calm. He knew and I knew that, despite the indictment, they had nothing whatever on him. The crew of the *Marshall* were in the Tombs. They had talked too much while drunk. Now they were held as material witnesses—Murphy, Pike, and Frenchy—with the prospect of remaining locked up until the case came to trial, if ever.

Clarence, the Senegambian cook, was the only man set free. He didn't know much at the best of times, but before the district attorney he was one black wilderness of ignorance. He knew the name of the schooner, and that was all. He had no idea what cargo she carried. Where was he when she was being loaded? "In town getting groceries." Who loaded the ship? "Niggers."

"What," the D.A. finally asked him, "do you know, anyway?"

"I know," said Clarence with dignity, "that I shipped as cook on that schooner, and if I didn't have meals on time the captain raised hell."

They turned him loose.

We got a lawyer. His retainer was the first of several hundred thousand dollars members of his profession chiseled out of me, directly or indirectly, in the next few years. A rum-runner in the average attorney's hands has about the chance of a fish in a hot frying pan. The first question they all ask is not, "Are you guilty?" but, "How much have you?" The more you have, the more difficult the case becomes, and the larger, consequently, the fee.

Ben was going to stay and face indictment. The Georgian skipped to Florida, and I sent the imprisoned crew word that if loyalty to me was keeping them quiet, they might as well answer all questions and come on out of jail. I had decided to dodge the law rather than face it. I had too many irons on the fire to remain in New York. The *Arethusa* was waiting for me offshore. If things got too hot for me in America, there were a lot of other places I could go. Nassau was a nice town. I could live there.

Murphy, Pike, and Frenchy eventually came out of jail. The first went to New England and, later, shipped with me again. Pike went to see the big Georgian, who was in Florida and was promised $1,000 to go to Nassau and stay there. He went.

Frenchy followed Pike south and also interviewed the Georgian, who told him to go to Nassau and collect half the $1,000.

Pike said he had received nothing but promises, but the Irishman could not convince Frenchy. The more he talked, the more certain Frenchy grew that Pike was holding out on him.

They fought all over Nassau about that thousand. Finally they shipped on the same rum-runner, and in a resumption of their quarrel, Frenchy shot Pike through the stomach and kicked him overboard.

Weatherly decided to go with me. He was a nice kid, but his fiber wasn't tough enough for the strenuous life of a rum-runner. I think he turned to me because I was calm and confident while his own uncle was so plainly frightened, and besides, there was liquor belonging to the Georgian still unsold on the *Arethusa*.

We went to New London together. I got in touch with my schooner that had been jogging patiently about off Nomans Land, and we sold some more of her cargo to Connecticut purchasers. I enjoyed myself in New London, but Weatherly was increasingly unhappy. The thought that government agents might be after us bothered him all the while. We registered under assumed names, but that did not keep me from being on good terms with everyone in the hotel. Weatherly insisted on acting the part of a fugitive from justice. He must have seen it in a play somewhere. If he appeared in public, it was with his hat pulled down over his eyes and many glances over his shoulder.

I was happy, but I played my hunches. Something woke me early one morning, saying in my ear "Time to get out of here." Fifteen minutes later we were on a launch, heading out across the Sound and, as I learned later, Jim Lynch, a Treasury agent's man was asking at the hotel for me.

From then on for weeks, the *Arethusa*, the government, and I played pussy-wants-a-corner. Lynch and his mate McAdam had been sent out to get me, and they did their best. We've had a lot of laughter, of late years, talking over the details of that chase.

CHAPTER IV

MY BED IN THE NEW LONDON HOTEL was still warm when the Treasury agent's men searched the room, but the launch into which Weatherly and I had jumped was spilling the miles over her stern en route for Gay Head, where a remnant of the Indians of New England still dwell.

Indians are ideal people for a rum-runner to live among. They don't ask questions. They don't talk to strangers. They haven't any particular use for law or the government. Weatherly and I stayed with them several weeks. The *Arethusa* still jogged about Nomans Land, and each night we discharged more cargo, the bulk of it going into New Bedford escorted by Indians or in fishermen's craft. The *Arethusa* was the first rum ship to work off the Massachusetts coast.

Lynch and McAdam had no idea what had become of me and ran in circles trying to pick up my trail, while rumors kept floating in about the "mystery ship" that was hanging offshore. The prohibition authorities turned on the collector of the port of Boston, demanding that a cutter track down the *Arethusa*. The cutter tried but couldn't find her, for my schooner went far out to sea before daybreak and did not creep in again till nightfall.

Then scandal broke. A New Bedford newspaper reporter disguised himself as a fisherman, chartered a boat, and went out one Saturday to find the *Arethusa*. He succeeded where the cutter had failed, boarded her, talked with the crew, bought some liquor, and spread the story of his exploit over an entire page. He certainly laid on the color. My *Arethusa* was a rakish, sinister craft manned by Wild Men of Borneo, according to the newspaper yarn. There was some excuse for the reporter. My crew all were American citizens who hoped sometime to return to their native land. To avoid recognition when their reprehensible past was behind them, they all grew beards of untamed luxuriance and, since the schooner had been out a long time and fresh water was scarce, they rarely washed. They looked like Airedales and smelled like camels.

When I saw that yarn I knew it was time to move again. I could almost hear the outraged squawk it was certain to draw from the authorities. The protests that poured in upon the collector of the port in Boston almost drove him out of his mind. He was compelled to issue a statement, denying the presence of any rum ship off the coast and saying the reporter had probably encountered some Canadian schooner that had sold him a few bottles. But he sent the cutter *Acushnet* after me again. I felt in my bones that it was time to say good-bye to Gay Head.

Weatherly urged me to stay another twenty-four hours. Here, where there were no strangers to peer at him, he was getting back his nerve, and he had arranged to sell 500 cases of his uncle's whisky that night.

That afternoon, while we were in our upstairs room in an Indian's cottage, strangers drove up to the door, thick, husky men whose appearance yelled "detective." I heard them ask our host where we were. They explained quite glibly that they were friends we had invited to go on a fishing trip with us. Our old Indian answered, quite as glibly, that there never had been any such persons as they described on Gay Head. The strangers left. Ten minutes later we did too.

My first thought was for my schooner; Weatherly's, quite naturally, for his hide. He scuttled away in the Indian's old flivver, bound for the east end of Martha's Vineyard, where I promised to pick him up. I chartered the fastest fishing launch in Gay Head, and, because my luck still was in, found the *Arethusa*. I told Captain Gott to make a wide circle out to sea, coming in at the end of three days to a point twenty miles southeast of the Cape Ann whistling buoy. If I didn't show up in a few days thereafter, he was to go back to Nassau.

On my way back to Gay Head I crossed the bows of the cutter *Acushnet*, coming down coast under a full head of steam and looking like a fussy old lady trying to find a runaway child. She ran up along side a little swordfisherman, hailed her, and then foamed away on her course. I drew up under the schooner's lee.

"What did the cutter want?" I bawled to her master. He was a lean New Englander, salt and dry as a split cod, and he spat over the rail before shouting back:

"Wanted to know where Bill McCoy and the *Arethusa* was."

I waited. He spat again.

"Told him I never heard of neither of ye," he roared. "Dinged fool!"

They don't breed squealers among those New England fishermen.

We picked up Weatherly in the launch, ran over to Buzzards Bay, and took the Boston train. We got off at a suburban station and taxied into the city. Three days later I chartered a car and went down to Gloucester.

Two staunch friends met me there.

"We've been readin' about you, Bill," they told me quickly, "and there's men in town lookin' for you. Best take to the water till they leave. There's a boat ready."

Once at sea again in this little motor skiff, I found I could relax. There is nothing that calms my nerves more than a big dose of ocean. Weatherly still fidgeted, but I dozed until, off the Cape Ann buoy, we raised the lovely white shape of the *Arethusa*, waiting with all sail set. I wondered at the spread of canvas until I saw between my schooner and the horizon, three destroyers puttering about on no perceptible mission.

I waved to Gott. He hove to and wrung my hand as I came overside. Above, the wind stirred such tumult in the slatting sails that he had to scream his message.

"Was goin' to leave in another hour. I don't like them warships."

The old ghost of navy interference was walking again. I didn't like them either. Clearly it was time to change scenes for a while.

"Halifax," I ordered. "Wait for me outside the harbor."

I was back in the launch. I saw the *Arethusa* shake her sails as though getting her directions straight. Then she seemed to make up her mind. Her canvas filled, she lurched, spun on her heel and was off, an eager slanting figure against the blue sky.

Going back to Gloucester, we faced the wind. The owner of the launch had his oilskins, but Weatherly and I were in street dress, and the bow kept digging up scoopfuls of spray and flinging them back on us. The engine room was the only protected place. Weatherly squatted to one side. I perched on the engine itself, with a foot either side of the flywheel of a ten horse-power Lathrop and a plank across the cylinder head for a seat, for four solid hours, while water crashed on the decking overhead. I have had more comfortable rides.

Returning to Gloucester was a risk, of course, but the rollers were too heavy for us to go on to Boston in an open boat. Once ashore, I changed all my money into $1,000 bills at the bank and then went to Boston. The following afternoon I took steamer to Yarmouth, Nova Scotia. Weatherly followed by rail. I breathed scarcely at all until my ship cast off, and then, when I had watched the salt water widen between her stern and the pier, I went to my bunk and slept fourteen hours.

On reaching Halifax I sought the harbor. There, offshore, like a patient dog before his master's closed door, waited the *Arethusa*. She had left Cape Ann barely twenty hours before I sailed from Boston. Twin screws and a locomotive had brought me to Halifax. She had only her sails, but she had beat me in.

I looked up Bill Acker, collector of customs, and came clean.

"Collector," I said. "I'm Bill McCoy. I've a rum-runner, Bahama registration, jogging off your harbor. I want to come in for repairs."

A genial, magnetic person is Bill, but blunt and hard as a caulking maul.

"Don't you bring that damned boat in here," he told me. "We're drier than America—a hell of a lot."

"But," I objected, "I'm cleared for Halifax."

"Yeh? I know all about you runners and your 'Halifax clearances.' You get her away from here."

I looked as indignant as possible.

"You mean," I asked, "that though I have a British ship and a British crew"—God forgive me for that one!—"that I can't come into a British port?"

"You can't," he snapped, and then corrected himself. "No, you can come in if you insist, but you'll have one hard time getting out again. I'm telling you for your own good, McCoy. Go away from here and stay away."

That was his last word. Halifax was too strict to have any dealings whatever with a rum-runner. Times changed at Halifax before I left the game. Shiploads of 20,000 cases left for New York in 1924. The racket was too profitable for even Nova Scotia moralists to keep out, but in 1921 no one had yet found out how much money there was to be made in shipping liquor to the United States.

For a moment, when I stepped out of Acker's office into a cold Nova Scotia drizzle, I was whipped. There seemed nothing to do but return the *Arethusa* to Nassau with part of her cargo still unsold. And then a hunch whispered to me. There was St. Pierre, port of the French island, of St. Pierre et Miquelon, four hundred miles east. I squared my shoulders and went to see the French consul, M. Gilbey. He was cordiality itself.

"Ah," said he. "You weesh to go to St. Pierre for repair. But certainly. You are not cleared for there? What does that matter? Go, m'sieu, and ask for Folquet Frères on your arrival. Go on your sheep. I will cable you are coming."

I promised to send him back some absinthe, of which I had a few cases on the *Arethusa*, and shut the door quick before he could kiss me.

Weatherly stayed in Halifax, but I chartered a harbor tug, put a few cases of fresh provisions aboard her, and started out to meet the *Arethusa*. The wind was out of the east and picking up force. You could see by the sky that a gale was brewing. The clumsy tug kept poking her nose deeper and deeper into the seas and heaving them up over herself. Twice the captain wanted to turn back. Each time I boosted his courage by raising the charter price.

The gale was getting into high, and the decks of the tug were all awash. We could see the *Arethusa* plainly enough but she was on the offshore tack under foresail and jumbo, riding like a gull over the gray seas through which we plowed and crashed. We were steaming full speed, and still we couldn't catch her. I yanked the whistle cord until my hand was welted, but the wind swept the sound away, and it was a long time, during which I had to boost the charter price again, before my schooner saw us. She came about and ran down toward us, buoyant and beautiful, her white hull sliding down the seas like a fish, her sails silver against the black of the approaching storm.

She got to windward of us and put over a dory. A yellow-oil-skinned seaman hopped in and rowed in under our lee, and I managed to get the provisions and myself into it. This was no small job, for the tug's deck was thigh deep in breaking waves, and I had to walk the rail from the pilot house back to the lee quarter. I shouted to the tug captain to wait for some liquor I had promised him and Consul Gilbey, jumped down into the dory, and looked for the *Arethusa*.

Gott handled her more as though she were a motor car on asphalt than a schooner in a gale. While we were loading the dory he bore away and ran down under our lee; the wind took the dory over to him. We sent the boat back with a case of absinthe, and two cases of Scotch for the tug crew, and when it had returned we set the riding sail and stood away on our course for St. Pierre.

First, however, we had a little argument. All hands were disappointed not to go to Halifax. One seaman in particular, a Newfoundlander who had joined us as thin as a snipe, had eaten so much he had swelled like a wet sponge. He had been obliged to put a twelve inch "V" in his trousers and was certain something was the matter with him, he was expanding so. He demanded to be put ashore at Halifax so he could consult a doctor. I told him there were doctors at St. Pierre.

The rest of the crew were still dubious. Each minute the wind was screaming higher through our rigging, seas were rolling larger, and storm clouds in the east had turned the sky into one big bruise. Halifax looked good to them.

But I talked about the glories of St. Pierre. I never had been there, but that only made my oration more eloquent. I reminded them it was a French island, and that the French were a gay people, fond of wines and dancing. They all had learned that in school, hadn't they? I spoke of the liquor, the women, the music for which France is famous. I pictured St. Pierre as a mariners' heaven, a Fiddlers Green. By the time I had finished, a hurricane wouldn't have turned them back. If we had decided thereafter to put in to Halifax, I believe most of them would have swum to St. Pierre.

When the crew went forward, Captain Gott pulled me aside.

"Bill," he confided, "those lies of yours sounded fine, but, Bill, how the hell are we going to get there? I was to Miquelon once, but that's years ago, and there isn't a chart on board."

Night and the gale were coming in. The sky was gray, and the sea a foam-streaked black. It was bitter cold. We'd been chased out of American waters. Halifax wouldn't have us. Nassau was far away. We were waifs of the sea, and my heart sank. For a moment, I wished I was out of it all and back in Florida, building boats for chicken feed.

We searched the cabin and found an old school geography. From its map of Canada, we determined the approximate latitude and longitude of St. Pierre et Miquelon and worked out a Mercator's sailing, thanks to Admiral Sims's teachings on the *Saratoga*. Then we put the *Arethusa* on her course.

She went like a thoroughbred in a steeplechase, alternately stabbing the sky and the bottom with her bowsprit as she climbed and slid down the hill-high surges. The gale mounted all the time, and my stomach, affronted by weeks of shore grub, mounted too. For a long time I clung to the lee rail and suffered. It did seem as though I had enough to trouble me without this.

I calmed at last, staggered down into the cabin, and rolled up in the lee bunk. As I lay there, I felt my worries one by one drop away. I was at sea, where I belonged, and on the schooner I loved.

The water mumbling against the *Arethusa*'s side, the keening of the wind in the rigging, creaking of tackle, and the sound of feet on deck were a lullaby. I dozed, roused again and again by the crash of seas on the planking above and drafts of the icy air of the North Atlantic that blew down into the cabin.

Presently old Captain Gott, his face wet, his sou'wester dripping brine, brought me more blankets.

"Going to blow the fillings out of your teeth, Bill," he told me. "Sleep well. We're making everything fast."

The cadence of seas, breaking on the deck above, quickened. The wind screeched louder, but in my bunk the motion was easy and slumber bringing. There were none of the jerks and catches and sickening lurches you have to endure on a rigid steel steamer, but a long, easy swaying. Through the open hatch, I had a framed picture of the man at the wheel, shadowy and rich in the glow of the binnacle lamp. There was a rope about his shoulders; another around his waist. Certainly, there must be dirty weather ahead. I didn't care. A big dose of sea water had wiped away all my worries. A sense of comfort and relief ran through me, lulling and warming, like wine.

They had the *Marshall*. Let that go. They couldn't convict Ben; they couldn't catch me. I had my lovely schooner and enough money to sail her to the South Seas for a year or so, if I wished, until things blew over. I hated to go to sleep and stop appreciating how cozy and happy I was.

I woke as they changed watches on deck. Seas were coming aboard incessantly now, with a steady rush and pounding through which I could hear the feet of the men, clumping, halting to hang on as the water swept past, pounding again.

Louis, a big German-American sailor, was making his way aft to relieve the wheel. Through the wind and the bursting seas I heard him singing as he came: "Feather your nest." He continued to chant it after he had been lashed to his post. I could see his face glistening in the yellow light of the binnacle lamp. One minute, his body would blur against the dull background of water as the *Arethusa*'s stern went down. The next, it would be clearly outlined against the lighter gray of the sky, as her bow fell.

Gott came down to report to me once or twice. The weather was still making, but everything was O.K. He stayed on deck all night. A grand good skipper, old man Gott. Louis still sang "Feather your nest." I dropped off again and woke with a start to hear Gott yell, "Here she comes. Look out!"

I leaned from my berth. By the light of the lamp Louis's face was stiffened into a snarl. His roped body was arched, his hands locked on the wheel. I knew what was coming, one of the great toppling seas that wait for unwary sailors. It broke on our quarter with a great sound. Louis went under, sou'wester and all, but I didn't see him vanish. The companionway was a square conduit, spouting sea into the cabin. A shoulder of the wave hammered upon the skylight, broke through, and the North Atlantic came down and sat on my chest.

I was washed out of my bunk into two feet of water that sloshed about the cabin floor and drained away through the scuppers into the bilge. I found my feet and started up the companionway. Beyond the hatch I saw Louis again, streaming with brine like old Neptune himself, but still holding her on her course. As I reached the deck, he picked up his song where the Atlantic had choked it off: "Feather your nest."

The force of the wind almost overthrew me. The deck was nothing but wet blackness and sound, and glimpses of foam flew past like streaks of luminous paint on the night Gott came aft clinging to the weather rigging and shouted in my ear that both dories had been smashed into chips but that no one had gone overboard and the schooner was unharmed. She was tearing along, sound and proud, logging 14 knots under foresail, jumbo, and jib.

I borrowed dry clothing from Gott and spent the rest of the night in the weather berth. No more seas came aboard. By morning the gale had passed and had been succeeded by a mild southerly breeze, though the rollers were still enormous. I drew down a lungful of the cold salt air. For the first time in weeks I was hungry, and Arey the cook's shout of "Time to mug up" was sweeter than any music. I stood in the reeling galley, wolfing doughnuts, beans, and coffee, and was perfectly happy.

By midnight our geography book reckoning proved itself. We raised St. Pierre and hove to until morning. At daybreak we stood in for the harbor entrance, flying our pilot signal. One already had sighted us and was soon alongside in an oversize dory. He was a whiskery Frenchman, garbed in heavy woollens, high leather hobnailed boots, and a fur cap, and had almost no English.

Tomoka was the name on my schooner's stern, but when the pilot gripped the wheel he stared about him as one recognizes a long absent friend, ran his eyes aloft over our tall masts and said in a tone of delight:

"This sheep *Arethusa*!"

I nodded. He became much excited and banged the palm of one hand with the other fist.

"Ah," he exclaimed. "*Arethusa* good sheep. Capitaine Morrisey. *Arethusa*, *Columbia*, bing, no hurt."

I knew to what he was referring. Captain Clayton Morrisey, while drifting along at a two-knot clip through a fog, had got out of his course and had run the *Arethusa* square into the sheer cliff of Columbia Rock. The schooner had bruised her bows above the water line but had suffered no other hurt.

We sailed into St. Pierre. It looked little like Fiddlers Green from the sea, a bleak village, with a stone scattered beach and little white houses and sides of hills white with drying codfish. The men looked at me reproachfully. They saw no signs of the rum and revelry I had predicted, and the smell of drying fish was powerful.

We anchored off the Governor's house, and the Folquet brothers, apprised of our coming by cable, were the first to greet us. That was the beginning of a friendship that endures to this day. There were more fair-dealing men in the rum running game than you will encounter in business anywhere. Foremost among all of these in honesty and trust I place the Folquet brothers.

Mine was the first rum running ship ever to reach St. Pierre. I opened up the liquor trade from that port. Since then it has brought the inhabitants of that formerly poverty-stricken island millions of dollars. My stay at St. Pierre was a peaceful interlude between trouble in the past and trouble ahead.

Pounding salt water ice from *Arethusa* on a voyage to St. Pierre et Miquelon for Christmas champagne. (*Courtesy of The Mariners' Museum, Newport News, VA.*)

CHAPTER V

I ENJOYED MY SOJOURN AT ST. PIERRE. My crew didn't. Not entirely unjustly, they blamed their disappointment on me. I hadn't lied to them entirely. In the first place, never having visited the town, I couldn't tell when I described its charms whether I was lying or not. In the second place, I had promised them plenty of wine, women, and song. The wine at least was there. Champagne was $1.25 a quart. Song, too, was theirs for the asking. I had pictured for the benefit of my crew a little mid-ocean Paris. I was bound to admit, myself, that St. Pierre did not live up to specifications. It was only a village, whose sole sources of dissipation were a few frostbitten little grogshops with grandiloquent titles like "Café de l'Universe," "Café de Paris." These closed early each evening and were no encouragers of revelry when they were open.

In the years immediately following, thanks to my having pointed out the way to wealth, life in St. Pierre increased in tempo and temperature. It became Nassau's chief rival for the rum trade and, I believe, has outstripped her of late years, but even rum running has been conducted decently and in order at St. Pierre. There never has been any of the violence and boom-town revelry Nassau saw.

I did not go to St. Pierre as a missionary of unrighteousness. My sole purpose was to find a dock in which the *Arethusa* could be refitted and repainted while I sat down and planned my future course. While we were making ready to put my schooner in the slip the whole island made me welcome.

M. Chartier, acting governor of St. Pierre et Miquelon, visited the *Arethusa* and bewailed the fact, after hearing me tell of the possibilities of the rum trade, that French law made it impossible for the inhabitants to export liquor. I told him of Nassau's experience, of the hostility that the first attempt to export rum had awakened and the prosperity that had come to the colony since then. He insisted that he would take the matter up with his government. I had this much share in opening up St. Pierre to the liquor trade.

It was against the law of the island to land any alcoholic beverages there unless they were direct from the mother country. The *Arethusa* still had about 1,500 cases of whisky and assorted liquors aboard. We repaid the hospitality shown us by the acting governor and the merchants of St. Pierre by inviting them and their wives to several dinner parties on my schooner.

Arey, my cook, outdid himself for these affairs, and although our crockery was only agateware, his food was praised and my liquor enjoyed. When each party broke up, I gave out bottles of absinthe as souvenirs to all my guests. No one ever offered the least objection to carrying these ashore, despite the law; which only proves that every human being is out to gyp the government.

There is still one sad spot in my memory of the hospitality St. Pierre showed us. A French family, the Leeties, to whom the Folquet brothers had introduced me, had been my guests on the *Arethusa* and immediately insisted that Captain Gott and I should dine with them in return two nights later. We accepted gladly, but in the turmoil of getting the schooner ready for the slip forgot all about it.

We sat down early that evening in my cabin to a fine meal. We were hungry, and we tucked away fried cod tongues and cheeks, boiled lobsters, home made bread, and a big dried-apple pie. When it was over we leaned back in our chairs, stuffed to the eyes. Gott, in the middle of a sigh of satisfaction, choked and said solemnly: "Oh, my good God!"

"Indigestion?" I asked.

"Indigestion," he gasped. "Bill, we're due to the Leetie's for dinner in just one hour."

"Oh, my good God!" I said.

Gott tried to fasten his belt and couldn't.

"We can't go," he moaned. "I'm a foot over the load line now. Send word we're sick."

"At this time of night?" I retorted. "Why, they'll have dinner all ready for us. We'll have to go."

"I can't," he puffed.

"You'll have to," I retorted. "The only thing for us to do is get ashore and walk about until it's time to show up at the Leeties. That may do some good."

It was night by now, and there were no street lights in St. Pierre. Gott and I climbed out of our dory and started on our shake-down cruise. The town is built on a hillside, and heavy rains had washed most of the dirt off the streets, leaving nothing but water-scoured stones that turned when you stepped on them. I fell down once and Gott three times. It wasn't walking, but a combination of mountain climbing and blind-man's bluff.

We scrambled and stumbled and sweated and swore, and our recent dinner continued to rest just below our ribs like so much lead ballast. At length we paused, brushed each other off as well as we could in the darkness, and marched to the Leeties.

One look at the table was enough. This wasn't to be the quiet family dinner our hostess had invited us to. It was a banquet. We sat while course after course was put in front of us and tried to conceal our lack of appetite with light conversation. Neither of us was in any condition to talk his best, either.

The soup, being liquid, went down. We sparred with the fish and managed to stow a little of it away. When chicken and great mounded dishes of vegetables came in, I saw old man Gott's lips moving silently. His eyes stuck out like a crab's. I think he was praying.

We were licked. I tried to eat chicken. I could chew still, but I couldn't swallow. Gott didn't even try. He only sat there, looking as though an amateur taxidermist had stuffed him. I hoped no one would notice him, but trust a hostess to see whether her guests are eating.

"I am afraid, Capitaine Gott," Mme Leetie said sadly, "that you do not care for our French cooking."

Gott gulped and said with difficulty:

"I am on a diet, madame."

That was too much. I guffawed. Then I explained to our hostess. She laughed too. No one looking at the supercharged Captain Gott could help it. We had another dinner with the Leeties later on and did it more justice.

We had to wait for the high run of tides to get the *Arethusa* on the slip. She was too deep to dock her otherwise. My crew, bored and resentful at the failure of St. Pierre to come up to my specifications, demanded to be paid off. I complied and sent them all back to Gloucester except for Captain Gott, Arey the cook, and a fine seaman, Olsen. I mistook seamanship for honesty and kept him with me. I suffered for it later.

Olsen was part of the plan I had been building in the relaxation and quiet of St. Pierre. It was simple and, it seemed, airtight. I would buy another schooner and, transshipping the *Arethusa*'s cargo, send it back to American waters on her. When this was sold, I would have a total of $60,000.

I inquired of Chartier who, besides being acting governor, was a distillery agent, what the price of Black & White was in Scotland.

"Sixty shillings," he replied, "but you are a friend, M. McCoy. If you wish to go to Scotland and buy, I will send you as my agent. You can then purchase it for forty-five shillings."

That meant, if I took the *Arethusa* across the Atlantic, I could buy 6,000 cases of Black & White for $54,000. It sold at $60 a case, off New York. I would come out of the deal with $360,000, enough for anyone to retire on. Then, away for the South Seas and years of cruising on my *Arethusa*.

Weatherly was in North Sydney, Nova Scotia. Two men to whom I had sold liquor off Newport joined him there and wired me to come over and negotiate for part of the *Arethusa*'s cargo. I prepared to leave on the old packet *Propatria*.

I was about to go over the *Arethusa*'s side when something made me call to Captain Gott.

"Captain," I told him, "don't you open a hatch while I'm away, and don't you leave this harbor till I'm here on deck again."

I met my would-be customers in North Sydney. I forget their names, and most people in the rum running racket did not use their own, anyway, but I do recall that both were professional gamblers and that one of them had an artificial hand. They were genial, but somehow I couldn't close a sale with them, so I dropped negotiations temporarily and went out and bought another schooner, a big black cross between a cargo carrier and a Gloucesterman, the *J.B. Young*. She was in perfect shape and cost me only $5,000, for there was a surplus of such craft in Nova Scotia then: winter was coming on and there was little or no freighting.

I kept my name entirely out of this purchase, buying her through a dummy and having him give a first mortgage on her to my attorney. It proved to have been a wise precaution.

Weatherly and the two gamblers decided to go back to St. Pierre with me. We waited while I made sure the *J.B. Young* had cleared for the French islands. Then, when I tried to buy return tickets on the *Propatria*, I was informed by the agent we would have to have passports and must get them from the American consul.

The last thing I wished to do was notify the United States government that I was in that part of the world. We packed our things, checked out of our hotel, which faced the pier from which the

Propatria sailed, and waited on the steps until she gave her sailing whistle. Then we ran for it and leaped aboard the packet as water was beginning to spread between her side and the pier. The captain of the *Propatria* knew me. He had smuggled some of my absinthe ashore. He made no objection to our passportless condition.

It was a rough passage. A first-class stateroom held six, and they all were filled. I went to bed early and woke to find myself roommate to five French men and women who were being seasick in chorus. I went on deck, crawled into the signal-flag box and slept comfortably all night.

Gott stared at me so strangely when I boarded the *Arethusa* that I asked him what ailed him. By way of reply, he handed me a cablegram from North Sydney, sent shortly after I had landed there. It read:

> "CAPTAIN Gott, Schooner *Tomoka*, St. Pierre:
> Have sold entire cargo. Provision, sail to point twenty miles SE St. Pierre then to point twenty miles SE Skataree. Federal agents after us. Weatherly and I under cover. Deliver cargo to party giving duplicate of this telegram sail for Nassau where will join you. BILL McCOY."

While I stared, Gott told me his story. He did not question the authenticity of the cable when he received it and got ready to obey. Then, all at once, he recalled my parting instructions: He was not to stir from harbor until my return.

Thoroughly bewildered, my captain sought counsel from Spurgeon, cashier of the St. Pierre branch of the Royal Bank of Canada, where I had deposited part of my funds. Spurgeon at once smelled fraud and wired to me in North Sydney as follows:

> "McCOY, North Sydney. Take receipt I gave you to Royal Bank of Canada and have them cable me, our code, copy your receipt. Have orders for *Arethusa* supposedly from you but doubt authenticity."

I never got that message. It was due to Gott's and Spurgeon's caution that I did not lose my ship and cargo. If my captain had obeyed that fake order, the *Arethusa* undoubtedly would have been pirated.

Who did it? I have always believed that my gambling friends from Newport were responsible. They denied any knowledge of the matter when I accused them, and left St. Pierre hastily after I told them what would happen if they did not catch the next ship back to Canada. Undoubtedly, through pretending friendship for Weatherly, they had got what information they required and had lured me to North Sydney so that they could steal my schooner's cargo.

I might have seen this narrow escape as forerunner of another streak of misfortune, but I still was full of the Scotch from Scotland plan. I shipped a crew on the *J.B. Young* and made Olsen her master. Then both the *Arethusa* and the *J.B. Young* ran three miles out to sea, so as not to offend St. Pierre law, and we transshipped the *Arethusa*'s cargo to my new schooner.

I ordered Olsen to take the *Young* to my old station off Nomans Land and wait for me there. Gott was to outfit the *Arethusa* at St. Pierre for the voyage to Scotland and wait for me while Weatherly and I made a quick run to the States. We returned to America by rail from Nova Scotia and into neck-deep trouble, all of it due to Olsen.

The first thing he did was to run the *Young* too close to Nomans Land by daylight. The cutter *Acushnet* chased him away.

Meanwhile, in New Bedford, I sold the *Young*'s cargo, both the Georgian's and the Italians' share, to a little Jew, one Schwartz. I wired the Italians that I had at last disposed of their shipment, and they sent to protect its landing the same detective agency operative who had guarded the liquor we sold the Connecticut prohibition official, some weeks earlier.

Schwartz, bearing a note to Olsen from me and protected by the agency man, sent his boats to Noman's Land to get the cargo. The *Young* was not there.

The little Jew returned to New Bedford, came into the room where Weatherly and I were sitting, and exploded like a bomb. He waved a blue 38-caliber revolver in all directions—I don't believe he ever had handled one before—and announced some forty times in one minute that he was going to get his whisky or our life blood. I held my breath. He was doing so many Indian club stunts with that cocked revolver that I expected it to go off.

Weatherly, who went all to pieces under the pressure of worry, was calm now and deadly quiet. He sat slumped back in his chair, black eyes narrow, one hand deep in the side pocket of his coat. I knew he had Schwartz covered. I knew he would shoot to kill, too, and that disturbed me almost as much as the way the Jew was juggling his own pistol.

The Italians' man, the agency operative, who had always posed as a hard guy whom no one could take, wilted under that flourished revolver. He cowered in a corner and kept begging Schwartz to listen to reason.

But the little man, a former pants presser who had hoped to invest all his savings in a cargo of whisky, would not listen to anything until he had talked himself hoarse. He had not paid for the liquor; but he had gone to big expense to charter and equip several boats to take the cargo off. And now he believed we had gypped him.

Presently he ran out of wind and words, slammed a chair against the door, and sat down facing us. I talked and calmed him down. He put his gun away, not in a side pocket, but in the breast pocket of his jacket, butt down, so that the muzzle stuck up like a fountain-pen cap and threatened at any moment to blow his own nose off. At length, he permitted the agency man to telephone the Italians. One of them came up the next morning and smoothed matters over.

Schwartz, by the way, died as a result of his next whisky venture. He chartered a Gloucester schooner, the *Natalie Nelson*, and sent her to the Azores for a load of rye. His love of a bargain caused his death. He hired the cheapest kind of crew and captain. They ran the schooner onto the St. Pierre rocks during a fog, and ship and cargo were a total loss. The shock killed Schwartz.

We searched for the *J.B. Young* off Nomans Land and could not find her. After two days we returned to New Bedford. The agency man called up the Italians in New York, and I was in the room at the time. The replies that someone was making to the detective's report seemed to me suspiciously loud and clear for a New York call. I clapped my hand over the mouthpiece and told him the wire was tapped. He hung up as though the receiver were red hot. I ran downstairs and talked to the switchboard girl. She told me one of her wires had been acting queerly all day and furthermore confided that two strangers had been in only a little while earlier and had asked the number of our room.

Five minutes later we had left the hotel. The agency man went back to New York, and Weatherly and I hired a car to take us to Boston. We motored to the South Station, disembarked, walked through the station, took a taxi at its other side, left it a few blocks from the hotel we had selected, walked to the hotel and spent several days there. I was certain that we had shaken off pursuit for a time, at least. Weatherly, however, was all gone to pieces nervously again. He would sit for hours, hunched up, silent and sick looking, and would only say when I tried to pull him out of it:

"I'm homesick, Bill. I want to go home. And I can't."

He had been raised in a little North Carolina town. He knew that his newspaper notoriety had spoiled his home for him forever. He was a nice lad, Weatherly, but he wasn't built of the sort of material that could stand the game.

While in Boston, I heard from the *J.B. Young* through a friend in Gloucester. Olsen had got word to him that she was waiting for me off Cape Ann. I hurried to Gloucester, chartered a schooner, and went out at once to find her. The Swede had her jogging about twenty miles off the coast. I ordered him to go down the coast and wait for me twenty miles off Long Branch. I had begun to wonder whether this tail end of the *Arethusa*'s first cargo were jinxed and I should be forced to go carting it up and down the Atlantic seaboard for the rest of my life. After death, too, my ghost might keep right on, a new variety of *Flying Dutchman* to warn sinners into obedience to the law of Volstead.

We went to New York. I wanted to get that hellish liquor off my hands and start my trip to Scotland. The Italians had sold their part of the load and chartered a former steam yacht, now masquerading as a tug, the *John Gully*, to land it. There are at least several hundredweight of papers concerning the *John Gully* in the hands of the federal authorities. She was a bad old tub.

We went to sea one bright October morning and soon picked up my schooner jogging about at her appointed station. The Swede had obeyed orders for once. I thought perhaps the jinx had broken. I suggested to the *Gully*'s captain that if he would pick up a tow it would serve as a good disguise for us when we returned, liquor laden, to New York. He agreed and hailed a four-masted barkentine, deep with lumber. They were some time making an agreement. The skipper of the barkentine didn't believe any tug master in his right mind would haul a heavy ship from off Long Branch to the Statue of Liberty for the price we suggested, but finally he agreed.

Our captain told him he would be right along as soon as he had given water to "that little fishing schooner on the horizon." We steamed over to the *J.B. Young* and were soon alongside, but did not dare make fast, for a heavy swell was running. It was short work, however, with the schooner's dories and the lifeboat from the *Gully* in action, to transfer 600 cases. We ran back, picked up the barkentine, and towed her into the harbor right under the nose of a revenue cutter. After dropping her we proceeded to the dock at Tarr's shipyard and stored the liquor in a small warehouse.

I went back to the rooms Weatherly and I had on upper Broadway, feeling that at last half my trouble was over. All I had to do now was dispose of the Georgian's whisky, and everything would be jake again. Weatherly was drunk. He had been that way every day for a week now. He was killing a quart of whisky each evening. He said he couldn't sleep without it. His nerve had run out.

"All right, Mac," he would say when I tried to hearten him. "You mean all right, but you don't understand. You're a freelance. Your father and mother aren't living. My home town is so small everybody knows about me and I can never go home again. I'm homesick, Mac."

Later, when I went to Montreal, Weatherly and I parted. He went south and eventually drifted into Nassau. I saw him on Bay Street during the boom. He looked like a lost dog, but when I offered him a lift he shook his head.

"No, Mac," he told me. "Everything's going to be all right, thanks."

I think I was the last person to speak to him, for a half hour later he went to his room in the Victoria Hotel and shot himself through the head.

That was the second death for which the *Marshall* seizure was responsible.

The day the *Gully* brought the liquor ashore, Weatherly drank himself to sleep early. I did not go to bed. I was jumpy, and along toward midnight I went out and bought an early edition of the *American*. When I opened it, something kicked me in the stomach. On the first page was a story about the seizure of the *Gully*. We had left a case or so for her crew. One of them had got talkative drunk and blown the works to the police.

I was reading when one of the Italians who owned the whisky came in.

"I don't feel right, Bill," he complained. "I thought I'd drop in and talk to you."

"You're going to feel a heap worse," I promised him, handing over the paper. He read it and turned green.

"Well," he said, dropping the sheet on the floor, "all that trouble for that liquor, and now it's gone."

"Listen," I said. "We don't know that. Cops work slow; maybe we can beat them to it."

He perked up a little when I told him my plan. We hailed a taxi and broke the speed law from West One Hundred and Eighteenth Street to the home in Brooklyn of our friend Fred, the boatman. He listened to our story and rushed for his boat, while the Italian and I headed for Tarr's shipyard. At the gates the watchman told us no one had been there. We entered, ordered him to lock the doors and open for no one without a search warrant.

The liquor was where we'd left it. Fred came roaring up to the end of the pier in his boat. We and his gang worked like firemen in a burning building, breaking out those cases, got them all aboard his craft, and jumped in after them. A half hour after we left, my old shadows McAdam and Lynch were searching the warehouse and swearing.

We landed the liquor before daylight at another shipyard where Fred was certain it would be safe. We were dead tired, and I went to a hotel and knocked off for a few hours. When I woke Fred had his boat ready, and we ran out to sea to find the *Young*. She had disappeared. I hoped that the Swede had taken her away, but something kept me from believing it. Next morning I learned that she had come into port and surrendered to the prohibition authorities.

Olsen, whom I had trusted, had sold the liquor remaining aboard my schooner to a crowd in Jersey, taken the money, and blown, leaving a dumb French crew in charge. None of them really was certain where they were, or how to get back home. They sailed the *Young* into New York harbor and told their troubles to the first prohibition agent who came aboard.

My schooner was held, and I was indicted all over again. Indictments can't bother you if the government doesn't catch you. I hopped a train for Montreal. All my plans were shot to pieces. My schooner and half the liquor she carried were gone, and Lynch and McAdam and the rest of them now had two reasons instead of one for catching me. The trip to Scotland was out of the question. From Montreal I wired Gott to sail the *Arethusa* back to Nassau and took a steamer there myself.

Even now, the jinx hadn't finished with me. During the voyage South, a case of diphtheria developed on the steamer, and the passengers due to land at Nassau, including Bill McCoy, were dumped on the quarantine island outside the harbor and kept there for ten days.

The Italians had hired a lawyer for me. He got the *J.B. Young* out of the federal clutches. It had cost me $5,000 to buy her, and I paid $20,000 to get her back. My attorney, I heard it whispered afterward, had to split his fee with one of the powers in Washington under Harding. I didn't believe it when I heard it, and the more I learned of lawyers, the less credible it sounded. That gag of bribing a government official grew whiskers before I left the rum running game. Every runner's lawyer told him that yarn and then collected a double fee.

The *Arethusa* sailed into Nassau while I still was marooned on the quarantine island. I saw her go by, gull-winged and graceful. She pulled me up out of depression. I'd taken some tough ones on the chin, but the future was still there. I was a new man when I stepped ashore at last in Nassau. And, believe me, she was a new town too.

Loading scotch at Hamilton, Bermuda, 1923.
(Courtesy of The Mariners' Museum, Newport News, VA.)

Loading with Canadian Club in Hamilton, Bermuda. According to Bill McCoy, American tastes at the time preferred bourbon and American rye. *(Courtesy of The Mariners' Museum, Newport News, VA.)*

Deck loading in Nassau, Bahamas.
(Courtesy of The Mariners' Museum, Newport News, VA.)

Loading *Arethusa* at Nassau, Bahamas, 1923.
(Courtesy of The Mariners' Museum, Newport News, VA.)

Down the hatch. Loading *Arethusa* at Nassau.
(Courtesy of The Mariners' Museum, Newport News, VA.)

Arethusa could hold upwards of 5,000 cases of liquor.
(Courtesy of The Mariners' Museum, Newport News, VA.)

Loading gin in Nassau, Bahamas.
(Courtesy of The Mariners' Museum, Newport News, VA.)

The "hams" containing six bottles, stowed better and were easier to handle on Rum Row. They also sank quicker than wooden crates in the case they had to be jettisoned.
(Courtesy of The Mariners' Museum, Newport News, VA.)

CHAPTER VI

NASSAU, IN THE FALL OF 1921, was well launched on her third and most prosperous era of activity. Pirate ships had lain in her waters, and buccaneers had squandered handfuls of doubloons ashore. Blockade runners had swaggered along her streets and had taken their swift steamers out of her harbor to return with wealth, if they returned at all, and an itch to spend it.

Now the town awoke to find herself involuntary hostess to a new group of wild ones, combinations of pirate and blockade runner with a few entirely individual traits of violence thrown in for good measure—the rum gang.

The call of big money had summoned them as the pibroch gathers the clan. Nassau suffered a variety of the stampede that always follows a gold strike, the opening of new diamond mines, the discovery of a fresh oil field. The big money clan rushed in upon her. Adventurers, businessmen, soldiers, including a renegade officer or so, sailors, loafers, and at least one minister, they sought to make their fortunes by keeping America wet.

These argonauts differed from kindred groups who had followed the call of big money in other quarters of the globe. In their ranks, it is true, there were many of the genuine adventurer type, but in general they were a harder, tougher, more entirely unscrupulous crowd. Other rushes drew their recruits from the open-air breed. Nassau's invasion was composed of city men, New York City men, for the most part. Big shots of the underworld with their escorts of gunmen and racketeers left their haunts in Manhattan and Brooklyn and moved to the Bahamas. The Nassau gang was largely made up of gangsters who knew gang procedure. They were not toughened and made reckless by what the boom compelled them to endure. They were more than adequately tough already. Big Eddie, Big Harry, Squinty, and Lefty, and the rest of them, poured in with their retinues of gorillas and for some vivid months proceeded to take Nassau apart and remould it closer to their hearts' desire.

Bay Street, the waterfront chief thoroughfare of the town, no longer was a sun-drenched idle avenue where traffic in sponges and sisal progressed torpidly. It was filled with slit-eyed, hunch-shouldered strangers, with the bluster of Manhattan in their voices and a wary truculence of manner. The faces that passed your shoulder in ten minutes on Bay Street would have given a New York cop nightmares for a week. Their owners, for the first few weeks, made existence a continual horror for the black constabulary of Nassau.

Nothing like these hard guys had ever crossed the trail of the gorgeously uniformed, pompous coons of the Bahama police force. The invaders had no reverence whatever for red and blue coats and pipeclayed sun helmets. These merely constituted excellent targets for fists or missiles.

To save themselves from ignoble extinction, the police finally reached a tacit agreement with the gangmen; a live-and-let-live policy. All fights, felonious assaults, breaches of the peace, mayhems, and disorderly conducts within the uproarious family circle of the mob itself were to be the mob's own private affair. No notice was taken of them unless some legitimate citizen of the colony was involved. If one were, no great amount of attention was paid anyway.

This truce endured while the gangs stayed. Repercussions of their revelry and business dealings disturbed the nerves of Bahamians, but they suffered, generally in silence. Part of their patience was due to helplessness; part to the prosperity that rolled in upon the island in the wake of the gangsters. The strangers had come to buy and ship whisky, and every case that left Nassau put $6 into the colony's treasury. Each time my *Arethusa* took 5,000 cases of Scotch to the Row, I left $30,000 in the hands of the customs authorities, and I was only one of innumerable shippers. Despite the outrages committed on the peace and dignity of His Britannic Majesty's loyal city of Nassau, protests from the sufferers were few. Nassauvian bankrolls were getting too fat for their owners to kick, no matter what the gangs did.

There were, of course, complaints now and then. One of Nassau's churches was adjacent to the Lucerne Hotel, hangout for all the gang leaders on the island. The police authorities were informed practically every Sunday by leaders of the congregation that it was impossible to worship in a satisfactory fashion when one could not hear what the minister was saying. One could not hear because next door, the big shots, the mugs and gorillas and gunmen at the Lucerne, were continuing Saturday night's drunk through the bright Sabbath morning. Whoops and yawps, singing that was not even remotely hymnlike, brawls, and now and then a general combat with much shattering of furniture, discommoded the worshippers in the adjacent church.

Every Sunday they told the constabulary all about it. Every Sunday the constabulary promised to investigate and did nothing more.

The Lucerne was a rambling frame hotel bowered in palm trees. Before the advent of the bootleggers, it had been a prim, quiet hostelry, precisely run by an elderly New England woman and her daughter. The chief justice of the colony and other folk of great respectability lived there. Most of these departed by one door when the bootleggers entered by the other, and sought more refined quarters. But the chief justice stayed on. No one ever understood why. For a servant of the law, it must have been a hideous existence. Nowhere, outside of a boiler factory, was there a less quiet building than the Lucerne during the gang's heyday.

The little old lady who ran it was the sole person in Nassau with any control over her guests. She was gray haired and withered, with mild blue eyes behind gold-rimmed spectacles. Her background should have been a garden in some quiet Massachusetts village. She belonged among hollyhocks behind a white picket fence. She had as patrons a riotous horde of veteran drinkers and lawbreakers, crooks from Hell's Kitchen and bigger shots from the white light district. They were forever scheming against each other, fighting for liquor, plotting for ships; individuals and groups tricking and battling. Murderers and thieves, hijackers and thugs swarmed in her lobby, jammed her bar.

Any man in the world who had tried to run the Lucerne would have seen his hotel pulled apart and thrown away and probably would have shared its fate. The little old lady went calmly on, beaming shortsightedly at men whose records would have made a jail warden shudder, gently chiding killers, correcting the manners of bad actors no male would dare cross. And that swarm of scoundrels loved her. They all called her "Mother." She insisted that, though maybe they were just the least bit wild, they were all good boys at heart.

I have seen a fight break out in her barroom. The gangs were always as explosive as gunpowder, and a spark would set them off. There would be a name uttered, or a blow, and in a minute the room would be boiling with battle. Tommy, the cockney bartender, would dive behind the dented mahogany barrier. Peace-loving citizens would flee into the night. "Mother," hearing the racket, would sigh, shake her head, and rush downstairs. Not much more than five feet high and weighing a scant hundred pounds, she would wade serenely into that welter of furious men, and at sight of the little black-clad figure and the sound of her dry New England voice the war would die away.

"Now, boys," I've often heard her say, "if you aren't going to behave yourselves you'll have to get out of my barroom. Right away, understand. I'm going to shut it for the night now. If you can't behave yourselves you can't have anything more to drink here. Everyone will have to leave. Tommy's going to close up."

And they would obey her. "Yes, Mother," they would mutter. "I didn't mean to, Mother. I'm sorry, Mother." Big tough men would grin sheepishly and ramble off without any argument. She was usually indulgent, but firm when matters passed a certain point, and they obeyed her like children.

Fire dances were one of the gangs' chief recreations, a pastime with no inhibitions that traced back directly to the African jungles from which so many of the Bahamian's forefathers hailed. The component parts of a fire dance were a score of Negro wenches, a drum fashioned from a keg by stretching a bladder over one end, a fire, and illimitable gin. Put these all together and they spell, after the fire and gin have melted away restraint, as barbaric an orgy as the stars ever looked upon.

Usually these revels were held in a clearing in the brush not far from Grantstown. Some bright spirit among the gang, one evening when Mother was absent temporarily from her hotel, suggested that a fire dance be staged in the Lucerne's yard, among the palms. It was well under way when the old lady returned, to find a bonfire blazing; a drum throbbing wickedly; dark, wholly nude bacchantes circling madly in the red uncertain light, and a ring of frenzied white men yelling and patting juba. It was not a scene that the entire police force of Nassau would have dared disturb, but the old lady broke through the ring of lustful men and confronted them. The drums stopped, the clapping died away, the wenches scuttled for their discarded clothing.

"Boys," the proprietress of the Lucerne said, "I didn't think you'd do anything like this. Would you want your own mothers to see you this way?"

That ended the dance. "Mother" was the only person I ever met who might have been able to suppress the rum running racket.

Her patrons were mild and obedient with her, but they spent their days and nights gypping and fighting each other and initiating square dealing and simple merchants of Nassau into all the intricacies of the double cross. Until their advent, the liquor dealers of the colony were willing to trust their customers, presuming that they were honest, too. It had been common practice to buy rum "on the cuff."

A schooner owner could purchase all the liquor he needed to load his craft for $5 a case. He would then take it north and sell it and, returning, pay the merchant who had trusted him, the Nassau price, plus the original $5 a case for the risk involved. One man in particular, Christie, a native of Nassau and a square shooter, had carried on a profitable business that way for a year, with no more security than his customers' word.

Such a soft spot was too easy to exist long. A gang member chartered a steamer and loaded it with 17,000 cases supplied by Christie in the usual "on the cuff" fashion. He paid $5 a case, went north with the shipment, and never returned. Christie naturally was ruined and died shortly afterward. Thereafter, liquor dealers abandoned their earlier trustful system and sold for cash only.

The gangs were past masters in the arts of crookedness. They knew all forms of cheating, bilking, and skulduggery. They were developing hijacking into a science and they were experts in strong-arm work. But of one matter, and a most important, they were ignorant. Seamanship was a closed book to them. Most of them did not know one end of a boat from the other. They could obtain plenty of liquor in Nassau. They could provide for absolute protection, once it was landed in New York, but on their stampede to the Bahamas they had overlooked the fact that an island is completely surrounded by water and that they couldn't ship their plunder by truck.

No one in the world, however, thinks he knows more than a New York wise guy. If certain Bahamians suffered through the mobs' crooked work, other natives revenged the victims by selling the ostentatiously canny gang members some of the most astonishing tubs in which anyone ever dared sail. And these wise men of Gotham took them to sea with the cheerful confidence of ignorance.

Big Eddie and Squinty were among the first to get stuck. Someone sold them a sharpie, a little flat-bottomed sailing craft. They loaded her with more liquor than a ship twice her size should have tried to carry and set sail from Nassau, expecting to make their way New York by the grace of God.

The sharpie cleared the bar, and at the first swell the trade winds sent against her, opened up like a water lily. Every seam was sprung, her bottom fell out, and Eddie's and Squinty's liquor went to Davy Jones, while they and their subordinates scrambled into a dory and made their way back to Nassau.

Shortly thereafter the biggest of the big shots on the island fell for a steel schooner yacht that was well into her second childhood. He bought her for no more than three times her value, loaded her deep, and with an assorted group of crooks on board, sent her north.

Off Hatteras, the schooner hit one of the storms that ranges that locality, and her crew, terrified, ran her into the lee of Bodie Island and cast anchor. Even there the swells were bad, everyone was seasick, and when a particularly big roller plunged her bow under and swept her deck, someone in panic cut the hawser.

Out to sea they were blown, traveling sidewise and threatening to roll over any moment, until someone with a little salt-water experience contrived a drag and put it out over her stern. For an hour or so that worked, and then a big wave climbed on her, smashed her overhang, tore away the drag, and crashed into her cockpit, breaking the bulkhead beyond and crushing cases of liquor.

The wise guys from New York huddled in the cockpit, which was knee deep in a cocktail composed of equal parts of champagne, Scotch and sea water, and gave themselves up for lost. So they would have been, too, if an oil tanker had not hove into view. She spread oil to windward of the crippled craft and ranged alongside her, smashing in the schooner's bow in the process, damaging her stern further as well, and scaring the half-drowned gangsters additionally, if that were possible. All of them were rescued, just before their craft breathed out its last wheeze and went down. The tanker's skipper raved when he learned what cargo the schooner had carried:

"A nice bunch of rats you are! I save your bloody lives, and you don't even bring a bottle aboard for me. To hell with you."

I was on excellent terms with Nassau's imported gangdom, but our acquaintance was only social and never too intimate. I liked my excitement more diluted and less erratic. They were quick with their blackjacks and, on occasion, with their guns, and since they were consuming personally almost as much liquor as they shipped, you never could tell when some innocent bystander would get hit by mistake.

Lefty, a crook physically, mentally, and morally, had been gypped by one of his erstwhile friends and determined to get even. He was an artist with the blackjack, and choosing this as his weapon of assault, he slipped into the bar of the Lucerne one evening, venomously drunk, marked a big man lounging against the bar and smacked him down. When Lefty smacked them, they stayed smacked. This particular man went to the hospital for months with a crushed-in skull. Unfortunately for him, he was not the man Lefty had been looking for at all, but the pilot of the Nassau-Miami plane, a pleasant, inoffensive citizen. Lefty was quite regretful but explained that it was just a case of mistaken identity.

Fights of no discernible ancestry to the uninitiated frequently raged on Bay Street. They were private combats, and the Nassauvians walked wide around them and let them roar their course. Usually they were conducted with fist and blackjack though guns occasionally were drawn.

I saw Big Harry and another rum-runner, both drunk, collide one day, draw off reeling, and begin to pump lead at each other from automatics. Each fired an entire clip and, thanks to the alcohol inside them, neither was hurt. Later, I found them standing shoulder to shoulder in the Lucerne bar, buying each other drinks, and the best little pals in all the world.

Another bootlegger, a tough little Jew, staged the first air battle ever held over the Spanish Main, and I was partly responsible for it.

He came tearing into my rooms at Mrs. Kemp's one day, raging and sputtering. He had hired one Sudsey Finnegan, a Bostonian and a schooner owner, to take a load of liquor north and had seen Sudsey clear the bar two hours before. Now he had been tipped off that Finnegan was double-crossing him, had contracted to deliver the load to clients of his own, and never intended to return to Nassau.

"My lovely rye," he almost wept. "And that low-life pirating it. What'll I do, Bill?"

"I know," I told him, "what I'd do. I'd go after Sudsey. I'd take a fast boat and a rifle, and I'd overhaul him and make him come back and land my whisky."

"I'll do it," he exclaimed, and left, but he didn't take a boat, he chartered a plane. They roared out over the Main and circled Finnegan's schooner until the Jew managed to drop a message aboard her demanding that Sudsey put about and return to Nassau. Finnegan read it and wiggled his fingers at his nose. The Jew rested his Winchester on the edge of the cockpit and whaled away. I don't believe he ever nicked the schooner, but Finnegan and his crew shot back, and after a bullet had cracked close to the aviator's head he swung his plane wide and, despite his passenger's bereaved screams, went back to Nassau. The Jew never saw his liquor or Finnegan again.

Mike Calahan sold a load of whisky to Big Eddie and Harry, two of the big shots of the rum mob. Business ethics among the gangsters had become so scrambled by this time that it was impossible to determine who really was guilty in any controversy.

Calahan, at any rate, came to my rooms one evening, tense and apprehensive, with a .38 on his hip, and told me that he had just learned that the liquor had been bad and that Eddy and Harry were gunning for him. I calmed him down, persuaded him to leave his revolver in my desk and went with him over to the Lucerne Hotel. Neither Eddie nor Harry was there, and we went upstairs to Calahan's room, which was directly across the hall from the suite occupied by His Britannic Majesty's chief justice in the Bahamas.

While we were talking, Calahan's door was kicked open. Harry stood there, drunk. Liquor never made him boisterous. The more he took the more quietly dangerous he became. Now his face was wicked and his voice softly threatening. He held a Luger automatic in either hand by the muzzle.

"Now, you so-and-so-forth," he said. "I gotcha. Take one of these, you thus-and-such, and we'll shoot it out."

He meant it. Calahan had jumped up when the door opened. Now he backed up against the wall, his eyes on the guns, but he made no movement to take one. He didn't stir while Harry, lifting his voice, proclaimed to the entire hotel what sort of a rat he believed Calahan to be. The chief justice, across the hail, opened his door and peered out. He certainly heard an oration.

Harry was working himself up into a frenzy. He spun one of the Lugers in his hand and fired. The bullet smacked into the floor between Calahan's feet, and the clap of the explosion nearly deafened me. Like its echo came the slam of the door across the hall, and thereafter the sound of furniture being frantically thrust against it as the chief justice of the Bahamas barricaded himself in.

Calahan was weeping with a combination of rage and helplessness. I managed at last to soothe Harry. I left them together talking things over. They reached some sort of an agreement and were apparent friends thereafter.

No one except the chief justice paid any heed to the shot. Gun explosions were too frequent in those days for anyone to be inquisitive. I have sat in my room in the evening and heard regular Fourth of July salvos booming out along Bay Street to the accompaniment of yells and whoops. It was merely the bootlegging mob feeling merry or celebrating something.

I had numerous offers from the various gangs to charter my schooner, but I refused them all. The Italians were loading me with all the liquor I could handle, and I knew they were square. I knew most of the Lucerne's clientele wasn't.

The demand for ships and trustworthy men to handle the rum money was so great, however, that men from strange walks of life were drawn into the trade. A white officer of the Nassau Constabulary threw up his post and went to sea, serving as supercargo on a rum schooner, until he made a fortune and retired.

The Reverend Mr. Dunn, a minister who had striven for a number of years to make Nassau a godlier community apparently appreciated after the advent of the rum gangs that his was vain endeavor. He told his congregation farewell, abandoned his calling, and became a rum-runner. I met him several times thereafter in St. Pierre, Halifax, and New York. He was bronzed and hearty and did not seem to be grieving over his sanctified past and sinful present.

Another former servant of the church backslid into the liquor traffic. She was the *Messenger of Peace*, a bluff-bowed, beamy old craft, employed by the Church of England bishop in making missionary journeys to the far-flung islands of the Bahama group. She had almost outlived her usefulness when Captain Louman, a Cockney seafarer, bought her from the bishop, installed a 45-horse power motor, and put her into the rum trade. He was commander of the *Messenger of Peace*. His wife was his mate, and two darkies her crew. He never changed her name. As the *Messenger of Peace* she dumped much illegal liquor into America. Usually she ran from Nassau to the inaccessible inlet of Okracoke, just south of Hatteras and a haunt of the pirate Blackbeard, and made a number of most profitable trips.

I knew that Louman knew nothing of navigation and asked him one day how he made his landfalls.

"Ow," said he, "I just generally goes up the Gulf Stream till it's time to 'aul in. Then I 'auls in, and there I am."

It wasn't the perfect system for navigation, however, for he went aground in Okracoke, and the Coast Guard had to haul him off. He gave them a case or so of whisky as reward and was promptly arrested by the county authorities. He was sentenced to six months in jail. Louman talked them into a compromise. It was decided eventually that if he promised to sleep in jail every night and keep the lock-up clean, he and his wife might work about their ship during the day, provided they fed themselves.

The skipper served his term with two months off for good behavior. The entire town assembled on the dock and cheered the *Messenger of Peace* as, with the captain at her helm and his wife as engineer and crew, she waddled out to sea, bound for Nassau and another cargo. The Loumans cleared about $100,000 and then retired from the game for good.

Not all the Nassauvians who went on rum craft fared so well. Harry Rowes, son of a high official in the Bahama government, signed on as supercargo of a schooner bound for Rum Row. The craft was pirated soon after she reached the coast, apparently with the collusion of the captain and mate.

Members of her crew testified that they saw the pirates force the lad into the boat in which they were carrying the plunder liquor ashore. He was never seen again.

The rum mob may have known what became of Rowes, but what the rum mob knew or did was no outsider's business. They were sensitive about inquiry of any kind. During their reign, newspapermen were about as popular on the island as cases of bubonic plague. One reporter from the United States landed, marched up to the Lucerne, and sought out Big Eddie.

"Brother," he told the big shot, "slip me the dope on this rum running thing. I'm a reporter, and I'm here to investigate it."

"Yeah?" Big Eddie said. "So you're a reporter, eh? Well, here's the dope. That steamer you came on goes back to Miami this afternoon. You be on her when she sails, and don't you never come back as long as I'm here. Get me?"

The reporter obeyed.

It was into this hard, suspicious, quick-acting mob that Pete Sullivan, Treasury agent, thrust himself. He came to Nassau disguised, with express orders from Washington to trail me, stay after me, and, at the first opportunity, arrest me and bring me back. I was in the lobby of the Lucerne, and Pete was hanging about in the offing when one of the crowd of crooks recognized him.

"Gang," he squealed, "I know this guy. He's a government dick. A spy."

Chairs scraped back. Feet scuffled across the floor. The gang closed in on Pete, shooting questions through clenched teeth. Sullivan is a good actor, but he was in a tough spot, and he knew it. I liked the way he kept his head up and his voice level, though his face was white. He will never be closer to dying without making the big jump than he was that minute. I felt in my bones that he was after me, and yet I liked his spunk. I shoved my way through the crowd about him.

"Easy," I told them. "Easy. I know this baby. He's a friend of mine."

"He's a dick," someone yelled.

"He's an Elk," I came back—I had noticed his button— "and so are a lot of you boys."

"Show your card," one of them demanded. Pete got it out. His hand shook as he passed it around.

Big Eddie asked me: "Bill, you're sure he's straight? If he's a copper he doesn't get off this island till after he's embalmed."

"Copper, hell!" I snorted. "Why, he's a customer of mine."

I marched Pete out of the Lucerne with the mob still growling behind him, shoved him into a hack, and took him to my rooms. There he came clean, showed me his credentials, and told me why he had come to Nassau.

"I'm going back without you," he told me. "I couldn't take you now, McCoy."

He had guts. He made me laugh.

"You bet you're going back," I told him. "The boat leaves in the morning. If you stay any longer I can't keep those hyenas off you. They know who you are."

He stayed in my rooms that night. I put him aboard the Munson liner in the morning. He looked haggard, and I didn't believe he had slept much. Pete since has told me he sat up all night with his gun in his fist.

He wanted a quart of whisky that morning. I said to a liquor dealer standing by: "Burnside, get me a quart for my friend here."

Burnside looked at Peter with stony eyes.

"Any quart I give a spy," said he, "will be poison." I got the liquor elsewhere.

Just before the liner sailed, Burnside came rushing aboard again, grip in hand. He had received a cable from New York that his schooner, the *Bertha A.*, had been captured by a cutter and towed in.

Sullivan gave a hard little grin when he heard this.

"Fine and good," he said to me. "When that baby does get to New York I'll damn well pay him back for the quart he wouldn't give me."

"Pete," I told him. "Lay off. Burnside is a good guy and my friend."

"Kayo," Sullivan acknowledged after a moment's thought. "I lay off. I owe you a heap more than that, Bill. Sometime, maybe, I'll have a chance to pay you back."

His promise was just so much talk to me then.

Sullivan went north, and I returned to riotous old Nassau. While the rum mobs were making whoopee day and night, I was laying plans. They seemed so simple and airtight that I did not see how I could help becoming a millionaire in a short while. Then I'd leave the game and refit my *Arethusa* and go to the South Seas forever, or at least until the government had had time to forget there was a person named Bill McCoy.

I was determined to go into rum running in a bigger, more businesslike fashion. Everything looked promising. I didn't see how I could be tripped up.

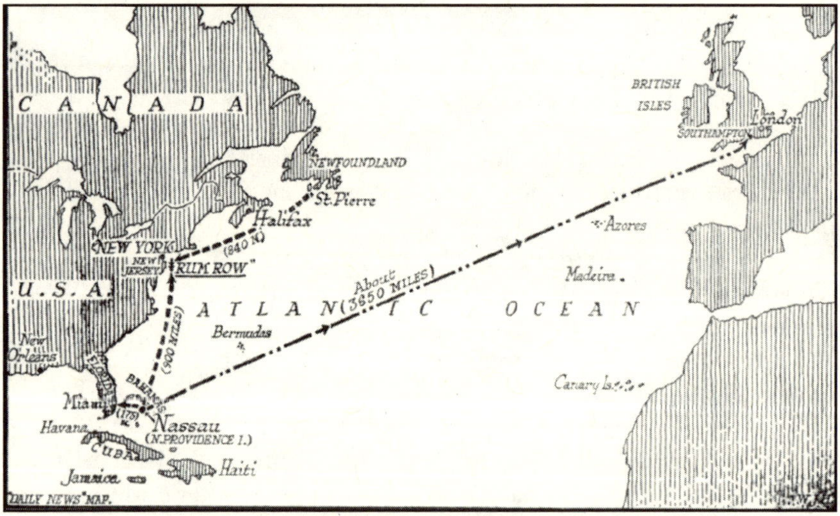

Map of the rum trade, circa. 1923, as depicted in *London's Daily News*.

CHAPTER VII

THE RUM RUNNING GAME, in my time, wasn't the cold business proposition it is today. The element of chance was its controlling factor in 1922. The racket then was like roulette. You sat down and evolved an unbeatable system. Then you tried it out and found yourself next morning with a bitter taste in your mouth and all your pockets turned inside out.

In my rooms at Mrs. Kemp's I had sat and figured out things. Sullivan's trip to Nassau had proved that the government wanted me badly. My former scheme of sending a schooner north and going up by train myself to supervise her unloading was out. The risk was too heavy. I had had my fill of being chased all over New England by Treasury agents. There was too much exercise and too little profit in that game.

I decided that hereafter I would remain in Nassau and become a shipper instead of a runner. I would attend to the assembling of cargoes and the chartering of my schooners, sending these north by steady, reliable captains whom I could trust. Captains I could trust! That was the weak spot in my plan, but I did not appreciate it then. My scheme eventually blew to bits, not because of my liquor or my ships. These both were the best that money could buy, but I couldn't, no matter what I paid, purchase human nature as staunch as my schooners or as straight as the whisky they carried. Square skippers in the rum running game were scarce as flying fish off Labrador.

While I still was working out my plans, trouble began again. I might have taken it as an omen, but I didn't.

When I bought the *Marshall* and the *Arethusa*, I placed them both in the name of an Englishman living in Nassau, paying him $3,000 to act as dummy owner. After the *Marshall*'s seizure he was indicted along with the rest of us and rushed at once into the arms of a lawyer who took all his cash and then asked for more.

The *Arethusa* was lying off Salt Cay at the rum-runners' anchorage. After the trade had got thoroughly under way, schooners and erstwhile yachts, former submarine chasers and tugs had packed Nassau's little harbor so full that the Bahama officials had cleared them out and made them anchor elsewhere.

One morning the dummy owner of my ship appeared in Nassau, rowed out to the *Arethusa*, and informed her captain and crew that the schooner was his property and that he had come to take her over.

When I heard this, I hotfooted it to my own lawyer in Nassau. He interrupted me when I began to tell my story.

"Johnson?" said he. "Oh, yes. I know all about that, Bill. You see, he has retained me."

"Now, wait a minute," I begged. "Aren't you my lawyer?"

"Oh, yes," he replied, and didn't have even the grace to look embarrassed. "It's better for me to represent both of you, Bill. We can reach some settlement more quickly that way."

"Settlement," I said. "Settlement, hell! He was nothing but a dummy and got paid for his risk. You know that."

"Quite true," he replied, beaming. "It's a nice question of law, Bill, but I've no doubt we can adjust it amicably."

I wasted no more time listening to a lecture on the niceties of law. I rushed to the waterfront and sent Pilot Brown out with a note and clearance papers to Captain Gott, ordering him to take the *Arethusa* to sea and be off the bar the following morning.

I did not return to the lawyer's, but went to my rooms and sat in the window with my glasses, watching my schooner and waiting for her to get under way. There was no bustling about her decks. Hours passed, and still she remained at anchor. I stormed back to the harbor and found Brown.

"Certainly," he reported, "I gave Captain Gott your orders, but the crew refuses to sail, Bill. They say it isn't your schooner and they aren't taking their orders from you."

I returned to Mrs. Kemp's, buckled on a long-barreled Colt, and ordered a boat to take me out to my schooner. I found poor old Gott on the verge of hysterics.

They didn't make better seamen than Captain Gott, but he was elderly, and the tension of rum running was telling on him. He was not the sort of man a crew would fear to defy, and now he explained that when he had tried to carry out my orders they had refused flatly to obey.

I went forward. The men squatted on the hatch covers and looked up at me from under their brows, but never stirred when I told them to get under way. One of them said:

"This is Johnson's schooner. He's got papers to prove it. She ain't going to move till he comes back with an attachment."

"Ain't she?" I asked. I eased on the windlass to the thirty-fathom shackle and knocked it loose. "Now," I told them, "we're going to sea the minute a government boat puts out of the harbor yonder. You tramps can go along or swim. I don't care which."

I waited aboard the *Arethusa* until night had fallen and I was certain no official with an attachment would appear. Then I went back to shore and settled this "nice question of law." I met Johnson on the street and backed him up against a wall with the point of my gun.

"Now," I told him; "You listen. If you lay a finger on my schooner I'll shoot your guts out. Get that straight, because I never meant anything quite as much."

He trembled and gulped up his story. His lawyer in Florida wanted another thousand dollars right away. Otherwise, so the attorney said, Johnson was bound to go to jail. It had been the lawyer, of course, who had suggested the seizure of the *Arethusa.*

I gave the dummy owner of my schooner $200.

"Give your lawyer that," I said, "and give him a message for me, too. Tell him that if he makes another move against me, or that if you go to jail, I'll send a gang over to Florida and fix him so he'll be practicing law from a hospital for the next six months. I've got a dozen friends over at the Lucerne that would ask nothing better than to beat up a lawyer."

Johnson must have told his attorney, for he never went to jail, and there was no further move to attach the *Arethusa.* I fired her crew, with the exception of Arey and Captain Gott. It was just as well in rum running to change crews frequently, anyway. You had fewer men floating around who knew all about you and your affairs under that system.

I shipped a new mate for the *Arethusa*, an Englishman, hired a fresh crew, and sent her North under a $20,000 charter from a Nassau liquor firm. Meanwhile, my lawyer in New York had got the *J.B. Young* released, and she returned to Nassau. I made Arey her captain. He had shipped as cook on the *Arethusa*, but he was a seaman and a navigator, and, I believed, loyal.

Now that the Johnson interlude was over, I started to put my plan into effect. I organized the British Transportation and Trading Company, with an impressive list of dummy directors and officers, and Bill McCoy as actual owner. I was going into the trade on big lines. I saw myself owning a fleet of vessels and filling the Royal Bank of Canada at Nassau so full of money that they have to add a couple of wings to the building.

Schooners, I knew, were cheap in Nova Scotia. I could buy one there for not more than $5,000, but I was too busy to make the trip myself. I gave Arey $1,000 for expenses and sent him off to start the expansion of the British Transportation and Trading Company. He got as far as Miami and returned by the boat he had taken over. His thousand was gone. He said someone had picked his pocket right in the railway station.

I did not fire him, though I did decide that he was much too careless with cash to be captain of the *J.B. Young*. Thus, the first man on whom I had depended failed me.

On the heels of Arey's ignominious return I received word that Captain Gott had been stricken with heart disease on Rum Row and had been taken into New York, where he had died. This was the second wallop luck handed me. It sent me back on my heels. Gott had been my right-hand man, absolutely square, and a most lovable personality. The English mate took his place and eventually brought the *Arethusa* back to Nassau with her cargo sold and receipts correct.

Meanwhile, the yacht of a Canadian asbestos magnate touched at Nassau. One of her officers, a young, finely built sailor, sought me out and asked me for a job. He was square shouldered and level eyed. He knew the sea and had served as lieutenant commander in the British navy during the war. That in itself seemed to me sufficient recommendation. I sent him to Nova Scotia on the mission Arey hadn't accomplished. My fingers were crossed all the while he was gone, but he cabled from North Sydney that he had bought the *M.M. Gardner*, a fine big schooner, and shortly thereafter sailed her into Nassau. The British Transportation and Trading Company had a $33,000 charter ready for him. He loaded and went north the day after he had arrived, sold the cargo, and was back in harbor in three weeks. I began to believe that I had found not only a successor to but an improvement on Captain Gott. I gave my Canadian a bonus of $3,000. His astonishment and delight seemed pathetic. Actually they were ominous. There could be no mistaking his love for money.

Rum Row, on which I had been first settler, was growing now into a long and strenuous marine thoroughfare. Pirates were beginning to range its length. The *Gardner*'s skipper built a wooden gun which he set up on her bow. Under the canvas cover he contrived, it looked exactly like a quick firer. He went back to New York with 4,400 cases.

The British Transportation and Trading Company had not only been sailing its ships profitably, but it also had been on the outlook for new markets. The duty at Nassau was still $6 per case. At Jamaica, there was no duty at all. I pointed this out to the Italians. We conferred with Jamaica liquor dealers and were promised a cargo of 5,000 cases.

Meanwhile my English mate had brought the *Arethusa* back to Nassau. She was in need of overhauling, and I made him captain and sent him on her to Cuba with instructions to drydock and refit at Cienfuegos. I had another good man in this Britisher, I thought.

The Italians brought down with them to Nassau a young American seaman and urged me to make him captain of the *J.B. Young*. Since they intended to charter her and I was none too certain of Arey's integrity at this time, I gave him the job. He had brought his wife along with him. I know of only one woman who ever mixed with rum running and did not cause trouble. The Italians' man and his wife sailed on the *Young* for Jamaica, with Arey still a mate. I went by steamer to Kingston with one of the Italians and supervised loading her cargo.

But the wife of the *Young*'s new skipper apparently thought she was on a sightseeing tour. She liked Jamaica and wanted to stay there for a while. Accordingly she prompted her husband to complain to me persistently about his new command. He said the schooner was unseaworthy He objected to the crew. He insisted the *Young* needed refitting, and managed, by one protest or another, to delay her sailing a full week while he and his wife motored about the island.

At last I lost my patience, and when he appeared one morning on the *Young*'s deck with an entirely fresh batch of reasons for not leaving, I said: "You either sail today or get the hell off here and stay ashore." He went ashore, and, after talking with the Italians, returned to beg for reinstatement. I gave it to him, but he fiddled about and did not sail that day.

Next morning, one of the liquor dealers who had cargo on the *Young* came to me in agitation, saying that an American revenue cutter was putting into Kingston with the crew of one of the Vance steamers. He urged me to get the *Young* away before she arrived. The schooner's skipper was out motoring with his wife. Arey and the crew and I tried to put the *Young* out to sea. The tide was low, and she rested on a mudbank. With foresail and headsails set, she would not budge. The captain and his wife came aboard while we were working. I think he had a brand-new set of objections to file, but he took one look at me and refrained. I was in the mood to chase him up a mast and knock him off its truck.

The wind was blowing strongly. I took the chance of tearing a stick out of the *Young* and ordered her mainsail up. For an instant, after it filled, I believed everything would carry away. Then she came out of the mud with a tremendous sucking sound and a rush of dirty foam. Her captain said he wanted to talk to me.

"Shut your damned trap," I told him. "Get her out of here."

She had dropped over the horizon when the cutter entered Kingston harbor, with Vance's crew. They were all blacks or yellows. Colored men never were successes in the rum trade. Vance's steamer had been overhauled on the high sea. The approach of the government boat scared the darkies so thoroughly, pier head gossip said, that they let their ship founder in water miles deep.

I returned to Nassau, weary and yet triumphant. The *Arethusa* had completed a successful voyage and was refitting. The *Gardner*, under the former British naval officer, was on the Row. The *Young* was on her way there. When these two schooners returned, I would have $85,000 and I would put half of this into rye, which, at Rum Row prices, would bring me back $120,000. I would reinvest that and, in a few more months, pull out of the game. Then, after selling my other ships, away to the South Seas on my *Arethusa*! The British Transportation and Trading Company was sitting on top of the world.

The first discord in the harmony my heart had been singing came in a cablegram from Cienfuegos. The skipper of the *Arethusa* had found she was six inches too deep to get into the drydock there and was bringing her back to Nassau.

So much for trusting to a captain's initiative. He never thought of removing the 125 tons of pig-iron ballast in her hold that would have let her into the slip with a couple of feet to spare. He dumbheadedly returned to Nassau. I said a lot of things to him and then sent him and the schooner on to Jamaica, where the Italians had another cargo waiting.

Thereafter I suffered everything that Job did, except boils. Before I followed the *Arethusa* to Kingston by steamer, I got a cable from New York. My schooner, the *M.M. Gardner*, had been seized and towed in.

Her capture was due entirely to the spinelessness of the former

Bill McCoy's schooner *Henry L. Marshall.*
(*National Archives Photograph*)

Bill McCoy's schooner *J.B. Young* anchored off Paradise Beach at Nassau, Bahamas.
(*Courtesy of The Mariners' Museum, Newport News, VA.*)

Bill McCoy's schooner *Vera Thornhill* off Newfoundland.
(*Courtesy of The Mariners' Museum, Newport News, VA.*)

Bill McCoy's schooner *M.M. Gardner.*
(*National Archives Photograph*)

naval officer, whom I had trusted. In 1922 the ships of the rum fleet on the Row were all lying twenty or more miles offshore. The year before they had crept in at night and trans-shipped into lighters. Now that prohibition enforcement was growing more strenuous, they stayed far out to sea and let the buyers come to them.

A group of prohibition agents combined to see if they could not run a bluff on some rum ship. They piled into a government launch and went to sea. The first victim they picked was a steel former yacht owned by Symonette of Nassau and captained by a hard-boiled old British skipper. The prohibition man ranged alongside of her and told her captain he under arrest.

"Am I?" he retorted, dived into his cabin, and came out with a Winchester in his hands. "One of you bleedin' blighters just put your 'ands on my rail and I'll show you whether I'm under arrest or not."

"We're agents of the United States government," they roared. Simonette's man shone his searchlight squarely on the red ensign at his ship's stern.

"An' this 'ere is one of 'Is British Majesty's merchant ships on the 'igh seas," he yelled back. "Just you come aboard, and we'll start another war."

He saved his craft, but he lost the *Gardner* for me. The agents next ran over to her and ordered her to follow them into the harbor. My captain, a former naval officer, meekly obeyed. Thus another man I had trusted failed me, and I had lost my ship and her cargo.

I took the boat for Kingston where the *Arethusa* was loading. Luck hadn't finished rubbing my nose in the dirt yet. I had been ashore at Jamaica only an hour when a British sailor, spruce in pillbox cap, white coat, blue trousers, and bamboo stick, walked in on me at the hotel and told me I would have to go back on the steamer that brought me. Since I had no passport, he said, I could not remain on the island.

Two large black policeman guarded the ship gangway lest I try to land again. It was some hours before the Italians had got to the liquor dealers and the liquor dealers had obtained permission from the governor for me to come ashore. I found out later that Consul Lathrop at Nassau had cabled Jamaica that I was a dangerous rum-runner, twice indicted in the States, and should be refused permission to land.

When I returned to my hotel at Kingston I had further news. The *J.B. Young* had been run down by a liner on the Row and had been so badly damaged that she was going to St. Pierre for repairs. This threw me against the ropes, but it completely floored the Italians. They refused to charter the *Arethusa* and went hurrying north to look out for the shipment on the *Young*.

It was not my ships but my men who had failed me again. In the *Young* case, Arey, her mate, on going off watch, had called the captain but had not waited on deck, as he knew he should, until the skipper took over. Instead, he had gone to bed, and the captain had not got up. An incoming steamer had smashed into the *Young*, carrying away her bowsprit, though not injuring her severely. But her captain, egged on by his wife, who was having hysterics, insisted that they would have to run in somewhere for repairs and, because he was afraid to touch at Halifax, took the *Young* and her cargo all the way to St. Pierre. While she was refitting there, he and his wife went to North Sydney, "to get charts," and never came back. Arey eventually brought the schooner back to the Row and got rid of her cargo. She had sailed in July. She returned to Nassau December 1st.

I got the *Gardner* back, eventually, but it cost me $22,000 in lawyers' fees to free her. Her captain, who had sold almost all the liquor she carried before he wilted under a bluff, vanished. I think I got back about $6,000, eventually, out of a cargo I had planned was to clear me $46,000.

The British Transportation and Trading Company, which had started out that season to make its owner independently wealthy, was a leaky and battered craft by the end of the year.

My plans had been well laid. The only trouble was that they could not be carried out unless you had men you could trust. I hadn't. They weren't plentiful in the rum running game.

I accused Consul Lathrop of having deliberately made trouble for me at Jamaica. He did not deny it, and chuckled.

"I'm getting old, Bill," he told me, "and I like to have my friends about me. Load your whisky here. You'll find that Murphy has excellent rye. I'll I able to keep my eye on you, then, and let Washington know exactly what you are doing."

The *Arethusa* was the only ship I had, now. The hundreds of thousands I had hoped to make had dwindled until I had barely sufficient in the bank to buy a thousand cases. I was in the game to stay, however. I was keeping the resolution I had made when I entered it. I limited my smuggling to liquor, and only the best of that. Other men dropped out of rum running for the darker and more profitable enterprise of landing drugs and Chinese on American soil. But that's a phase of the situation of which few hear.

The pious American government has been so intent on spending hundreds of millions to keep its citizens from drinking what they please that it has had little cash or personnel remaining to check worse evils.

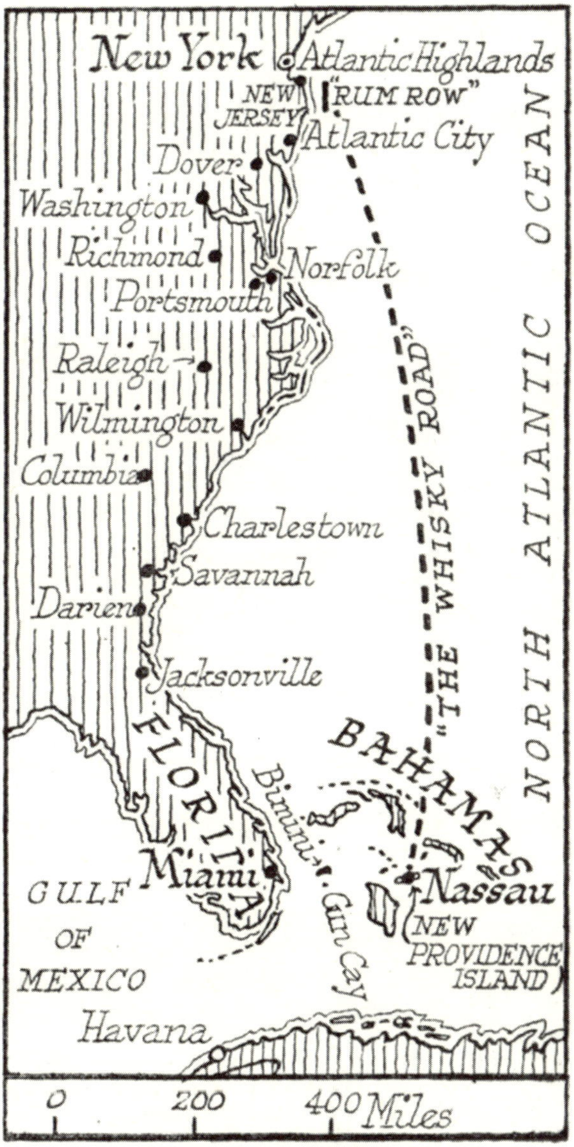

"THE WHISKY ROAD."

Chapter VIII

ON MY SECOND TRIP TO JAMAICA I received a definite offer to enter the Chink-running business. On the steamer *Canadian Fisher* were a half dozen Chinese girls. They had been stowaways on the ship's last trip to Montreal, had been caught, and were now being returned to Jamaica.

One of them approached me and urged me to take her and her companions north on one of my schooners. Their friends in New York, she said, would pay me passage of $2,000 a head, and, if I cared to enter the business, I would get more passengers than I could handle. I didn't care to.

Others did, however, and for all I know still are running yellow men and women up from Cuba and Central and South America to the United States.

It is a foul game, as rotten and unscrupulous as ever the old slave trade was. Only the hardest and crookedest go into it, but there are plenty of these knocking about the blue water of the Main with the sole purpose in life of making money, no matter how.

Because a hundred rum-runners are taken for every Chink carrier the government nabs, this does not mean that the latter are few. Many a man is suspected of having had Chinese aboard but never captured. A Chink leaves a smell behind him. But your nose may tell you much that can't be proved in a law court.

Many things have happened, are still happening, for that matter, on the Spanish Main which are set down as mysteries because no one concerned therein dares speak. Ships still sail from the islands and never come back. Not all of them founder. Piracy, in spite of the smug claims of civilization, is not an entirely dead profession.

The brilliant, wicked seas that lap the West Indies have seen more of horror than any like stretch of water the world over. And even now fresh chapters which no one reads entirely are added to the gruesome record each year.

Chinese who seek to enter the United States by boat pay half their fare in advance. Thus, whether the runner is able to land his cargo or not, his voyage is not a financial failure. If he is hard pressed, he destroys the evidence against him.

Rumors float about the Main, thick as the big orange patches of Gulf Stream weed. Many are utterly false, yet I have heard tales so typical that I have known they must be true.

There is one about a schooner captain who loaded twenty Chinks in Cuba and set sail for New York. The yellow men were packed, sardine-tight, in his hold. None was allowed on deck, and the embarkation had been at night, yet something went wrong.

Off Hatteras, with a half gale blowing, a cutter appeared from nowhere and swung into the schooner's track. They clapped on sail. The white craft astern hourly loomed larger. Capture was imminent and there were those twenty Chinese below. The schooner's skipper threw her off her course and slanted away on a long tack, so that the lee rail went under, and the other, riding high, hid the deck from the oncoming cutter.

One by one, the twenty yellow men were summoned from below. Ax in hand, the skipper stood beside the hatch. One by one, the Chinese were knocked on the head and pitched overside into the violent sea.

When the last had vanished, the schooner resumed her course, and the revenue cutter, crawling up astern, finally halted her and sent an officer aboard, demanding her clearance papers.

"Havana to New York in ballast."

The officer sniffed. "You're carrying Chinese."

"Not any."

"I've got a nose, man."

"We carried a batch downcoast to Neuvitas before we left Cuba. The stink sticks. That's all. Look for yourself."

He looked, found nothing but a smell, and the schooner went free. It had not been an entirely unprofitable slaughter, for each of the twenty yellow men had paid half his passage money—$1,000—before he had come over the side.

Bits of unfinished stories bob up now and then to demonstrate that rum is not the only thing against which America needs protection. A few years ago, misty dawn revealed to men of the revenue service a Bahama sponge schooner, the *Mary Beatrice*, adrift midway between Rum Row and New York's harbor mouth. No sail was set. No one was on her deck. She slowly swung about, end for end, in the suck of the tide.

They boarded her. Forecastle and cabin were deserted, but lights shone down into her hold revealed seven slit-eyed, bloodstained, impassive Chinamen, who said nothing, who knew nothing, who had forgotten even how they came to be aboard the schooner. Newspapers thereafter for several days spent much space on this "mystery of the sea." I know the solution of that "mystery," because I had a part in it.

The *Arethusa* was on Rum Row at the time, with her British skipper Hall and me aboard. One afternoon a dory rowed toward us from a ship anchored farther down the line, and a Bahamian mulatto boarded my schooner. I knew him. His reputation was bad, even in tolerant Nassau. He was nervous now and explained that his craft, whisky laden, had run short of water. He wondered if I could let him have a little.

We went into my cabin, and there I made certain of what I had suspected on deck. The man reeked with the pungent, unmistakable odor of Chinks.

It was a gaudy fight while it lasted, but it didn't endure long. While my skipper looked on in growing horror, I downed the mulatto and lashed his hands behind his back. Then I locked him in a closet.

"Do?" I answered my bewildered captain "I'm going to see if I can swap a Chink runner for couple of indictments."

By the first bootlegger who reached the *Arethusa* that evening I sent a wire ashore to Colonel Hayward, federal attorney, telling him whom I had caught and offering to turn my captive over to the authorities.

The bootlegger insisted afterward that he sent the wire. I have never learned whether Hayward received it. By next morning the whole affair was out of my hands. During the night, while business was briskest on the *Arethusa*, Hall sneaked down into my cabin and released the prisoner. He slipped into bootlegger's craft and vanished. At daylight authorities found the *Mary Beatrice* adrift off the harbor.

It was easy to imagine what had happened aboard her. She carried a Negro crew, and when her captain rowed away and did not return they frightened and attempted to follow the tradition of the Chink-running trade by destroying the evidence. But the Chinese outnumbered them. Exactly what occurred that night on the *Mary Beatrice* is known only to seven bloodstained survivors who all through the ensuing inquiry professed to know nothing. How many yellow men were killed in the battle and went over the side with the corpses of the blacks is part of the mystery. The survivors, as I recall it, finally were deported.

When I discovered that my captive had been released, I fired my captain on his own quarterdeck.

"You cawn't do it," he defied.

"Cawn't I?" said I. "Who says so."

"The Board of Tryde regulations. No captain of a British ship can be dismissed while 'is craft is on the 'igh seas. It's never been done, and it never will be."

"You," I told him, "take your Board of Trade regulations and get off this schooner, or I'll jam them down your throat."

It may never have been done before but I did it.

There was, as far as I am aware, never any Chink running out of the Bahamas. Drug smuggling also was taboo. The colonial government, which the prohibition authorities liked to picture as descendants of the Forty Thieves, actually was most strict and upright concerning trade from the islands. Any irregularity was punished heavily. What American officials overlooked was that the Bahama Islands, in selling liquor for export, were conducting a legal business under sanction of the laws of the British Empire. Traffic in Chinese and narcotics was flatly illegal in the Bahamas. I do not believe it was attempted.

Havana was, and as far as I know still is, a prime market for illicit drugs. Trade between there and the States is heavy. Little enough has been said in praise of rum-runners, and perhaps they deserve no more approval than they have received, yet they were not the completely depraved folk the moralists said they were. If they had been, they would have quit handling bulky cases of liquor and turned to narcotics.

Some of them did, a good many, perhaps, but the bulk of the rum fleet left that dirty game alone. Ethics, of which the prohibitionists in America said we had none, prevented us from running narcotics. The rats that went into that racket made, and are still making, fortunes and taking not one tenth the risk we liquor carriers ran.

The activity of the drys has been almost humorously lopsided. Hundreds of millions of dollars have been spent to parch an increasingly wet nation. Only the smallest fraction of that amount has been used to fight a far more deadly menace. Prohibitionists have been like policemen who spend so much effort enforcing parking ordinances that they have no time left to protect their community against yeggs and murderers.

Traffic in drugs has grown tremendously. I know that is so, and statistics will bear me out, although statistics can deal only with the drug runners who are caught, and they seldom are captured.

It is easy to see why the narcotic trade is increasing. Liquor still flows into America in an undiminished stream. Rum is bulky stuff. You must have a big ship. You must have a loading organization and an unloading organization. You must have clearance papers from the port you leave. You cannot sail without them.

Drugs are compact. Cocaine or heroin or morphine to the value of a schooner load of Scotch can be carried in a suitcase or so. Where tons of liquor can be loaded and discharged, drugs can be put ashore with not one tenth the difficulty. The liquor runner is not the worst and most unscrupulous of his breed, by a long jump.

When the *M.M. Gardner* had been captured and the *J.B. Young* had been run down, and all the other woes to which the British Transportation and Trading Company seemed permanent heir had showered upon me, I appreciated that there was something wrong with my plans which had looked so unbeatable on paper. If I ever were to get that cruise to the South Seas I must go after it in some other way.

The end of the summer in which I had hoped to make my fortune found me with two of my schooners seized, a third in St. Pierre for repairs, and the fourth and last, *Arethusa*, waiting empty in Nassau with the hurricane season coming on and her owner almost broke.

All this was due, directly, to letting other men handle my ships. Even a fool, after he has tried to enter a door several times and has been socked on the nose each trial, starts to look for some other, safer entrance. I determined that hereafter I would take my own risks whenever possible. From now on I would sail my own schooner and carry my own liquor. The only way to be a successful rum-runner was actually to run your own rum.

The *Arethusa* had a capacity of 5,000 cases, but my bank roll would purchase only one fifth of that. I bought 1,000 cases of Murphy's rye, the best in the world, and with Captain Crosby as skipper and a hardboiled, willing crew, we took her out of Nassau that October and went north through the Gulf Stream. I had no consignee waiting for my cargo at the other end. I had to depend on shoppers along Rum Row for my trade.

The *Arethusa* went like a gull, and in eight days we had taken our place in the Row off Fire Island lightship. This marine liquor market of which I had been founder was growing in size. It was not yet in its heyday, but the number of craft that joined it was increasing monthly. Our legal position had not been clarified in 1922. We all lay twenty miles offshore, and fishing boats and other small craft came out, had a meal aboard, loaded, and returned to the beach. Occasionally, a cutter would wallow down the line, sniffing suspiciously at our heels, but supervision in that day was only nominal.

Most of the craft on the Row rode at anchor. I rarely did. The *Arethusa* sailed so sweetly that I found it better to jog back and forth under foresail and jumbo, logging not more than two or three knots. The motion was easier, both for us and for the craft that came alongside to buy, when my ship was under way. And besides, in case of pirates, or kindred danger, we wasted no time sweating over an anchor. We clapped on more canvas and slid away.

I found the *J.B. Young* riding near the lightship. Arey had brought her back to her station from St. Pierre, and the Italians were supposed to be taking off her cargo, but he complained at their slowness. They would come out, get a load, sell it ashore, and then spend their proceeds painting Broadway brighter before returning for more. The *Young* was in poor condition, having been away from her home port for months. Her crew was bearded, dirty, and sullen, her sails little better than rags. I told the supercargo the Italians had aboard that he could either land the thousand cases remaining within a week or else ride back with it to Nassau. I also gave Arey orders to sail in seven days.

At this time, when I had begun to believe that loyalty was just a word in the dictionary, Arey brought me a new shipmate, the best, the most unwaveringly faithful with whom I ever sailed.

You could have put him in your hat when he first came to me; a fat, black, rubbery Newfoundland puppy, with a curly tail, oversize paws, and hopeful, trusting brown eyes. Arey had brought him down to me from St. Pierre. He was my buddy and best friend as long as I sailed.

He was a lonely little cuss at first, until he got used to the ways of my ship and me. He whimpered softly at night in my cabin, so I would take him into my bunk. Then he would curl down between me and the wall, give a long contented sigh, and go to sleep at once.

He grew rapidly, but my bunk didn't. When it became a

question of which of us would sleep on the floor, I dodged the problem by having a double bunk installed instead.

He became a big, deep-chested, strong-bodied dog, with eyes that were always soft brown when they looked at me, but glinted green if a stranger entered my cabin. He knew his place. He would make no protest unless the visitor moved toward my desk. He knew his job, too. My money was in the desk. He would thrust himself between it and the intruder, not even growling, but with his lip curled back from great white fangs and the green devil flickering in his eyes. Always the visitor backed hastily away.

When trade was brisk and I had to be on deck, I would leave him in my cabin beside an unlocked drawer that sometimes contained more than a hundred thousand dollars in cash. It was perfectly safe. If anyone had touched it he would have had to kill or be killed.

"Old Faithful," I called him. The schooner was his home, and my cabin his and my personal room. There was only one thing in it on which he looked with suspicion—the stove. Shortly after he came to me, we rode out a terrific storm one night. He was curled up close to me in bed, and a fire was going, for it was bitter cold. A sudden lurch of the schooner threw a red-hot lid into the bunk on top of him and me. We woke before either of us was more than scorched, and I wrapped the lid in a blanket and got it back where it belonged. He never quite trusted the stove after that. It was a strange animal that threw things at one.

His devotion to me was so constant that sometimes I forgot it. At Bermuda, the *Arethusa* lay a mile out in the harbor, and I went ashore by boat to make arrangements for loading her, leaving Old Faithful aboard. I stayed that night at the hotel. Next morning a darkey hallboy poked his head into my room.

"Boss," he asked, "does you own a big black dawg?"

I said I did and asked him why. He grinned and answered:

"He been layin' out in front, jes' under your window, all night long."

I looked out. There he was. He had swum ashore and was patiently waiting for me. That afternoon, in the haste of getting back to my schooner I forgot him again and did not miss him until I climbed overside and he was not there to greet me. I looked shoreward. He was halfway out, his big black head cutting through the waves. I rowed back and got him. There were plenty of sharks in those waters.

He stayed aboard the *Arethusa* until I went to jail. Then I gave him to a shore friend to keep for me, but when I came out again he was dead.

Arey's loyalty, the way he had stuck to the schooner and handled her after her captain had deserted, gave me another and better impression of him. He had lost the thousand dollars I had entrusted to him, and he later had been partly responsible for the running down of the *Young*. I was willing to wipe that all out now. I made him captain of the *Young*. He served with me for the rest of my career. I never had a better assistant.

The *Arethusa* hung around the lightship for a day or so and did not sell a bottle. The retailers did not know me. Heretofore my ships had carried consignments almost exclusively. We left our position and ran down the Jersey coast to a point off the Highlands. The steel schooner *Jeanette* lay there, and her crew were friends of mine from the Bahamas. She was loaded with a cheap grade of rye from Cuba and reported poor sales, but her supercargo, Bob Cameron, an old friend, confided:

"Stick around, Bill. If they don't like our stuff, I'll send them over to you. I'll tell the gang you've got the real McCoy goods."

That day and night we made our first sales to the Jersey sea skiffs. At this time, these craft were Rum Row's chief contact with the shore. They were open boats, high bowed and about 28 feet long, with the engine—usually a 60-horse-power, 6-cylinder Pierce-Arrow lifted from an automobile—installed in a watertight box. Empty, their maximum speed was 15 miles an hour, and laden, about half that.

They were tubs compared to the craft that later came to the Row, when government supervision stiffened. Only seamen could have brought them out through the weather they often encountered. Wind and waves never stopped them. In storms there were always two men aboard them, one to steer, the other to pump and keep her afloat. Any other breed but these Jersey lads would have added a third to holler for help, but they were reckless, and seamen to the backbone. They always came out full speed ahead, and you could hear the old wagons smacking along over the waves a mile away. Their exhausts were under water, and when running slowly, no one could hear them.

The first few who sampled my whisky spread the word ashore. From then on I had no complaint about the number of my customers. Despite the storms that kept hammering us all this voyage, in two days of reasonably clear weather I had sold my entire cargo.

The last few cases were taken off my ship by a big Jerseyman who ran his skiff solo. He paid me in twenty-dollar bills. To a rum-runner, small denominations were a pest, and I asked him if he had nothing larger.

"Nope," he said, "but I got plenty of these," and showed me a coat pocket packed with more twenties. He got under way and went squattering shoreward while we made sail for our return to Nassau. There was a stiff wind, and a storm was gathering in the northwest. I went into the cabin and began to count the twenties. There was something about the feeling of them that bothered me, and when I looked closer the shading on the reverses did not seem quite right either. I yelled to Crosby:

"Overhaul that mug who just left."

He was bouncing through the waves at 10 knots, but under full sail we came up on him as if he were anchored. He tried to bluff it out for a moment, then wilted and paid me in legitimate cash. I had only half enough time to tell him what would happen if he tried that racket again, for the wind was mounting. We squared away for Nassau with a gale driving us from astern.

Captain Crosby had been bred to square-riggers and yachts. He was not used to the rig of a Gloucesterman. An error in maneuvering found us running off, wing and wing, before a screeching nor'wester. Only a seaman can appreciate the jam we were in, the 70-foot main boom, the 45-foot main gaff with a 60-foot hoist stretched out on one side the full length of the main sheet and the foresail spread on the other.

Something had to be done, and done quick. We were going like a destroyer, literally crucified to our course. Crosby was steering her like an artist, yet the least error or inequality, and one of the booms was bound to jibe and quite probably rip the sticks right out of her. The gale beat on her sails till they boomed like drums, and the *Arethusa*'s hard-driven hull was throwing aside great welts of foam. We had to work fast and take a chance.

All hands were on the foreboom tackle. Crosby eased her around a little. We got the foresail in and had slacked on the tackle when what we had dreaded happened. As the fore gaff came across the deck the fore tackle parted. The boom swung like a lightning streak. Sparks flew. Boom, sheet, and tackle went across. The *Arethusa* brought up with a jerk, as though she had hit a wall, but everything held.

She ought to have been torn to pieces, but there she was, sound as before. Those Gloucester fishermen are built to stand anything. They are the one-horse-shays of the sea. I presume that when they do go, they fly all to pieces in an instant.

We rounded to and took in the mainsail, but the canvas was old and split from gaff to main boom in an eighty-foot rip. The wind was mounting, but it was fair. We put my schooner under jib, jumbo, foresail, and riding sail and let her go for Nassau.

All night long the nor'wester sang in her rigging, and under partial canvas she went like a flung spear. By next afternoon we were well into the Gulf Stream. Only a light easterly breeze was blowing, the weather was warm, the sky and water blue. We took in the riding sail and bent spare foresail to the main gaff, set flying jib and fisherman's staysail, and we were rolling home to Nassau, happy, relaxed, with $50,000 cash in my cabin.

We repaired the rip in the mainsail, with all hands plying palm and needle, and about sunset bent the mainsail and maintopsail and under light airs quickened her speed from seven to nine knots. I lay on the deck. Above me the big sail bellied and muttered like a circus tent, the lofty trucks swept the heavens, and the wind played through the rigging with a pleasant sound. This was the game I liked. This was what I had been looking for. I was perfectly content.

In the morning, when I went on deck, the sea was flat, the air still. The water, so blue the day before, was sepia, and all about us, as far as we could see, were great sodden patches of brown weed with lumps of driftwood here and there. We were barely making steerage way with all sail set. It was so still that I could hear the fingers of weed rasp along the schooner's sides. This was the Sargasso Sea, legendary yet actual. All morning, while the *Arethusa* crept through the sluggish, tanned water, dolphins played about us. We caught a dozen on hook and line and took them to our cook, who would not broil them until he had placed a silver coin in each fish. The metal did not tarnish. That, he said, proved they were edible.

For twenty-four hours thereafter we lay becalmed in the Sargasso Sea with a flawless hot sky like a cover set over the watery brown floor. We whistled and stuck our sheath knives in the main boom. This is an old sea tradition to bring a breeze and skippers never object, even though the boom be varnished. Obedient clouds poked their heads over the horizon. They sent us a wind that pushed us out of the waste of weeds and freshened all afternoon. That night we logged 44 knots in a four-hour watch and arrived at

Nassau exactly eighteen days after we had sailed, a record for a trip to the Row and return.

On the morning after my arrival I drifted down into Murphy's liquor warehouse. He and his secretary, Marcus, welcomed me and inquired about my trip. I told him I had come to invest the proceeds in his rye, and while yarning about the voyage, dived into my pocket and pulled out the wad of counterfeit twenty-dollar bills the bootlegger had tried to shove on me.

"What do you think of these?" I asked, tossing him one. He was a big, florid man, but as he looked at it he grew pale. His breath whistled as he glanced toward the door and tore the rest of the wad out of my hand.

"You great big blundering jackass!" he gulped. "Where were you when they were giving out brains?"

"The guy didn't stick me. I saw they were queer," I protested.

"Sure," Murphy hissed, "and what do you do? Isn't there enough against you in the States? Do you know that William J. Burns and Colonel Nutt of the secret service are on the island now—that they're due here any moment to look over my plant? And you, you big goop, have to come in here with your big hands full of phony twenties, so as to make a good impression on government agents."

He spun about and thrust the wad of bills at Marcus.

"Tear them up," he ordered, "and throw them down the sewer. Fast."

He was still mopping his forehead when Burns and Nutt, who had come to Nassau ostensibly to look for drug smugglers but actually to investigate the rum running traffic, entered Murphy's office. Neither knew me by sight, and I kept well in the background.

"Mr. Murphy," said Burns, "have you any objection to permitting us to see your plant?"

The liquor dealer froze up. He was angry, and when Murphy got mad he always grew polite. Usually he was a blustering, rough-tongued, genial citizen. Now he was coldly courteous.

"Certainly, gentlemen," he replied. "Perhaps you would care for a sample first."

He filled glasses and offered them.

"You understand, gentlemen," he continued, "that this is just business. I am not drinking with you socially."

Nutt and Burns glared, but Murphy's face was entirely impassive. He led them on a tour of his plant. There were tiers on tiers of casks, each containing the best rye America ever produced. The liquor was from seven to ten years in wood and had evaporated down to about twenty-eight gallons per barrel. Whisky to me is just so much unpleasant medicine. I rarely touch it, but I loved the fragrance of Murphy's old rye. Rubbed between the palms it exhaled a soft, pungent aroma like old rose leaves. It was smooth and dense as oil.

Murphy reduced this liquor to 100 proof with distilled water and had installed a modern bottling plant. When the quarts were filled and labeled they were carried to the packing tables. Murphy was one of the first of the liquor dealers to abandon the old-fashioned whisky case, bulky and rigid, for burlap-wrapped packages of a half dozen bottles each. These were far easier to handle and to stow, and took only about half the room necessary for case whisky. In the trade the packages are known as "hams."

At the packing tables were scores of negresses, sheathing each bottle in corrugated paper, stacking them into pyramids of six each, packing straw about them, wrapping them in burlap, sewing the cloth fast with double sail twine—preparing more emissaries of the Demon Rum to corrupt further the morals of America. They sang as they worked. Probably Burns and Nutt, watching their labors, considered the songs blasphemous, for they carolled: "Jesus Loves Me," "Nearer My God to Thee," "Jesus, Lover of My Soul," and kindred hymns.

Murphy politely led his unbidden guests from the bottling plant to the end of his pier.

"My liquor," he explained, "is purchased, and I load it into lighters at the end of this pier, which is well inside Bahama waters, as you can see. At the end of this pier my responsibility for it ends, and here my responsibility to you gentlemen ends also. Good-day."

When Burns and Nutt had departed I invested the proceeds of my first personally conducted trip to Rum Row in another shipment of his rye.

CHAPTER IX

ONCE AGAIN I HAD THE WORLD BY THE TAIL and felt I could tie a knot in it. I had completed the fastest trip ever made from Nassau to the Row and return. I had money, and had just purchased 2,000 cases of Murphy's rye. My *Arethusa* had a good captain and an able crew, and, to me, sailing her to and from the Row was sheer delight. Lorin A. Lathrop, the American Consul, meeting me on Bay Street, looked at me with quizzical eyes from beneath his sun helmet and said: "Bill, you look happy."

I told him that I was and explained why. He sighed.

"Well, Bill, the wicked shall flourish like a green bay tree, I suppose. Personally, I am delighted that you are prospering. Officially, however, Bill, I deplore it; I deplore it."

He went on, shaking his head in mock despair. The government of the United States was never represented anywhere by a better and squarer man. He and I understood each other perfectly. He did everything he could legitimately to help the authorities collar me, and I knew it and respected him for it. But he never stooped to snooping or spy work of any sort. He fought square and never landed below the belt.

Nassau became so important a spot in the estimate of the government that an assistant consul was sent down to lighten Lathrop's labors. He did not follow the code of his superior, but spent much time snooping about the docks and drinking with schooner captains and rum-runners—always permitting someone else to pay. We did not blame him for that, for we knew his salary was small, but I began to suspect that he was confusing an assistant consul's duties with those of a detective. I proved to my satisfaction that this was so.

He was an inquisitive cuss, forever asking questions. Shortly after I bought the *Arethusa* and changed her registered name to *Tomoka*, he asked me with a tremendous air of indifference:

"By the way, McCoy, how do you spell your schooner's name?"

"T-a-m-a-k", I lied. In the copy of the next confidential report

Bill McCoy helps heave up anchor at Nassau, Bahamas.
(Courtesy of The Mariners' Museum, Newport News, VA.)

Bill McCoy insisted his vessels be kept in "ship shape." Here he paints his cabin on *Arethusa*.
(Courtesy of The Mariners' Museum, Newport News, VA.)

Bill McCoy, right, and an unidentied crewman, mug for the camera while on Rum Row. (*Courtesy of The Mariners' Museum, Newport News, VA.)*

Bill McCoy makes a model of *Arethusa* on Rum Row while the mate checks the chronometer. (*Courtesy of The Mariners' Museum, Newport News, VA.)*

sent by the consulate at Nassau to Washington and relayed back to me by my still unknown friend, I read that Bill McCoy had changed his schooner's name from *Arethusa* to *Tamak*.

I said nothing of the matter to Consul Lathrop, but soon the assistant was transferred elsewhere. Some time later Lathrop said to me, during a conversation and referring to nothing that had gone before:

"Bill, I'm not a prohibitionist or a spy. I never go to the waterfront to snoop, nor will I tolerate it in my office."

"Yes, sir," I agreed gravely, and I knew why the assistant consul had been withdrawn. His successor was not much more of a help to Lathrop. He was a youngster with a fully matured taste for booze who tried to prevent rum running by drinking up the island's entire supply. Whisky and the tropics had their way with him. He lost his post, landed in the gutter, and eventually shipped as cook on a rum-runner and left the island. The Consul's assistants were more hindrance than help.

Though it was early December now, and storms were plowing back and forth between Nassau and New York, I was looking forward to my next trip North and itching to get under way. News that I was running my own schooner to the Row spread about Nassau and one evening, when I dropped into the Lucerne to watch the $1,000 a point crap game the mob staged almost every evening, I was greeted as though I were Johnny Walker or Old Granddad himself.

A dozen of the gang begged me to take shipments north for them. "Bill, carry a hundred cases for me." "Big boy, let me put five hundred aboard."

They were so eager and I was so contented with the present and the outlook for the future that I agreed right and left without considering the size of the *Arethusa*. It was not until I got back to my rooms at Mrs. Kemp's that I sat down and began to check up on my promises.

I found that I had agreed to take enough liquor to sink my schooner at her anchorage and fill another as big as she to the loadline besides. The next day I spent in hunting up my would-be consignors and getting them to scale down their shipments. Eventually, I reduced the total to 3,700 cases.

The *Arethusa* would be loaded pretty deep for a winter voyage with 5,000 cases aboard her. She had my 2,000 rye already in her hold. I knew 5,700 was an enormous cargo, but, as I have said, I was riding the crest of the wave again and felt my luck was in. I let the gang load her. They made their purchases, and it was almost dark when the cargo began to arrive by lighter.

All night whisky kept coming aboard, while the darkey tally man and I checked off. We filled the hold till we could scarcely slide the hatch into place. More boats kept arriving to be unloaded. We packed liquor in and under the forecastle, beneath my cabin floor and under the cabin bunks, before the last of it was stowed. Then, just before dawn, with my 5,700 cases stowed, I went home and rolled into bed. We planned to sail at noon the next day when there was high tide at the bar. We needed it.

Mrs. Kemp came out to confront me as I was going downstairs next morning. Her hands were on her hips, and there were scandal and fright on her face.

"My fathers above!" she exclaimed. "You aren't going to sea on that schooner the way she's loaded? Everyone in town says she's unsafe."

While she argued with me, the parrot in her living room kept screaming, "Unsafe, unsafe!" His rasping voice pursued me down the street. The news apparently was all over the island. Friends stopped me on Bay Street and said: "Bill, you're never going out of harbor with your schooner laden like that."

I replied that I certainly was and that I'd trust the *Arethusa* with double that load. When I saw my schooner I wished I had not boasted so loudly. A Conch boatman sculled me out to her. She seemed to lie pretty low. When I stepped over her rail and onto her deck I splashed in water. Her scuppers were awash.

My crew sat moping on the hatches. Captain Crosby came up, shaking his head.

"Bill," he suggested, "she's loaded too deep. We'll never make it."

I could not go back on the boasts I had made.

"Why?" I told him. "We'll make a record trip out of it."

"It's the stormy season," he said.

"We'll pass right between the storms," I retorted. He shrugged and surrendered.

"All right. You're the owner, but I've got a mean feeling in my bones, Bill."

The crew had gathered around us.

"We'll be laying on the Row in January," one of them ventured. "She'll ice up and sink under us."

"Any of you boys afraid?" I wanted to know. Each man of them was, being a seaman, but all had too much guts to admit it.

"I tell you what I'll do," I said at last. "I'll ship three more forecastle hands. That'll make the work easier."

"Captain Bill," one of the crew answered. "If you put three more men on her she'll sink right here."

I went ashore and got my additional seamen, big rawboned Finns who had deserted a lumber schooner to enter the rum trade. For fear they would change their minds when they saw how deep the *Arethusa* lay, I made them bring their bags along when they went aboard, and we cast off immediately afterward. We went out over the bar at high tide and headed north with a fresh sou'easter.

With all sail set, we drove at 12 knots across the Northwest Providence Channel, straight for Hole in the Wall at Abaco. Beyond Abaco, we knew we would face our battle, and before we reached there we had lashed everything movable to the bulwarks and covered the hatches with double tarpaulins soaked in tar and oil. I set in front of the helm the rack that it was becoming customary for all rum-runners to carry in winter-time and filled it with the usual four bottles—rye, Scotch, rum, and wine.

So we made ready an overladen schooner to fight the North Atlantic in December. Below her deck was one of the most valuable cargoes ever to leave the Bahamas. At Nassau the liquor on the *Arethusa* had cost me and my bootlegger friends a total of $171,000. On Rum Row it would sell for $342,000. Once landed, it was worth $684,000. Dealers would cut it, one part liquor to three of water and grain alcohol. Ultimate consumers would pay $2,000,000 or more for the *Arethusa*'s load.

The broad gray Atlantic swells shouldered into us by the time we were clear of Hole in the Wall. The *Arethusa* did not rise and slide over them. So heavy was she that she drove through the surges, cutting a path for herself on level keel while water came green across her deck.

"Boy," I heard one of the new hands say, "this ain't no ship. She's a fish."

In spite of the half-submerged condition of the *Arethusa* the first few days were pleasant, with satisfactorily mild winds. We slugged along up through the Gulf Stream, decks awash most of the time, and in warm, sunshiny weather. Each watch we tried the pumps, and each watch they sucked dry. The *Arethusa*'s topsides and decks were as tight as her under planking. Flying fish lit in the water on deck, thinking it was the sea.

I began to believe that my prediction that we should dodge all storms was a true prophecy. Then, my punishment for overloading my schooner caught up with me.

Three hundred miles off Hatteras, the sou'easter died, and a heavy squall came out of the southwest, advance guard for a wind that blew ever harder. We were too deep to carry much canvas in this blast. Before we could get in the mainsail, water was rolling over her decks, mid-thigh deep. Frenchy Rivert, my cook, summoned at the cry, "All hands on deck!" emerged grumpily from his galley, was tripped by a roller, caught up, and carried toward the rail. One of the Finns grabbed him and hauled him back spouting sea water and cuss words. If the cook's rescuer expected gratitude, he got none. Frenchy only glared as though he had been the victim of an inane practical joke.

The seas were getting up, and the overladen schooner submerged herself in every one that hit her. Sea did not wash her decks, but literally buried them in a tumult of water that swirled over hatches and foamed about the masts. It was past time to heave to, for you could see her sticks bending in the ever mounting gale and there was no spring or give in her hull to relieve them.

Buffeted by the invading seas, we all hung to the shrouds and waited, hearts in mouth for the three big waves whose aftermath would give us opportunity to heave to. Crosby, clinging to the wheel, handled her with the sure touch of an artist. Three big ones crossed our deck, nearly pulling some of us overboard with them. Crosby jammed the helm hard down, screeched: "Stand by the main halyards. Grab that sheet."

The *Arethusa* came into the wind. We fought and cursed as we got the mainsail in. It bellied and tried to evade our wet, clutching hands, but we stowed it, half of us under water most of the time. The wind in her rigging was a high steady yell. A sea climbed over our bow and came sternward, high and gray, rolling over the dories and smashing them to bits in its progress, immersing us and nearly drowning us before it passed. On a sailing craft you never appreciate the force of the wind until you heave to. Now, it swept our breath away and thrust its chilly fingers deep through our sodden clothes.

A mass of gray clouds like dirty cotton waste had wiped out the sun. The cheerful blue of the Gulf Stream had changed to lead. Foresail and jumbo still were set. The helm was hard down, and we were no longer sailing but simply drifting to leeward. We floundered about her deck, battening down the forecastle and cabin hatches, and then, because the water swept across the schooner as though she were a derelict, we perched when everything had been made secure on top of the furled mainsail. There, until nightfall, we stayed, a long, silent line of sodden men. No one said anything. We watched the *Arethusa* buried over and over again by the swarming seas; we looked at the hungry water swirling beneath us and clung to our perch.

None of us was happy, but no one, I think, was quite so wretched as I. The rest of them had only their own lives to worry about, which was enough, but I, with my boastful overloading of my schooner, was responsible for them all.

The sou'wester, blowing up out of the tropics, was not cold, but its blast made wet bodies shiver. The Gulf Stream, too, was warm. Otherwise, one by one, we miserable perchers on the main boom would have become numb and dropped away into the expectant seas.

Clinging to the furled canvas, I cursed myself heartily but uselessly. My infernal greed and my willingness to oblige a gang of bootleggers had made me overload my beloved schooner and take her to sea with men who of their own will had trusted their lives to me. It would serve me right if I did drown. I had always told myself that I was in the game for the adventure it afforded, and here I was, roosting on a boom with the crew I had imperiled because of nothing but my hunger for dollars.

I wondered why some of the men I had brought into this predicament didn't push me off into the water as a Jonah. I marveled that none of them at least said, "I told you so"; but no one spoke. I was perched next to a big Norwegian. When the gray water immersed the schooner and reached up toward our dangling feet, we held our breaths, wondering whether the schooner would emerge from that one. And when she did reappear, the squarehead would look at me and grin, saying worldessly, "Not that time, anyway."

I stopped my self-reproach and embarked in futile calculation. The hold was filled with whisky; the forecastle was jammed with it. There were 5,700 cases aboard, and beneath them, 125 tons of pig-iron ballast. The *Arethusa* was built of heavy white oak. I tried to see just where she retained the buoyancy that kept us afloat and I could discover no mathematical justification for it.

The wind was still mounting, and the seas rose with it. We watched the continual burial and resurrection of the *Arethusa* and wondered just how many times more she could go under so deep and still return to the surface. One great wave smashed against the jumbo and burst it out of the bolt ropes. Thereafter, the schooner lost all headway and lay broad side to the seas that climbed higher toward us. When they came aboard they drowned the hull of the *Arethusa* entire. Nothing remained but two masts sticking up in the turmoil of water. Then, while our hearts stood still, streaming bow and stern would emerge, to go under again a moment later.

In the late afternoon I saw a large steamer hove to on our lee and drifting along broadside with us. I knew then that the storm was as bad as it seemed to us main-boom roosters. Big steel ships depending on engine power only heave to in this fashion when the waves are so high that they threaten to break a craft's back if she heads into them.

Dusk came over the horizon, turning the ocean black in the twilight, the breaking seas began to gleam with phosphorescence, and in the dropping temperature my teeth chattered. I knew if we spent the night where we were there would be fewer of us there in the morning. I broke the silence that had endured for hours.

"What do you boys say," I asked, "to going down into the cabin and getting a drink?"

It was true that if we were below when the *Arethusa* went down and forgot to come up again, we should all have no chance, but we had little more than that on the main gaff.

"Let's go, Bill," the others chorused. Their teeth were chattering too.

It was easier to agree than to go, however. It meant playing tag with the enveloping waves. Each must wait until the schooner shook herself almost clear and then dive for the cabin hatch, slide it open and jam it shut behind himself before the next surge caught him. If he was tagged, he was out of the game permanently.

One by one we stumbled down into the cabin just ahead of the returning surges: water-soaked, dripping men, hair wet and lank, faces pinched with exhaustion and cold. We lighted the swinging lamps, looked at each other, and grinned weakly. I got a bottle of Murphy's rye, and we killed it. Never was liquor needed more.

Now that we could think of something besides our own immediate misery, we all spoke of the schooner's seaworthiness. Here in the cabin with a living gale blowing above, the motion was so easy that our glasses did not slide from the table, and the brand-new jumbo had been torn off her without the stay breaking. I knew there never was a better ship. I knew I had abused her with too heavy a cargo.

"If you boys say so," I proposed, "we'll dump all these cases in the cabin overside. That will lighten her a little and give us a better chance."

But the liquor was working in them too. A half hour before, they would have asked nothing better than to see every last case jettisoned. Now they said:

"We'll take a chance, Captain Bill." "She'll stand it." "Let's hang on now we've gone this far."

The light, the warmth, the liquor transformed us all. Trapped in this cabin, with the North Atlantic hammering and washing overhead, we sat about and told stories and laughed. Along about eight bells it seemed to me that the cadence of breaking water above was slackening. I laid my watch before me and counted the crashes. Gradually the intervals between them grew greater. The force of the attack was dying. At last I took the chance of opening the hatch slide and looked up into a dark blue sky, set with stars. The seas were still enormous, but the wind was dropping fast.

By nine o'clock we dared return to the deck. The water still ran across it, and we had to work slowly and cautiously to keep from being swept away, but we managed to set the riding sail, which gave us a little headway, unlashed the wheel, and eased it a few spokes before making it fast again.

Presently the steamer on our lee got underway and came sliding past us, a long dark form with seas exploding ghostly white about her bows. Her siren roared: "That was a tough one," and we waved a lantern and shouted:

"All right."

We set the watches, and I went below and turned in, certain that our troubles were over. Men sleep soundly because we do not know what fate still has up her sleeve. At seven next morning, when I went on deck, the sun was sparkling on an ocean that was blue once more and ruffled by only a gentle west wind. We had all sail set and were loafing along our course at 4 knots.

We sounded the well, with a good deal of eagerness and uncertainty. The pumps sucked dry. I didn't believe it, sounded myself, and when the washers only wheezed and brought up nothing, primed the pumps with a bucket of water. We managed to draw three or four buckets of thick black bilge from the hold, and then she was dry again. Through all that long, brutal, ordeal, with the Atlantic doing its worst, the *Arethusa* had not taken in a teacup of brine. That performance gave me a greater kick and boosted my spirits higher than any liquor ever made. A hot breakfast on the cabin hatch of biscuits, ham and eggs, and coffee, the bright sunlight, and relief from the worries of yesterday, cheered me still more.

The night before, I had sworn that, if I got out of that jam, this would be my last rum voyage. Now, with the back of an old chart spread on the hatch and the crew standing about, I drew plans for another and bigger rum-runner, a super *Arethusa*.

We had been cemented into a unit by what we had gone through. We argued and suggested and revised those plans like kids. When they were completed, everyone was satisfied.

She was to be 175 feet over all, regular Gloucester fisherman model, with a 30-foot beam and 15-foot draft. She was to have two more feet freeboard than the *Arethusa* and two 100-horse-power crude-oil engines. There were to be an electric-light plant and a fine roomy forecastle, a large pilot house, a chart room, three staterooms aft, a living room with a fireplace and space for a piano.

"We'll build this baby," I told my crew, "and we'll run rum till I'm a half million ahead of the game. Then we'll outfit her for a long cruise and bear away to the South Seas."

"We're with you, Captain Bill," they shouted. "We'll sign on now."

Crosby was more thrilled over plans for the new ship than was I. He took them carefully down into the cabin and tacked them up on the wall. I found him sitting in his old armchair before them and smoking soberly.

"Bill," he said as I came down, "are you on the level about building that ship?"

"You bet I am," I replied. "We'll unload this cargo in New York and then go to Canada, have her built, and bring her out next spring."

"And this South Sea voyage, were you kidding about that?"

"Not a bit."

He sighed happily and knocked ashes from his pipe.

"Count me in, Bill," he said. "Some way, I've always thought I'd like to see the South Seas."

The Gulf Stream was swarming with sharks, big, savage gray boys that attacked anything in motion on the water. We killed a great number of them. One of us would shake an oar overside, and when a big fellow came to investigate, four of us would whang away at him with Winchesters. Sharks are a sailor's bane, and we watched them with satisfaction as, after their death flurries, they turned over and sank, white bellies glimmering down into the depths.

Crosby stood at my shoulder watching the slaughter. I remember saying to him: "That's the way we'll all go if we follow the ocean too long."

Next morning, on his way on deck, he paused in the cabin again and looked over the plan he had tacked on the wall.

"She'll certainly be a daisy," he said wistfully and went on up to his death.

The preventer backstay must have been weakened by the *Arethusa*'s late ordeal. It carried away as Crosby emerged from the cabin, and the heavy block, falling plumb, struck him on the back of the head. I heard it thunder on the deck, ran up, and found my sailing master sprawled on the planking. He was moaning, but he was unconscious, and there was a great dent in the back of his skull.

I carried him to his bunk and shouted to the cook to bring the doctor book, sole medical aid to seamen who ply the ocean on small craft. It was only a slim little volume, and a single paragraph alone applied to Crosby's plight. For concussion of the brain, it said, one should keep the victim's feet warm and his face bathed with vinegar and cold water.

I sat by Crosby's bunk, while one seaman kindled a fire in our little cabin stove and the cook ran for the vinegar. The captain breathed thickly and did not stir. I got up and pulled the plan I had drawn off the wall where he had pinned it.

"By God,' I said, "I'm through with the sea!"

What little we could do for the injured man did not seem to help. We put his feet close up to the stove, and I sat and alternated with the cook in bathing his face. Late in the afternoon Frenchy said something about getting supper.

"Every man cooks for himself," I told him. "You and I stay with Crosby."

The wind rose again. We hove to under foresail and spare jumbo. Toward midnight, while the seas were breaking once more on our deck and the gale was yelping through our cordage, Crosby died.

The wind blew itself out before dawn. Day brought a quiet sea. We went about the schooner numb and silent. Each of us, I believe, had secretly resolved to quit the ocean forever. Sailors make such a vow a thousand times.

Two of us sewed Captain Crosby's body into a sail, with 100 pounds of iron at his feet. We carried him to the rail on a plank and covered him with our American flag. I tried to read the burial service but finally handed the book over to the cook. When he said: "I commit thy body to the deep," we tipped up the board.

Crosby slid into the ocean with a little splash. The sea was quiet and clear. I watched him going down through the water, a white gleaming that grew dimmer and dimmer; that faded into a momentary flicker of blue and was gone.

Chapter X

I FORGOT MY RESOLUTION to quit the sea in the more immediate and pressing matters that faced me. We were somewhere between Nassau and New York, and I was the sole navigator on board. A poor sort of a navigator at that, for I had not worked a sight since I was graduated from the school ship *Saratoga* twenty years before. I shut myself up with *The American Practical Navigator* and studied it harder and more faithfully than ever preacher did his Bible.

With Crosby's sextant, at noon I was lucky enough to get a good meridian shot, but clouds rolled up, and I got no P.M. sight. All I could do for my *Arethusa* was to place her somewhere in the Gulf Stream on a certain latitude.

My only course was to follow the Stream northward and, when I judged I was far enough along, run in and pick up some light. If I were lucky enough to get a Sumner's line, I could then keep well off shore until abreast of New York and haul in.

We stayed in the Gulf Stream all that night, but a wind that blew against its current kicked up so choppy a sea that at daybreak I feared it would shake the already overtaxed *Arethusa* apart, and I gave orders to haul in for the beach. I turned in after instructing the watch to keep testing the temperature of the water every quarter of an hour and note the exact time when it turned cold.

When I took the deck again we were out of the Gulf Stream and with the wind on the port quarter we were tearing in for the coast at a smart rate. If there is anything lonelier and more nerve-racking than to be a skipper, with no idea of his location, rushing on through darkness blacker than his own ignorance, I don't know it, and of course I kept the lead agoing.

Finally, our lookout thought he saw the masthead light of a steamer ahead. I clapped my night glasses on the pinhead of glow and identified Bodie Island Light with a great sigh of relief. We jibbed and ran along up the coast. Morning was clear and cold. The wind swung into the West, and there was only a mild sea. We set all sail for Rum Row and boiled along at 12 knots with our lee rail under, overhauling several steamers whose crews waved as we tore by.

I knew where I was. My schooner was winging it like an albatross. The day was bright, and I was coming into Rum Row with the cargo all my friends in Nassau had said I never could carry north. I had forgotten all about my determination to quit the sea.

Off Barnegat a thick fog came rolling in. We were outside the main steamship tracks, but we kept our foghorn blatting. The air grew so dense that I was about to heave to and wait for it to clear when the man at the wheel said: "Captain Bill, I've fished out of Fulton Market thirty year. I can take you right up to Rum Row along the Gully."

He showed me on the chart the narrow ribbon of deep water where the current of the Hudson River has cut a submarine gorge far out to sea.

"Hold your course," said he, "and swing the lead every quarter hour. When she drops off from fifteen to thirty fathoms we'll be in the Gully. There we'll jog around for the rest of the night and run right up to the Row in the morning."

We followed his directions and arrived as he had predicted in the twenty-mile offshore liquor market, where boats from all parts of the world had gathered for the Christmas trade. It was a week before we tossed a single "ham" of whisky into a sea skiff. The weather saw to that.

Gale followed gale. We fought a nor'easter and rode through it, only to turn about and battle with a nor'wester that was worse. It was a whole week of utter misery and nerve strain, with the possibility of wreck, or of icing up and sinking, always leering at my shoulder. We were cold and haggard and dirty, for our water was none too plentiful, and even the food was running short. There were moments when I wondered whether our nerve or the bad weather would break first, but we held on and were at length rewarded by a clear, calm day.

Sea skiffs clustered about the *Arethusa*, and she regained her buoyancy as the liquor went ashore in 50- and 100-case lots. My brother Ben appeared with fresh water, a hind quarter of beef, which we hung in the rigging, and crates of fresh vegetables. He carried no liquor on the trips he made to the Row but continually watched out for our comfort, bringing us not only supplies but newspapers and magazines whenever the weather was fair enough to permit him to venture out.

That was seldom enough. For every day that was calm enough for unloading we had three when the wind was savage and the seas brutal. There was also, during a storm, the additional hazard of being run down by some liner. We lay off the harbor, directly in the path of incoming steamers from all quarters of the globe. It was about as safe to remain there in a snow as it would be to wander about in a railway yard under similar conditions. More than one rum running craft was rolled under and sunk with all aboard her by a liner groping her way into the harbor through a storm.

When the wind brought snow I left the Row. I had picked a spot about a hundred miles offshore, outside the transatlantic and coast traffic lanes, and I would run the *Arethusa* out and heave to. And there we would stay until the wind blew itself out, secure and comfortable on the staunch little schooner.

I sent word ashore to the New York mobs that I was on the Row with liquor from their friends in Nassau. They took this off as rapidly as possible, but as a preliminary precaution, sent out two gunmen to protect their cargo. They were about as much use or protection on the *Arethusa* as a pair of wheels.

They were tough guys ashore, hard men. They told me so themselves, and I have no reason to disbelieve them. The trip to Coney Island was the longest sea voyage either of them had ever under taken hitherto. Both were seasick when they came aboard the *Arethusa*, and both were frightened sicker most of the time they remained on her. When it began to blow—and it blew aplenty that trip—these hard-boiled gun toters would turn a grayer green than the waves themselves, moan, and crawl into their bunks. I tried to get them to come on deck, but you might as well have tried to persuade the *Arethusa*'s keel to come up.

One day, while we were returning to the Row after having ridden out a particularly violent storm, I spoke to the larger and professedly tougher of the pair. He lay in his bunk, alternately sick and scared to death.

"Jake," I persuaded, "you'll feel much better if you'll come up. You'll get a kick out of the waves. They're running big."

He gave a quavering moan. "Waves," he shuddered, "damn 'em, I can't see nothing else. Leave me alone."

He pointed to a mirror on the cabin wall. This was placed just opposite the hatch and as the *Arethusa* rolled, revealed now and then, a reflection of gray, tumbling water. The tough guy pulled the blanket up over his head and remained where he was.

Given a single week of fair weather, we could have unloaded completely. Blizzards and gales kept us on the Row four weeks. Whenever there was the slimmest chance of making the trip successfully, sea skiffs came out from the Jersey shore to my schooner. I was selling my rye for $60 a case. On the beach it was gobbled up eagerly at $120 that made these fishermen willing to take all sorts of risks.

They would come wabbling and bouncing out in their little open craft, one man steering, the other pumping for dear life, and swing in under my schooner's lee. Usually it was too rough to tie up. Four of us would hold the skiff away from our side with oars and boat hooks, and we would throw the "hams" of liquor out to her crew.

The buyer would toss a roll of bills to me. "Twelve thousand dollars for 200 cases, Bill," he would shout. There would be no time to count it then. I would stow it away in my desk drawer and leave my dog on watch. When the customers had gone I would check up. Apart from the one man who had tried to pass counterfeit $20 bills, no one who traded with my schooner ever attempted to cheat me. I don't believe any so-called legitimate business can equal that record.

My sales were made in the midst of confusion and haste, often after nightfall, and to men I had never seen before and might never encounter again. It would have been easy to cheat me, since it was known that I did not count the cash I received until later. There was no possibility of reprisal if I did discover fraud. Yet at the end of a sojourn on the Row, when I totaled the proceeds on the way home, the result always was correct, or more than I had calculated I should have.

The cash, nearly always, was in large denominations, usually $1,000 bills with a sprinkling of $5,000 and 10,000 notes. If a bootlegger handed you $100 certificates, he apologized, as the average man might if he paid a debt in pennies. The larger bills I usually slipped between the pages of Bowditch or my Bible. The rest I stuffed into my desk drawer. I always dreaded the task of sorting and counting these yellow and green slips and postponed it as long as I could. You may think a job like that would be thrilling and exciting. It wasn't. It was confusing, tedious, down right hard work. The joys of riches are overestimated if you have to sit down and count them.

Most daring of the sea-skiff men who worked off New Jersey's shore was Geriard Haldenbach, a lad who would ride his little boat through a yelping nor'wester as calmly as a nurse guides a baby carriage. Frequently we would be hove to, debating whether to stay in the Row or run before the storm, when the lookout would shout:

"Boat coming."

I would know it was Geriard. He drove through weather that kept all other sea-skiff owners ashore, thanking God they were there. With the sea bursting into foam about him, with the planks of his skiff's bottom smacking the waves like giant handclapping, he would come roaring out to buy.

The first day I saw him was one of the dirtiest during which we hung onto the Row. He came under the lee of the *Arethusa* with a foot of water slopping about in the bottom of his skiff and a boy working a pump.

"Fifty cases," Geriard yelled and tossed payment aboard. The rollers were running short and high against the ebb tide and the sea skiff and the schooner were rising and falling as though they were on alternating elevators. I said: "Son, you don't want to try to haul more than twenty-five cases today. If you had any sense you'd be ashore, anyhow."

"Fifty cases," he repeated. "I know my boat."

We were holding him off with oars and boathooks. A big wave lifted the *Arethusa*, and as she dropped into its trough the same roller heaved the sea skiff aloft and literally floated it onto our deck. Waist deep in water, we got it clear before the schooner rose again. Geriard only grinned while we cussed him plenty, but we all admired his nerve. He got his fifty cases and made shore. Thereafter he was one of my steady customers when I was on the Row. He told me he was in the game and taking the chances he did because he had just married a girl and wanted her to have the best of everything in the world.

"I make $3,000 a trip," he said. "She's worth taking risks for."

He died a little later with a Coast Guard's bullet through his brisket; died on the sea skiff we had grown to know so well. He was taking his chance, and the Coast Guard was following orders.

And let an ex-rum-runner say right here that those men of the cutters who made life misery for me were and are fine, square seamen who did a dirty job most of them didn't like, as cleanly as it could be done. Rumors of all sorts floated around the Row about the men of the service. I never believed them, and I never heard of any of them being proved. There are crooks even in the ministry. I have no reason to love Coast Guards, Treasury agents or Department of Justice men. They combined to put me in jail. I do say, however, that no government in the world has gamer, fairer servants than these. Prohibition enforcement agents are something else again.

Coast Guards in small launches frequently would pursue sea skiffs on the way back from the Row. Such a chase was under way one day when Geriard crossed its line and started to pick up one of the cases the fugitive had flung overboard. The pursuer fired at random and shot the lad dead. He had only meant to scare him away.

We spent Christmas on Rum Row that voyage. Ben came out Christmas Eve, which was calm and clear, with two great turkeys, cranberries, celery, nuts, and candy. We opened a case of champagne I bought from another rum-runner and had a gorgeous dinner, Christmas noon. That afternoon, however, the barometer began to drop and a nor'easter came snoring in to drive us out to sea to our safe spot, where we rode out the storm. We returned to do a brisk business all Christmas week. A few days before New Year's a neighbor on the Row ran his schooner alongside mine and confided that she had sprung a leak and would have to go into the harbor for repairs. He had still a hundred cases of champagne and sparkling Burgundy aboard, and he asked me to take it off his hands. I bought it.

At midnight of December 31st we welcomed in 1923 along the Row with burning flares, pounding of ship's bells, snorting foghorns and the bang and clatter of rifles and machine guns. Most of the vessels on Rum Row were armed now, for New York gangs were learning that there were softer pickings out to sea than they could find even along Broadway.

I had given the forecastle hands a case of Burgundy, and no ship greeted the New Year more boisterously than ours. I turned in soon after midnight and went to sleep almost at once. Three hours later, I woke sitting up in my bunk and vaguely worried about something. I can't explain what alarmed me, except that when anything was wrong with the *Arethusa* I always roused.

I went on deck. It had been snowing softly, and the ship stood out white against the black seas. Not a man was to be seen. There was no one at her helm. We were sailing about Rum Row risking collision with some other ship, square in the lanes of incoming craft, with my entire crew full of Burgundy and sleeping it off below. I got two of the more nearly conscious up on deck and remained on watch the rest of the night myself. We would have been an ideal victim for a rum pirate.

These gentry were becoming troublesome and grew increasingly menacing during the remainder of Rum Row's existence. I had heard of their raids in Nassau and before coming north on this run had shipped a couple of Lewis machine guns, several Thompson sub-machine guns, a half dozen Winchesters, several sawed-off shotguns, and a Colt .45 for each member of my crew. While selling liquor on the Row all of us went armed, and sub-machine guns were hidden in the furled sails. I also had given orders to my men never to bunch when strangers were on our deck but to keep scattered so that it would be impossible for pirates to hold us all up at once.

Only once did I graze actual trouble with these "go-through men" as the raiders were called, their boast being that whatever job they undertook, they did it and came back with the loot.

Three boats, two men on each, came alongside us one day. I did not like the looks of the visitors and warned my men to be on the alert while they were aboard. I don't think the "go-through men" cared for our looks either, for we had been at sea a month then, had not shaved since we left port, and each wore a heavy Colt on his hip. There might have been trouble, but it was averted by the arrival of other customers. They recognized the crooks and told me who they were. I ordered them off my schooner, and they went, growling, but obediently enough.

Another evening, on this same voyage, we saved seven "go-through men" from drowning, which probably won't be set down to our credit in Judgment Day Book. We marked them drifting past in a snow squall, one man working the hand pump of their sea skiff, another vainly cranking the engine, and the rest squatting miserably about. We ran over to them and picked them up. They were half frozen and seasick, with the dazed look of men who had been rescued after they had given themselves up for lost.

No harder-looking mob ever assembled in Blackbeard's or Harry Morgan's cabin than I had in mine that evening. Faces that never could have been admired for their spirituality or intellect had been further distorted by the scars of knives and bullets.

There was a large representation of cauliflower ears. My visitors moved quickly, and their eyes, until the drinks I poured them began to take effect, were narrow and alert. They were well armed, each man carrying at least one gun and a blackjack and having as well several pairs of handcuffs. These, when they had taken a ship, were to be used to tether the members of the crew with their arms about a mast until the craft had been unloaded.

They stayed all night, for a stiff wind was blowing and it was too dark to tinker with their boat until daylight. We all sat up together, largely because none of us dared to go to sleep, and yarned the hours away. I never had more courteous and proper guests. At midnight we grew hungry again, despite the supper we had stowed away earlier, and we made pancakes over the cabin stove.

One of my visitors then prepared a chicken salad and taught me how to make the dressing, which I use to this day. He explained that he had learned it while warden's cook in Sing Sing. Toward morning I broke out a can of molasses, and the pirates and their host had an old-fashioned candy pull.

By daylight the wind had died down and we were able to get our visitors' skiff to running again. They went aboard her after thanking me profusely and chugged away. Later, they reappeared.

"Hey, Bill," one of them called. "Can you handle 3,000 cases of champagne?"

I said I couldn't and asked why.

"Oh," they replied, "we've just taken a nigger schooner, and that's what she has aboard. Thought you might be able to use it. We can get rid of it all right."

Frequently, on subsequent trips, fast, suspicious-looking craft would bear down on me. "What schooner?" they would hail.

"Bill McCoy's," I would yell in return.

"Oh," they would reply and I always grinned at the change of tone. "Hello, Bill. How they coming? Our mistake," and the pirate craft would slide away into the darkness. Word had been passed around that I was right and was to be left alone. This, and our armament probably saved me a battle, first or last.

These marine hold-up men did not extend their protection to cover my customers. On this same voyage, one night, a lad from Freeport, Long Island, came aboard from his sea skiff cursing like an angry cat. He had been held up on his way out to the *Arethusa* and his craft had been searched by a launch full of men who said they were Coast Guards. He had hidden his money, $3,000, in the pump, and they had threatened to throw him overboard when they could not find it.

He was certain, and so was I, that they were pirates and would jump him again on his way back to shore with his cargo. I lent him a sawed-off repeating shotgun with six loads of buckshot in her magazine and told him to burn them up if necessary, for it was always open season on hijackers.

The lad was game. I stood beside our forward machine guns and watched him cast off. As he slid away from the *Arethusa*'s side, the pirates' craft, which had lain in the oiling, invisible in the darkness, crossed our bow in pursuit. I could see neither boat nor men, but only the swift white blur of water thrown up by her bows. I cast loose the machine gun and let him have it. Above its hammering I could hear yells and curses. They sheered away, and the Freeport lad escaped.

To the inexperienced and unwary, the pirates were always a menace. Several times, at night, we heard the far-away sputter of pistol shots and the accompaniment of yelling that told us the "go-through men" were in active practice.

Norwegian neighbors of mine on the Row were victims in November of this year. Theirs was a high-sided, ketch-rigged old craft and her owner, his son, a cook, and one seaman had brought her across the Atlantic with 500 cases of Scotch. They all were mild, rather bewildered squareheads, and when they were offered a charter to bring 1,000 cases up from Nassau, they took it gladly, for the pay was to be $3,000—a fortune in Norway.

The charterers had taken most of the liquor off and had not paid the old squarehead a cent. He asked for his money. That night his ship was pirated, all her remaining liquor but thirty cases which the captain had hidden beneath the cabin floor was taken, with what money the old man possessed as well.

We heard the racket during the night, and next morning my mate and I rowed over to investigate. The poor old captain was crying. He wore strange, stiff Norwegian fishing clothes, and high leather sea boots in which he shuffled about the deck rather than walked. He was a whole ocean away from home and had lost everything but the hidden thirty cases. I bought these from him for enough to get him back to Norway. I knew the charterers of the ship had pirated him to keep from having to pay the $3,000.

Rum Row was never a safe place, but we soon came to regard the risks as part of our business. All sailors, by the nature of their calling, are fatalists, anyway. They have seen too much of the whimsicalities of Fate not to believe in her. "What is going to be, is going to be," they say, and let it go at that.

Soon after New Year's, two big Newfoundlanders—Gilletts and Hickey—boarded the *Arethusa* one night. They had been ashore from their schooner *Jeanette*, and now, in the darkness, could not find her. We bade them welcome and, since the wind was making

Arethusa/Tomoka loaded to the gunwales in Nassau, Bahamas. (*Courtesy of The Mariners' Museum, Newport News, VA.*)

A Jersey Sea Skiff arrives on Rum Row. McCoy thought these the best contact boats.

A calm sea and some French visitors on Rum Row. Visiting fellow rum running vessels was a common practice. (*Courtesy of The Mariners' Museum, Newport News, VA.*)

The transit from Nassau, Bahamas, to Rum Row off the New Jersey Highlands, took about one week. (*Courtesy of The Mariners' Museum, Newport News, VA.*)

While on Rum Row, a lookout was always posted to look for customers and hijackers.

The crew of a mackerel boat come shopping for whiskey. Rum running vessels on Rum Row would trade liquor for fresh fish. (*Courtesy of The Mariners' Museum, Newport News, VA.)*

The *Tomoka/Arethusa*'s deckload of rye

The pirated Norwegian craft

The poor old captain was crying

Life on Rum Row included doing laundry, airing bedding and washing dishes.

Tomoka/Arethusa rides out a noreaster on Rum Row with a deck load. (*Courtesy of The Mariners' Museum, Newport News, VA.*)

and it was beginning to snow again, I ran out to my haven of safety in the Atlantic. There we rode out the storm, and, about noon next day, when the gale had abated, returned to our station off the Highlands. A rum-runner, empty and outward bound, hailed us as she passed.

"Hear about the *Jeanette*, Bill?"

"No"

"Run down in storm last night. Cut in half. Most of her crew drowned."

Gilletts and Hickey in all probability had saved their lives by losing track of their ship. They did not seem specially impressed by their escape. What was going to be, was going to be.

If there is anything in the favoritism of Fate, she is saving Hickey for great things or a hanging. He and his partner Gillets signed on with me. They were splendid sailors both, and I made Gilletts mate of the *Arethusa*, on which Hickey was one of my best seamen.

The following October the *Arethusa* was trapped close inshore on the Row by a sudden gale from the southeast. The Jersey and Long Island coast lines form a right angle, with New York harbor at its apex, and we were off the harbor mouth when the storm hit us. The wind blew directly toward Manhattan, but we did not want to visit New York. We were literally in a funnel neck, with Jersey and Long Island forming the flare of its sides. To get out of our trap we would have to beat offshore almost into the teeth of the gale. This was coming in so strong that its force kicked the crests off the mounting seas and set them flying in showers of spray. We were in too close to anchor. We had to claw our way out. If we were blown back on the beach we lost our ship and, if we didn't drown, we went to jail. It was up to the schooner to rescue us.

Foresail and jumbo were set. We battened her down, set her on the port tack and, huddling abaft the mainmast, watched the battle. The wind grew stronger. Presently rain came, wiping out visibility with a cold, stinging flood. The harder it blew, the heavier the seas became, the better my *Arethusa* behaved. She was one of the truly game whom heavy odds only inspire the more.

Masts slanting, sails straining, rail awash, and seas ranging across her to smash and spout at the break in her deck, doused by rain and buffeted by wind, the *Arethusa* fought her way to sea into the face of the storm. In moments like this a ship ceases to be a structure of wood and canvas. She becomes a creature. You feel that she is alive. You almost believe in the existence of her soul. And like a mighty soul, my schooner went forward against imminent disaster and battled her way offshore.

We could see nothing, but we knew we were winning, for Hickey was swinging the lead, and his voice chanted the deepening fathoms. I watched him prepare to heave again. One minute he stood, the six feet, two hundred pounds of him gigantic through the wavering rain. The next he had been erased by a sudden great sweep of water.

The *Arethusa* had taken a heavy lee roll, and a monster wave had leaped and caught him. He was gone. No one said anything. We heard only the clash of water and the screaming wind. Search for Hickey was impossible. He was gone.

The same sea that abolished him had washed the main sheet overside. It trailed in the tumult of water, and through that gray confusion, hand over hand along a dragging rope, came Hickey. He stood on our deck once more. Fate had calmly disregarded all the probabilities and had saved him when the odds were ten thousand to one against him. Was he grateful? Not perceptibly. He coughed up sea water and swore between heaves.

In January, 1923, the weather finally eliminated all further traffic on Rum Row. Storm followed storm so rapidly that it was impossible to get any liquor ashore. I still had 800 cases of my own aboard, but I decided to end my season now. I was tired of being chased out to sea, returning only to be chased out again by another gale.

Ben brought out a new sailing master, a young man from Gloucester and a sailor from boot soles to sou'wester peak. I determined to go to Halifax and refit during the rest of the winter. On the day the *Arethusa* started north, my schooner *M.M. Gardner*, illegally seized by the government, was at last released and sailed from New York, en route for Nassau.

The mass of currency in my cabin worried me. I wanted to get it into a bank as soon as possible. I packed a suitcase full with it and went ashore with Ben, telling the *Arethusa*'s sailing master I would meet him at Halifax. I banked $127,000 and went to Canada by train.

CHAPTER XI

I HAD BEEN IN HALIFAX A WEEK and was beginning to worry about my schooner when I had a telephone call from the hospital. My schooner's captain explained over the wire that the *Arethusa* was in the harbor, having fought head winds all the way up the coast, and that he himself was laid up with a fractured jaw caused by a swinging jumbo-sheet block.

I went to see Bill Acker, collector of the port. He was less severe than on our former interview. Nova Scotia was gradually drifting out of prohibition, but the law had not yet been repealed. I was permitted to bring my schooner in and refit her, despite the 800 cases of liquor in her hold, after I had given Acker my word that I would dispose of none of it while in port.

We put the *Arethusa* on the Halifax Shipyard Corporation ways, replaced worn tackle and wormy planks, and installed a 100-horsepower Fairbanks-Morse crude-oil engine that Ben had shipped up from New York, and a large fuel tank. I also reduced her sail area by having ten feet taken off the main boom and five off the main gaff. This rig made her steadier and easier to handle.

While on the shipyard ways, the president of the corporation, McClerg, asked me if I could let him have a few cases of champagne for a party he planned to throw. I was more than glad to oblige him, and told him so, but added that he would have to square matters with the collector of the port and the prohibition authorities first, for I had given my word not to break out a single quart while I was in the harbor.

One afternoon he sent over a boatman with the message that everything was fixed, and I let him have eight cases. Two weeks later, the prohibition director, Tracy, notified me that my ship had been seized, and Bill Acker sent for me. He and Tracy both were in his office when I arrived. Acker said:

"Bill McCoy, I'd have bet my bank roll on your word, and now you've broken it."

"Will you wait a minute," I asked, "and let me tell my yarn?" They heard me through, and then looked at each other. Both denied that they had given McClerg permission to get the champagne.

"All right," I said at last. "I'm the goat. That's that. Now what happens?"

We talked it over and decided to get rid of the case with as little publicity or pain as possible. It was arranged that my captain should take the blame and my name be kept out of the affair. The trial was held next day in the local court. When called, my captain stood up. The judge asked: "Are you guilty or not guilty?"

This was a new racket for my captain. He looked about helplessly until his eyes lighted on me.

"Which am I, Bill?" he asked.

"You're guilty," I informed him. "Tell the judge so."

"Guilty, your honor," said the captain.

"Two hundred dollars fine, one dollar costs," the judge answered. I paid the fine, later had to pay an additional $600 penalty imposed by Ottawa, and the matter was ended.

The *Arethusa* lay all winter in Halifax, but the newly freed *M.M. Gardner* was on the Row with 5,000 cases of Spay Royal and Strathmill Scotch whiskies which I had purchased jointly with the Italians in Jamaica. She had a long and miserable time unloading, for it was brutally cold with many storms. Ice lay thick in the inlets and floated out to sea, and the lightly built shore boats had to pick their way with care. Several boats cut their planks through on the sharp ice and were lost. One 60-footer ran into drift ice and sank with all on board in the North River off Hoboken. Five hundred cases of rye still lie beneath the river where commuters ferry daily.

I wanted to get out of the fog and bitter cold of Halifax and back to Nassau, but business made it necessary for me to go by way of New York. I knew they were more anxious than ever to lay hold of me there, but I decided to risk it.

I cleared the *Arethusa* for the Bahamas under the same sailing master and took passage on the Red Star liner for New York. The purser and I made an arrangement whereby I was stowed away in his cabin during the voyage, and he guaranteed to get me safely ashore when we reached the pier in Brooklyn. I went down the gangplank there in a waiter's coat and cap, put in at a saloon several blocks away and exchanged garments with the waiter, who presently arrived there with my own hat and coat and my suitcase.

I was tipped off before I started south by train that government agents were on the watch for me in Miami. I got off at Fort Lauderdale, twenty-five miles north of Miami, took an automobile to the Miami waterfront, and went to sea in a launch. When the *Mystery J.*, the little Miami-Nassau packet came out of the harbor, I boarded her, and the following morning reached Nassau.

It was a real homecoming for me when we entered the loveliest harbor in the world, with the white light at its entrance, the big white bulk of the Colonial Hotel looming on the opposite point, and the flocking buildings of Nassau beyond, with rolling hills in the background capped by the old gray Spanish fort.

The welcome I got when I stepped ashore warmed me like a jolt of rum. The customs men wrung my hand and then waved me through. Niggers on Bay Street grinned and shouted to each other, "Heah de sure-enough boss man!" Mrs. Kemp greeted me as though I had been her son. I bathed and shaved, changed my heavy clothing for pongee, and then wandered the rest of the day about town. Liquor dealers, bootleggers, and private citizens made much of me. The rumor had got about that I was dead, inspired no doubt by the death of Crosby. I wondered, as I strolled through warm-hearted, open handed Nassau, if perhaps I weren't dead and had arrived at the rum-runner's heaven.

Consul Lathrop, during my days in Nassau, used to ask me almost every time I met him:

"Bill, when are you going back home?"

I would answer: "Never, Consul. Why should I? I have right now what most Americans work three quarters of their lives to get. I'm on a permanent vacation, and to make it better, I've got a job that is more fun than a goat."

Those years in Nassau were the happiest of my life. They were too good to last.

I had got my business affairs well straightened out by the time the *Arethusa* came into harbor to receive the welcome that the waterfront always paid a rum-runner returning from a successful voyage. These greetings were worth seeing, and the *Arethusa* was received with more enthusiasm than other craft, for she was the best of the rum fleet and the darling of Nassauvians.

Pirates returning from a profitable cruise, blockade runners coming in, cotton and tobacco laden, probably received duplicates of these welcomes. The waterfront would be packed with cheering people. Mulattoes and octoroons, dressed in all their finery, would squeal and make eyes at the seamen. Runners eager to guide the returning sailors to the not inconsiderable merriment that Nassau in those days afforded would be there to pick up their convoys. Darkies would sing impromptu songs in honor of the returning ships. Some of them were genuine folk songs, original in words and tune. Several became so popular that the band used to play them at the receptions in Governor's House. The greatest and best of all rum running ports was Nassau.

I went ahead with my determination to reduce my fleet, and sold the *J.B. Young* to Johnson of Nassau. I intended to continue to sail the Arethusa myself, and one other craft, the *M.M. Gardner*, was all I felt I could handle safely and efficiently.

Much to the resentment of rum-runners in general, Nassauvians were not content merely with selling liquor, but were beginning to transport it to the Row, as well. This, many runners felt, was an infringement of their rights and a deliberate attempt to drive them out of business. In consequence of this hostility many Bahama-owned craft suffered when they got to the Row. Not a few of them were pirated, and the rest were discriminated against whenever possible.

The *J.B. Young* was lost on the first voyage she made for Johnson. He loaded her with 3,000 cases of rye and sent her to the Row. One night, while I was there on the *Arethusa*, a launch load of "go-through men" slid under my lee, and one of them called to me:

"Bill, is it true you don't own the *J.B. Young* any more?"

I admitted it and asked why they wanted to know. He made no direct response.

"We're set, then. Come on. Whoopee! Let's go!" The launch's wide open engine kicked her away into the darkness. That night the *Young* was pirated.

Three "go-through men" took her. They boarded as buyers and one of them began to pass out cigarettes. Of course, the entire crew of the *Young* bunched about him and were easy marks for the others, who held them up, marched them to the forecastle, and locked them in. They were kept there a whole day while the liquor was transferred. The pirates then unlocked the forecastle hatch and told their prisoners that the first man to stick his head outside within an hour would have it blown off. They made a clean get-away, with liquor worth $90,000, Nassau prices; and $180,000 on the Jersey beach.

I've always suspected what gang did it, but it was none of my business. The general opinion of rum-runners was that Johnson only got what was coming to him for trying to be liquor dealer and rum-runner at once.

Murphy was a liquor dealer who never tried to infringe upon a rum-runner's business. I visited him as soon as I returned to Nassau and found that his supply of gorgeous rye was almost exhausted. He had only three loads remaining. A Jewish mob who had chartered a big Lunenberg schooner and I each wanted it all. Murphy arbitrated. The Jews were loading one shipment, now. I could have another. The remaining 5,000 cases would go to the vessel that returned first to Nassau from Rum Row. It would be the prize for a race to New York and back.

The *Arethusa* began to load as the black British craft left Nassau harbor. She had a twenty-four-hour start on us, but we reached Rum Row only a little behind her. Within sight of each other we unloaded. Word spread of the contest, and when buyers learned that these shipments were almost the last of Murphy's rye, the best of such liquor in the world, we had no lack of customers. We worked day and night getting our cargo overside. The crew of the Lunenberger labored equally hard.

Late one afternoon I saw the black schooner get up her hook and make sail. She was sold out and on her way back for that final precious load. I still had fifty cases aboard unsold and could expect no customers until after nightfall. I hailed a rum running friend on a neighboring vessel, ran down to him and gave him the last fifty cases on consignment. The Lunenberger had gone over the horizon when we turned the *Arethusa* toward Nassau.

Clouds in the east told us wind was coming. My crew all were on their toes, my sailing master out of Gloucester was in his element. He knew what it meant to race for market, but he was trying this time to beat an opponent for a liquor cargo, not to be the first to sell his fish.

The wind came and stayed with us, a nor'easter that blew ever harder, and with full mainsail, foresail, jumbo, and jib filled with its pressure, we took all it could blow and asked for more.

With two men fighting her helm, with masts raking across the low flying storm clouds, with rigging singing like plucked fiddle strings, and a great angle of phosphorescent foam spreading from her eager bow, the *Arethusa* went south. All night long she plunged along like a runaway horse, and all night long my Gloucester skipper perched on the weather rail and, clinging to the main rigging, sang to her.

Through the tumult of the wind, the deep bass undertone of the taut wind-smitten canvas, the crash and wash of surges, I heard him singing in crooning, soothing monotone, urging his ship along. He took no relief from the mate, but watched over her and sang. Only when the gale blew itself out next morning did he go below.

We ran our latitude down with the help of that nor'easter. At noon, we were sixty miles ahead of our dead reckoning. Wind and her captain's song had brought the *Arethusa* 280 knots in twenty-four hours. We reached Nassau in five days from Rum Row and beat the Lunenberger in by a wide margin. Murphy grinned when I stepped ashore.

"The Jews said, Bill, that you weren't coming back but had gone to St. Pierre. I knew better. As a matter of fact I had a piece of change that said you'd beat them in."

I bought his last cargo of rye and took it back to the Row.

The summer of 1923 was the busiest and the happiest of my rum running career. It was also the era of Rum Row's greatest prosperity. My trips to and from Nassau went on with the regularity of a train schedule—one week to load, one week for the journey up, one week to sell, one week to sail home. On the 4th of each month I cleared from Nassau. Three weeks later I would return, with a suitcase packed with cash. I had grown to know the harbor so well that, if it were night when we reached the bar, I would not wait for morning and a pilot but would sail her in myself. Then I would go ashore, wake up Pilot Brown so that he might go down and touch the *Arethusa*'s rail and claim the pilot's fee, report to the medical officer, carry my cash to Mrs. Kemp's, throw it into the closet, and sleep until morning.

I was carrying the proceeds of a voyage to the bank one morning when I encountered Consul Lathrop, striding along as usual in impeccable starched white.

"Consul," I hailed him, "want to hold $130,000?" He hefted the bag and then asked: "You really mean you have that much in there?"

"You bet," I told him. He twisted his gray mustache thoughtfully for a moment.

"Bill," he said at length, "I'm in a quandary. I love this island. When I retire, I want to spend the rest of my life here. I'm building, as you probably know, a house out west. One of my neighbors is a most unpleasant person. So unpleasant, in fact, that I don't want my house near his. Yet there we are. It bothers me a lot."

We chatted on other topics, and then I went on to the bank. Entirely without Lathrop's knowledge, I made inquiries concerning the house of his distasteful neighbor. I found the man was only renting it and that I could purchase it for $500. I bought it and declined to renew my involuntary tenant's lease.

"Consul," I asked him the next time I saw him, "would you rather have so-and-so or a rum-runner for a neighbor?"

"That depends," he replied, looking at me keenly.

"You haven't any choice," I told him. "So-and-so is moving, and I've bought his house."

He was silent for a minute, and then said quietly: "Thank you, Bill."

I intended, eventually, to live in that dwelling, but fortune and the United States government had other plans for me. After my release from jail I sold the house for what it had cost me. I took the money back to Florida and stuck it away in a bank that promptly blew up, and I lost every penny.

CHAPTER XII

RUM ROW, IN THE SPRING OF 1923, in accordance with one of the many rulings laid down by the government, moved in to within seven miles of shore. That, in itself, helped to boom trade. For a time, save for pirate raids now and then, everything progressed smoothly and profitably under the supervision of revenue cutters.

Toward the end of the summer the government went actively to war against us. Cutters that heretofore had been content just to see that ships on the Row preserved the proprieties, began to intrude on their business. Rum-runners were chased and fired on, first with blanks and then with shell. Destroyers were turned over to the revenue men, and a horde of 75- and 36-foot speed boats were being constructed for their use. It was these last that finally scattered the old Rum Row. They became so thick and active that shore boats feared to venture out for a load of liquor.

But in early 1923 Rum Row was in its heyday. I used to look at that long line of craft, anchored all the way from Montauk to Cape May, with the pride a first settler would feel in the growth of his town.

Schooners and yachts, windjamming square-riggers from Scandinavia, tramps from England and Germany, converted tugs and submarine, chasers, anything with a bottom that would float and a hold that could be filled with booze, they stretched away in a long line, bowing to the surges, swinging with the tide and wind, waiting in apathy all day for the strenuous activity that began as soon as night fell. Up and down that long line white cutters plodded, surveying the old-timers, inspecting new arrivals. Dories floundered across from ship to ship as the captains and crews of the fleet exchanged visits. It was a roaring, boisterous, sinful-and-glad-of-it, marine Main Street of shifting membership and continually increasing size, and I was its founder and first citizen.

Beside the rust-streaked iron square riggers and tramps and the black, frowzy schooners of the fleet, my *Arethusa*, with her white hull and slim, well kept lines stood out like a lovely lady in a slum. She was the most famous and the fairest ship on the Row. When we were there we sold out more rapidly than anyone else. She was McCoy's ship, and she carried the real McCoy liquor, genuine, the best procurable, and uncut.

My reputation was all the advertisement I needed. Until the cutters began to be annoying I sold my liquor almost as fast as we could bring it up from the hold. One night that summer, when the sea was calm and all America apparently wanted a drink, I set the Rum Row record by unloading into small craft 3,400 cases between 5 and 10 P.M. I could have sold twice as much that night if I had had it, but they cleaned us out, and at 10 we sailed back to Nassau for more.

When we reached the Row and anchored, my brother Ben would come out to greet us, bringing fresh meat, vegetables, tobacco, water, newspapers, and magazines. Now that the *Arethusa* had an engine to move her quickly when necessary, we would anchor if it were flat calm and prepare for business. Otherwise we would jog about. Anchor or not, the trade came to us fast enough.

My reputation and the white form of the *Arethusa* riding on the Row were all the advertisement I needed. I had an understanding with my customers that if the schooner were flying the British ensign, it was unsafe to come near her by daylight. If she flew no flag, we were ready for business. For the guidance of shore boats at night, I placed a brilliant electric light well up in my ship's rigging. We were one of the few craft on the Row to have our own plant. Unshielded, we found this rigging light made our decks as bright as day and gave our operations undesired publicity. After one trial I put the bottom of a barrel underneath the lamp. It could be seen, thus, at a distance, but the disk of wood kept the deck and immediate vicinity of the *Arethusa* in deep shadow.

Business, as a rule, began at dusk and continued till just before dawn. Until the cutters began to be severe and inquisitive, boats would run out from shore at any hour, their crew would get a bite to eat aboard while we were loading and then would make leisurely return to the Long Island or Jersey coast. When supervision tightened, all the work was done at night.

At twilight we would get the hatch off the hold, buckle on the guns we never had to use, and prepare for business. My Gloucester captain had left me early, this year, and I had made Arey, skipper of the *Young*, sailing master of the *Arethusa*. Arey, as night fell, would climb aloft and, perched on the cross trees, night glasses in hand, watch for cutters or snooping revenue men.

"Boat coming," he would call down. We could see the craft just before it reached us, in the glow of our masthead lamp. Then it would slide into the great circle of shadow shed by the barrel bottom and come alongside. Someone would sing out, "A hundred Black & White" and toss up a roll of bills. Seamen, supervised by Gilletts, my mate, would pass "hams" over the rail. They would be stowed away in the shore boat, motors would roar, and she would be away, her crew happy in the possession of an extra case for themselves. I always gave the lads presents of whisky, and always a drink, whether they bought from me or not.

At times, when business was brisk, there would be fifteen skiffs, launches, and other varieties of motorboat lying alongside, side by side, at one time, each with its engine pounding until you had to screech to be heard. Wads of bills would be shoved at me from all directions. My pockets would jam so full that I would have to go below several times a night and empty them into my desk where Old Faithful mounted guard. Everyone was eager to get away. Everyone wanted to be loaded at once. The *Arethusa*'s deck would be as confused and noisy as the floor of the Stock Exchange on a busy day.

Men whom I knew loaded their own boats. A regular customer would cram his roll into my hands and shout, "A hundred Lawson's, Bill." I would screech back, "Port hold, Jake. Help yourself." No one ever took more liquor than he bought. No one ever shortchanged me in paying for it.

After midnight, as a rule, the trade would slacken. By 3 A.M., when the lights went out on the Asbury Park boardwalk, we knew our work was practically over. We would watch a new day come out of the sea, and then would roll into our bunks and sleep, utterly exhausted, far into the morning.

Accommodating customers on shore would send us off a boat with the morning papers and milk. We had all the comforts of home on the Row and some no home would harbor. Cash was so thick there and men so generous that daughters of joy actually started a navy of their own and embarked on Rum Row, sailing instead of street walking.

We lived high. Besides the food brought out to us from New York—we frequently lay so close to the harbor mouth that on clear days we could see the white spire of the Woolworth Building shining above the shore haze—the mackerel fleet hovered about, more than willing to exchange a mess of fresh-caught fish for a few bottles of liquor. Lobstermen gave us their short lobsters for whisky. Scallop boats dredged back and forth. More often than not these last were semi-bootleggers who trawled industriously when the cutter hung around and bought liquor by the twenty-five cases when they were absent. Rum Row, incidentally, was the direct means of opening up several new vast scallop beds. While pretending to be fishing during the presence of cutters, the crews found to their surprise that they were trawling scallops where they had never known they grew. The cream of seafood and the best of shore supplies were ours. We lived well and were happy.

As surveillance grew more severe, larger and faster boats replaced the sea skiffs that, up to then, had carried most of our cases ashore. Speed craft were snapped up by the bootleggers, who also began to build their own.

For a time that summer an airplane plied between the Row and shore, carrying twenty-five cases and making, on a clear, calm day, one trip an hour. This was before the cutters began to use their guns, and the plane's pilot took great joy in rubbing in their helplessness. We called him "Music." I never knew his real name.

The plane came out to us one morning when the air was still and the sea like glass. The cutter *Seminole* was anchored two miles east of us, and Music went out of his way to circle over her and wiggle his fingers at her crew. He dropped gracefully into the water by my schooner and loaded his regular twenty-five cases. Then he started off. His motor missed, almost died, and limped on, and the plane trailed shoreward like a wounded duck. The skipper of the *Seminole* pricked up his ears, hove up anchor, and swung toward us.

Music kept his motor from dying completely, but he could not get off the water. The best he could do was squatter along toward shore at not more than seven miles an hour. The *Seminole* belched great clouds of smoke and set off in pursuit. Her speed gradually increased, but seven miles was the best Music could do. As she drew up on him, he dumped his twenty-five cases, and when she overhauled him and towed him into New York, they had to set him free. He made many trips thereafter, but he stopped kidding the cutters and paid strict attention to business.

The *Sagitta* was one of the first of the high-powered boats to be run by a rum mob. I knew her of old. She had been owned by the millionaire, J. R. DeLamar, and my brother Ben had been her skipper. She was the fastest thing of her kind on the Sound and used to carry her owner daily from Glen Cove to the New York Yacht Club landing on the East River, and return.

During a calm clear night, Rum Row sounded a motorboat regatta. The darkness shook to the sound of engines rattling and booming. The craft all naturally, ran without lights and now and again cut each other down. The *Sagitta* was streaking shoreward one night when another craft, also going at full speed, rammed into her, shearing off the overhang of her stern and taking one of her crew along with it. In spite of the injury and the fact that her rudder was gone, the *Sagitta* made shore, steering with her twin propellers, and protected by her aft bulkhead.

The *Rex*, a 65-footer with three Liberty motors that developed a total of 1,350 horsepower and drove her unladen at 45 miles an hour, was for a long time the king of the shore boats.

She was tied up alongside the *Arethusa* one night and we were loading her when Arey, from his roost on the main gaff, called down:

"Cutter coming, Bill!"

The revenue vessel was still a mile away and the *Rex* was almost loaded. Her captain decided he could finish his job before he ran for it, but she started her engines to make her getaway quick. We worked fast, with one eye on the approaching lights of the cutter while the Little Jewish supercargo of the *Rex* danced up and down on her stern and begged us to hurry, and the power boat strained at her lines.

The government vessel was not more than a quarter mile away when we completed loading. Not waiting to cast off, the *Rex* threw her engine into full speed, and as she surged on her hawsers we chopped them in two. She went away from us like a startled fish, with a blur and a white explosion of foam, and she started so abruptly that the dancing little Jew on her stern lost balance and pitched into the sea.

This was toward the latter part of the summer when the cutters were beginning to use their guns. The captain of the *Rex* made one of the most daring rescues I had ever seen. He swung his roaring craft in a wide circle and, while the government boat bore down on him, ran alongside the drowning Jew and hauled him aboard. There was a flash of fire from the cutter's quarter, but the bang of the gun was blotted out by the bellow of the *Rex*'s engines as she dived off into the darkness at full speed with another shell from the cutter skipping after her.

Rum smuggling by air. Planes would taxi to *Tomoka/Arethusa* and load a maximum of twenty-five cases. (*Courtesy The Mariners' Museum, Newport News, VA.*)

The young aviator, whom McCoy called "Music" was Ed Musick, a pioneer pilot who flew for Aeromarine. Musick went on to become the premier pilot for Pan American Airways. He died in a plane crash in January, 1938 and, at the time, was the world's most famous pilot. (*Courtesy The Mariners' Museum, Newport News, VA.*)

When I saw the captain of the big motorboat again I praised his gameness in rescuing his supercargo under fire. He snorted.

"Hell," he returned, "I'd have let him drown and welcome, but the little so-and-so had $48,000 of our money in his pants pocket."

The captains of the regular cutters who patrolled the Row were gentlemen. They had been educated to the sea for the purpose of protecting ships and saving lives. None of them relished, I believe, the role into which prohibition and the government's growing resentment of Rum Row forced them. The man who risks his life in keeping the sea lanes clear, locating drifting icefields, and sinking derelicts is going to take small pleasure in firing on helpless craft, no matter how much rum they have aboard. I met Captains Covell, Ahern, and Camden and Commodores Billard and Yeandle during my time in the game. They were gentlemen all, and their crews were clean, fine youngsters.

I had no love for the cutter men in those days or they for me. I was foolish and took a special delight in annoying them. I suffered for that later. Yet I respected them, and I think they all cherished an under-cover regard for me.

While coming north on one of my trips this summer, I saw, about nineteen miles off Barnegat Light, a derelict three-masted schooner lurching awash through the seas. I put out a dory, rowed over to her, and lashed my pet and only red tablecloth and a lighted lantern to one of her masts. On reaching the Row, I looked for the cutter *Gresham*, which was then on patrol. If I had wanted to dodge her, she would have been on my tail at once. As it was, I ranged along the Row for an hour or more before I picked her up. I saw Captain Covell glare down at me from the bridge as I ranged alongside. I think for a moment he expected me to board him.

"Bill McCoy," I hailed, "reporting three-masted derelict nineteen miles east southeast of Barnegat Light."

"Haw-haw!" Covell came back with no trace of mirth in the sound. "What are you trying to put over this time, McCoy?"

"I'm reporting a derelict," I shouted. "That's your job, isn't it? If you find her and she hasn't my tablecloth and lantern on one of her masts, you can tow me in."

Covell saw I was in earnest and headed the *Gresham* out to sea. I believe he found her, for, during the rest of my stay on the Row that voyage, he acted as though he did not see me at all.

It was during this summer that I brought up from Nassau on my *Arethusa* the only woman ever to sell her own liquor on Rum Row.

Gertrude Lythgoe was a tall slender girl of barely thirty, with black hair, a brain as steady as her own dark eyes, and a history that was nobody's business. She came to Nassau as agent for Haig and McTavish's Scotch whisky, no one knew from where. She made no secret of her background, but she told an entirely different tale to everyone who asked. She had been born in California. She had been born in India. She was a gypsy. She had been raised in the Middle West. You could take your choice.

Nassau was not the best place in those days for attractive unprotected women, but though Gertrude was the former, she certainly was not the latter. Members of the rum mob who drew their own conclusions concerning her and then tried to operate accordingly, probably still recall the breath-taking fury she could show, and one or two must remember the pistol jammed into their ribs by way of making things clear. An able, thoroughly competent girl was Gertrude; no twittery jane at whom one could make passes with impunity. She expected others to mind their own business as thoroughly as she attended to hers.

She worked at that overtime, and in its course she ran me nearly ragged. Her firm in England had sent her over 1,000 cases of American Bourbon, excellent whisky, but they had bottled it in fifths of instead of quarts, and she could find no market on the Row for it. She called me into her office one day and asked me to take her Bourbon north. I refused, but every day thereafter she approached me with a new argument. She was a good businesswoman. At last I said I would take it at thirty dollars a case on consignment and, if able to sell it on the Row for fifty, give her an additional ten a case. She cabled her firm. They wired they were sending out their representative.

I was bathing one morning in my rooms at Mrs. Kemp's when a little Englishman, withered, woebegone, and weighing barely ninety pounds, including the monocle and cane, walked in on me, was flustered to find me wet and naked and offered to withdraw. I told him to sit down, and he explained that he was the agent sent over by Miss Lith's firm to see about the Bourbon.

"I envy you your physique, Mr. McCoy," he said as the breeze dried me. "I do indeed. You see in me, sir, the remains of a misspent life in India."

He seemed at once melancholy and proud of it. We talked over details of my proposition. While I breakfasted he watched me sadly and said he envied my ability to eat. It was agreed that the liquor would be placed on the *Arethusa*. My schooner had just battened down her hatches on 4,500 cases, and it was arranged that I would carry the Bourbon as a deck load. I paid the duty on it—$6,000—for Gertrude was painfully short of funds, and delayed my sailing a day to load. Gertrude and the remains of the misspent life boarded us with a suitcase just before we sailed. I presumed, of course, that the little man was to come along as supercargo.

I saw him shudder as he looked us over. The deck, as usual at sailing time, was cluttered. There were cases of beer for the crew's consumption stacked here, a crate of chickens there, cakes of ice sweltering on the hatch. The men were just getting over their farewell drunk and with bloated faces and puffed eyes looked even tougher roughnecks than they were. By nightfall I knew the salt air would have cleared their heads and that the mess on the schooner's deck would all be stowed away, shipshape and proper.

With Pilot Brown at the wheel and the little agent and Gertrude under the awning, we started the engine, and the schooner went pounding out across the bar. We passed the lighthouse and Tony Rocks. Brown turned over the helm and said: "Good voyage to you, Bill."

"Miss Lythgoe," I told her, "here's where you go ashore."

She shook her head and smiled. "Oh, no," she replied, "I'm going with you."

"Not a chance," I answered, thinking she was jesting. "This gentleman will be your supercargo."

"Oh, my dear chap," the remains of a misspent life exclaimed "Absolutely impossible. I should be a hindrance. I should be seasick continually. I should perish, I assure you."

Brown was yelling from the boat, and overhead the big mainsail was flapping thunder. We couldn't argue it out, for the noise was too great to hear any thing less than a shout. The little man scuttled into Brown's boat, the painter was cast off, the *Arethusa* paid over on the starboard tack, and we were off for the Row at a ten-knot clip. Gertrude Lythgoe, looking fragile and lonely on this ship full of burly men, smiled triumphantly at me. The racket of our engine died away, and with nothing to disturb us but the wind in the rigging and the breaking water overside, I was able to pick up the debate where the noise had drowned it out. It was empty argument, because here the woman was, going with us whether we wished it or not

"It's a rough gang," I warned her, "and a rough trip. Furthermore, the captain and the mate have one stateroom, and I, the cabin. You'll have to use the bunk opposite me."

"That will be quite all right," she told me composedly. "Will you show me where I put my things?"

Her first act toward settling herself for the voyage was to hang a .38 Colt and holster inside her bunk. I laughed and told her that was one thing she wouldn't need on my ship.

"I believe that," she returned meeting my gaze squarely, "but I don't take chances, Captain McCoy."

The effect of a woman's presence aboard was laughable. My crew had stared while she was on deck. When she had gone below, without orders from anyone, they had fallen upon the littered deck and started to clear ship. When Gertrude returned to the poop again, the *Arethusa* was as clean alow and aloft as any yacht.

The rest of the men hung back a little, but Frenchy Rivert, my cook from St. Pierre, approached her at once with a prance in his gait and launched into an oration on the good things he intended to cook for her and the music he could play for her when she wished. He had actually brushed his hair and put on a clean apron, too.

Women on a ship sometimes are considered Jonahs. It was not so with Gertrude Lythgoe. It was plain to my crew at once that she was right. They liked her from the start, and as fair weather accompanied us all the way to the Row, considered her a mascot. We were able to eat on the after deck every day. Frenchy insisted on serving Gertrude's breakfast in bed and cooked new and amazing dishes which he had never bothered to serve his employer, for every meal.

In the balmy evenings, I would invite the crew aft, and with Frenchy playing his violin or his accordion, we would sing old sea chanteys, expurgating them out of consideration for our guest. With Gertrude Lythgoe aboard, we were more like a Sunday-school picnic than a gang of rum-runners. The sailors made her bits of drawn work and carvings. Frenchy presented her with a model of the *Arethusa* in a bottle. My hard-boiled crew watched its language and even refused to bathe out of consideration for our guest.

Usually, on the approach of a shower, we all assembled on deck, mother naked, and waited for the downpour to wash us. Gertrude tactfully went below when a downpour started, but the dread that she might reappear was too much for my highbinders' nerves. They shaved daily, but they did not get a full bath until the first storm broke after she had left the ship.

I sold her liquor overside on Rum Row, and soon thereafter, as the *M.M. Gardner* was sailing back to Nassau and Gertrude was anxious to return, I put her aboard and sent her back. She left Nassau a few months later and wrote her Rum Row experiences for a newspaper syndicate. I don't know what became of her thereafter.

Gertrude Lythgoe and the "Duke," on board *Tomoka/Arethusa* in Nassau, Bahamas.
(Courtesy The Mariners' Museum, Newport News, VA)

Gertrude Lythgoe's second floor office on Market Street in Nassau. The sign reads "Gertrude C. Lythgoe, Licensed to Sell Wholesale Spirits & Liqueurs in Bottles as officially supplied & To Retail Wine & Beer." The gentleman in the foreground is Lythgoe's colleague the "Duke." *(The Bahama Queen)*

The "Rum Queen" prepares to get underway on board *Tomoka/Arethusa*
(Courtesy The Mariners' Museum, Newport News, VA.)

Bill McCoy, with camera, and Gertrude Lythgoe. McCoy kept a photo album of his rum running days. *(Courtesy The Mariners' Museum, Newport News, VA.)*

Dining on deck. Bill McCoy captioned this photograph "Pumpkin Pie." *(Courtesy The Mariners' Museum, Newport News, VA.)*

Gertude Lythgoe hugging Bill McCoy's dog on board the schooner *M.M. Gardner. (The Bahama Queen)*

Gertrude Lythgoe on Rum Row
(Courtesy The Mariners' Museum, Newport News, VA.)

CHAPTER XIII

TROUBLE BETWEEN THE RESIDENTS on Rum Row and the revenue cutters that kept prying into our affairs started early in the summer of 1923, grew more intense as the months progressed, and reached its climax in 1924, when, with the weight of the whole American government behind them, the cutters literally starved out the old-time Row, broke it up, and chased it away.

From the beginning there was never any cordiality between the white plodding government vessels and the mixed assemblage of craft that anchored off New York. We felt toward our uninvited supervisors the same resentment that players in an entirely private poker game would show to some self-appointed snooper.

By the government's own admission, we were breaking no law. We lay the distance offshore that the State Department had stipulated. We sold our cargoes on what was then termed the high seas. Legally we felt that the cutters' intrusion was unjust. It was their business, we held, to keep boats from coming and going between the Row and the shore, not to sniff around pious rum-runners on their lawful occasions.

For a time, while the government was organizing its offensive against the Row with much revision of age-long law, stretching of statutes, and diplomatic agreements with foreign powers, the cutter captains and crews led a miserable existence. With their old ships that shook to pieces at more than ten knots, they had no more chance of catching the fast shore boats than a fat dog has of capturing a swallow on the wing. All they could do was patrol up and down the line of liquor ships and look dangerously official. Yet their presence bothered us, and we showed our resentment. That was a mistake. It never does any good to kid a cop. An official can forgive and forget almost any crime you may commit except that of laughing at him. If we had treated cutters and cutter captains with respect we should have had a smoother time of it, and the Row, probably, would have endured longer. But the temptation to outrage helpless authority was great.

We made the cutter captains angry by jeers and practical jokes. Their wrath got into the reports they forwarded to Washington, and the angrier these reports became, the more authority the government gave them. By the middle of the summer they were trying to frighten us by firing blanks. When that did not work, the government granted them the right to use solid shot.

That was what we got for kidding the cops, and I got it heavier than anyone else because I had kidded them most. I kept strictly outside the seven-mile limit. I sold, quite legally, only the best of liquor. If I had minded my business and had been polite to cutter captains, the government might not have come to regard me as the blackest crook who ever sailed the seas.

I committed the grave sin of making the revenue service look ridiculous, and with the furious reports of these gentlemen bombarding the State Department, the United States government entered into a special agreement with Sir Auckland Geddes, British ambassador, whereby the British Empire disowned all responsibility for me, despite the registry of my schooner, and I was caught.

I don't believe the game the cutter captains and I played was entirely, or even primarily, responsible for my posing as the subject of a special agreement between two world powers. There was something more behind it than just sailors' loss of temper. Ninety percent of the men in the rum trade were my friends, but there was always the other ten percent.

The racket was beginning to feel the pressure of big business. Mobs were organizing to handle liquor more efficiently and in larger quantities. One of these, which had its headquarters in New Jersey, approached me and wanted me to join with them. I declined. The sport of rum running lay in playing your own game. I did not want any gang directing me, and I told them so.

The mob wouldn't take no for an answer, and when I emphasized my refusal with profanity and my opinion of some of the gorillas and gunmen they were employing, I was threatened.

If I did not throw in with the mob, I was told, I would be "fixed." The political powers behind this gang had influence all the way up. I could take my choice: throw in or get off the ocean.

Whether there was anything more than the usual wind behind this threat I have never been able to prove. There is one significant fact, however. It was a Jersey mob that threatened me, and it was for a crime allegedly committed in New Jersey that I went to jail at last.

The cutters were a pest. I pestered them in turn, and they had the last laugh on me. Whether they, or the mob, or a combination of these influences brought about my downfall, I have no way of knowing. Whoever got me was welcome to his last laugh. Though I went to jail, I had my fun first.

The tricks the cutters tried to play and the traps they laid for me were so obvious that the temptation to humiliate them was more than a human being could resist. The captain of the *Manhattan* attempted over and over again to catch craft that were loading beside the *Arethusa* at night. He would sneak up on me with all lights out. This was absolutely contrary to sea law, and it never did him any good.

My captain or my mate, perched on the main crosstrees, always watched the *Manhattan*. He would call down to me the minute her lights were turned off, giving me her approximate distance. The *Manhattan* had to steam slowly while doing this cat-and-mouse act, for if she put on power you could hear her clanking engine miles away. I would continue loading my customers' boats until she was close. Then they would scatter, and I would turn off every light on the *Arethusa*, slip away, and we would all whoop and roar when we heard the *Manhattan* wheezing past the place we had been. That procedure did not endear her captain to me, and the way I tricked him did not make me any more popular with him and his crew.

I mocked the dignity of the *Seminole*, too. She came along the Row one afternoon, her decks crowded with civilians on an official junket of some sort. The other rum-runners she passed behaved like good little boys in the front row of the classroom. I gave the officials something to remember besides a long line of anchored shabby craft. As the *Seminole* drew abeam of us, not a hundred yards away, I picked up two champagne bottles, loosened the wires about the corks, and waved one in either hand as though they were Roman candles. In a moment, the gas in the bottles blew out the corks with a loud report. The wine squirted and foamed. The junket party waved and cheered, but I think the *Seminole*'s captain felt I was jeering at him, and maybe I was.

At all events, a few days later, he put four of his men in a little launch and sent them down one afternoon to circle about my schooner and watch us. We had brought up a big deckload from Nassau that trip, and in it were a dozen cases of Pilsener in big quart bottles. My crew were drinking it on deck when the *Seminole* launch began snooping. The four cutter men looked so thirsty that I threw them a bottle.

They caught it. They had to, for a quart bottle of beer, flung as I flung it, would have caved in their craft's side otherwise. The yell of mingled alarm and joy they gave when they saw the missile coming put evil thoughts into the innocent minds of my crew. In an instant we had laid down a beer barrage on that launch. Some of it the occupants caught. The rest splintered the craft's sides before it drew out of range. The cutter men lingered a while at a distance and drank up what they had saved.

I understand that, when they returned to the cutter with a banged-up boat and a brewery smell on their breaths, their captain was not pleased with them or with me.

We had the laugh on the *Seminole* again shortly after, but this time quite innocently. We always carried up from Nassau additional steel drums of crude oil for our engine. It was calm on the Row one afternoon and I decided to clear our deck by pouring the contents of the remaining drums into our tank. When this was done we dumped the empty containers overside and, as the tide was coming in, they drifted shoreward in a long black bobbing line athwart the bows of the French steam schooner *Goberville*, a sinister ship which the cutter was watching closely, for she was believed to be a narcotic smuggler.

The *Seminole* came puffing along, and seeing the line of drums apparently put out by the *Goberville*, imagined that here was a new method of sending drugs ashore. The cutter secured every one of them, hauled them on deck, and cut them open, finding, of course, nothing but oil impregnated air. She dumped them overboard finally and turned her one-pounder guns on them, while we laughed.

The *Manhattan* hounded me more than any of the other cutters. Her captain seemed determined to get the last laugh. We were jogging along under foresail and jumbo one night on the inshore tack with no shorecraft alongside when his cutter, all lights out, slipped up under our lee. He apparently hoped to catch us inside the seven-mile limit and capture us. Arey, on the main crosstrees, sang down softly and told of her presence.

The *Manhattan* continued to slide along, only a blacker shadow in the darkness until it came time for us to wear ship. We put her helm up and jibbed around on the offshore tack heading straight for the *Manhattan*, which we were not supposed to be able to see. Out of the darkness came the frantic jingle of the cutter's engine bell. She jammed on full speed and barely ducked out of our course. There was a good deal of swearing on her decks, and then, all at once, her lights popped on. We gave him the razz as we drove past his stern.

It was too much to ask a man for whom such clumsy traps were set not to trick the would-be trapper. On another night when the *Manhattan* was busy sniffing along the Row, I started down the beach to pick up any customer that might come off from Jersey. The cutter was occupied elsewhere, and as it had just captured a sea skiff and its bootlegger crew, her captain put a crowd of his own men in the craft and sent them down to supervise me. Two of my customers had just come alongside when Arey saw a sea skiff full of men creeping up on us in the darkness.

"Pirates," he sang out. I emptied a Colt .45 into the air. There were yelps in the darkness as though each shot had lodged, and the sea skiff put hastily about and ran back to the *Manhattan*. We finished loading the boats alongside, and they had just left when the cutter, lights blazing this time, ran down toward us.

She came alongside, looming high above us, and a voice yelled from her bridge:

"*Tomoka*, ahoy!"

"Hello!" I replied.

"What the hell," he roared, "do you mean by firing on my boats?"

"What the hell," I bellowed back, "do your boats mean sneaking about the high seas with no lights on?' How can I tell them from pirates?"

"You know damned well," he thundered, "what they're out there for. I've a good mind to take that schooner and sail her into New York."

"Try it," I invited. "Only you'll need something better than a pack of Swede squareheads, and what do you think of that?"

"I know you, Bill McCoy, you damned rum-runner," Blank bawled.

"Yeh?" I asked. "Suppose you keep your lights on after this, and how would you like to go to hell, Captain?"

I learned a little later that to the list of my sins already collecting in Washington had been added the offense of firing at the American flag.

The *Manhattan*'s captain was determined, after that, to get me. One night he felt he had hit on the proper way to spoil my business. He put a fast sea skiff, with a powerful searchlight in her bow, after me. This craft followed as I jogged along, and occasionally threw its light on my stern. It was a black night with a good breeze blowing, and as we went down the Jersey coast we made about seven knots with the sea skiff pounding along in our wake and now and then flooding us with light. I paid no attention until a couple of customers brought their boats alongside. Then, while they loaded, I turned my searchlight, which was much more powerful than the sea skiff's, upon my pursuers. It outshone theirs and blinded them.

We continued to move along at seven knots while my customers' skiffs matched their pace with ours and kept their craft about fifteen feet from our sides. We tossed the "hams" of whisky to them. They threw me payment. All the while the cutter's boat was following us in the glare of our searchlight.

"Throttle down," I called to my customers, "while I lead this guy offshore."

They obeyed. I sang out, "Starboard the helm!" The *Arethusa* swung out to sea, and her light-dazzled pursuers, sticking to our trail, passed within a stone's throw of a couple of liquor-laden shore boats and never knew they were there. After ten minutes run we hove to and blinked out our searchlight. The following boat drew abeam, and it was filled with angry men. We talked back and forth for some time until they grew too furious for more words, fired a burst from their machine gun into the air, and scuttled back to the *Manhattan*. I suppose I should have reported to the King of England that a government craft had fired on his flag. The *Manhattan* was the only sneak cutter on Rum Row. *Gresham*, *Seneca*, and *Seminole*, the real old-time large cutters, with old-time captains, did not sneak. The *Manhattan* was a reconditioned tugboat.

Toward fall of 1923 the cutters got permission to fire solid shot at shoreward-bound rum-runners. Thereafter things grew grimmer, but there was still opportunity for many jokes and a good deal of laughter at the expense of cutter captains and rum-runners alike. As usual, most of the Row's humor was spent on the *Manhattan*.

A new speedboat especially designed for bringing liquor ashore was being sold at this time. These craft were big and seaworthy, long and low, with a flush deck and three Liberty motors that drove them along at 36 miles an hour empty and 25 loaded.

One of the first purchasers of this type was a guileless spirit who was not familiar with Rum Row kidding and believed what he was told ashore. Someone with little regard for the boat buyer's safety instructed him how to bring in liquor. The captain of the *Manhattan*, this practical joker said, was a good-hearted old scout who liked to see the bootleggers get along. All the boat buyer had to do was run alongside his cutter, hail him, and ask where the best whisky on the Row could be bought.

The victim, I have been told, did just that, and fled gasping and breathless from the flood of information and direction the frantic captain shouted at him, followed by rapid gunfire.

Sammy Randell, a friend of mine and an active bootlegger, bought a new powerful craft with twin engines and ran out through a fog one night to the Row. The weather was so thick that he mistook the cutter *Gresham* for a rum ship, ranged alongside her, and yelled: "How much for your Scotch?" The *Gresham* cut loose at him with a quick firer, and Sammy was so fright palsied that he threw one engine into full speed forward and the other into reverse. He circled the *Gresham* twice, screeching blue murder and with shells kicking up about him, before he came out of his fright sufficiently to get things straightened and go away from there.

Most craft depended on their speed to dodge the cutters but a few of the bootleggers went in for subterfuge. One man traveled out to the Row and back in broad daylight for months before the authorities identified him as a rum buyer. He had a big slow-power yacht with a "V" bottom. She had all the appearance of a rich man's pleasure craft, and this disguise was increased all that summer by the presence of two daintily dressed women who lolled in the craft's stern while its owner, in white duck trousers, blue double-breasted coat, and yachting cap, guided her along the Row until he was sure the cutter was elsewhere.

When certain, he would swing in alongside a rum-runner, lift the false flooring of his craft, and stow 200 cases of liquor in the "V" bottom. No one ever suspected him, thanks to the presence of the women aboard, until he put his boat into drydock for over hauling. Workmen, discovering the false bottom, talked too much to the wrong people, and the next time he put out toward the Row with his girl friends aboard, he was run down and captured by one of the new 75-foot speedboats the government was putting into commission to supplement the cutters.

These craft eventually killed Rum Row, for in time they became so plentiful that one could watch each rum running craft, keep trade away, and literally starve her out. At first they were far from effective, for a number of newcomers, principally Swedes, were assigned to command them. Big operators compiled a directory of these men and their peculiarities:

No. 0—Captain Jonson, can be fixed with ten cases.
No. 00—Captain Janssen, a double crosser, watch out for him.
No. 000—Captain Yensen, square but stupid. And so forth.

Toward the end of the summer of 1923 the *Arethusa* entertained distinguished callers. We saw a fast skiff coming out toward us one bright noon, boiling along through the sea, as those wild Long Island and Jersey boatmen always insisted on traveling. These men would go to infinite pains to camouflage their craft and reduce visibility against a background of water. After all their trouble they would tear out to the Row at full speed so that the cloud of spray could be seen miles away, like a ball of white cotton on the horizon, advertising to everyone that a bootlegger was on the way for a load.

When this particular craft bore down on us I saw that she was a sea skiff belonging to Jean Perry, an active customer, and that besides my brother Ben she had as passengers two other men and a woman.

The passengers came overside, which was an easy climb, for we had just come up from Nassau with a heavy load and were riding very low. Ben introduced Dr. Blank of the Postgraduate Hospital in New York, his wife, and Judge P. M. Black, a marine attorney. We unloaded the supplies that Ben had brought, and Perry ran his skiff over the horizon because the cutter *Seminole* was bearing in our direction.

The Blanks and Judge Black had come on a sightseeing tour at Ben's invitation, and we did our best to welcome them. We opened champagne, which Dr. and Mrs. Blank relished. Judge Black climbed upon the deckload we carried and demanded:

"Bill, do you mean to say that all this under me is whisky?"

"We'll open a case," I replied, and a seaman quickly revealed two dozen curved pint flasks of Lawson's liqueur Scotch. I told the Judge to help himself. He put one in each hip pocket and immediately pulled the glass stopper out of a third. By the time the *Seminole* drew abreast of us, he mounted his rostrum of liquor cases and, shaking the now emptied flask, delivered an eloquent oration toward the cutter on the rights of man and marine law.

He picked up another pint, went aft, and told Dr. Blank that he intended to steal the physician's wife and that he was not really Judge Black but Romeo Montague. He then recited long excerpts from *Romeo and Juliet* while Dr. and Mrs. Blank shook with laughter.

It was a fine calm afternoon. We had our anchor down and all sails furled. We spread an awning for the comfort of our guests and opened the ice-cream freezer Ben had brought aboard. We desperate, piratical rum-runners stowed away vanilla ice cream while our guests sampled our cargo.

The *Seminole* went on down the Row, and about four o'clock, Jean came back, full speed ahead as usual. Dr. and Mrs. Blank got into the skiff with no difficulty whatever, but we had a hard time persuading the Judge that the boat really was there. I saw that the cutter was bearing down on us again, and she fired a signal shot from her forward gun.

"Mrs. Blank," I said, "open your parasol and wave it. Doctor, have you a card with you? If you're overhauled, show it to Captain Ahern and tell him you came aboard to see a sick seaman."

The cutter fired again as the skiff darted away, but Mrs. Blank stood up on the back deck waving her parasol, and there was no more shooting.

The U.S. Coast Guard Cutter *Seminole* comes down Rum Row to look *Tomoka/Arethusa* over. (*Courtesy The Mariners' Museum, Newport News, VA.*)

Bill McCoy eats ice cream while his guests drink whiskey on board *Tomoka/Arethusa* on Rum Row. (*Courtesy The Mariners' Museum, Newport News, VA.*)

The Coast Guard would make regular rounds of Rum Row collecting information on vessels. (*Courtesy The Mariners' Museum, Newport News, VA.*)

CGC *Seminole* returning to port. There was little the Coast Guard could do as long as *Tomoka/Arethusa* remained in international waters. (*Courtesy The Mariners' Museum, Newport News, VA.*)

CHAPTER XIV

THE SUMMER OF 1923, the boom time of Rum Row, drew to a close. Winter and its storms were ahead of us, and my *Arethusa* was in need of refitting. She had been worked so hard and so fast all summer that we had taken time for only the most essential repairs. I determined to put her into drydock and prepare her for the winter campaign. She cleared from Nassau, August 4th, on the last voyage she ever was to make from that port. I had no suspicion, as she went to sea, with cheers and darkey singing bidding her farewell, that she and I both were saying a permanent goodbye to our foster home.

Nova Scotia had at last gone wet. Rum-runners were beginning to ply between Halifax or Lunenburg and the Row. When the *Arethusa*'s cargo was discharged we set sail for the latter port.

Fog swept in upon us off Cape Sable, dank and impenetrable. It had been cloudy for several days, and we had not been able to take an observation. We had only the vaguest idea where we were or how far offshore. We all were weary and nervous after our hard summer, and the tides off Sable are treacherous. We leaned on the rail, peering out into the gray, muffling blanket, and winced as we felt the schooner lunge and jerk as the eddies tugged her.

Suddenly, the wind whipped about, and I sniffed something beside the cellar reek of the fog—the perfume of fir trees. I told the men that we were close inshore and that I could smell land. They laughed.

But when my Newfoundland dog came bounding up out of the cabin, placed his forefeet on the rail beside me, sniffed, and then barked joyously, they began to believe. There was too much conviction in that sound. My old pup smelled his former house.

While we watched him, the wind thinned the fog, blew it away, and off our quarter lay Nova Scotia's beautiful shore, only a few miles away.

We reached Lunenburg that night. Her little harbor held a half dozen rum craft, either outfitting for their first voyage or overhauling for winter work. Nova Scotia, lately so prim, was going into the trade in a big way. Halifax grew rapidly into the trade's chief port of call for Scotch. I have run many a load out of the harbor into which, a few years earlier, I had been forbidden to enter because I had liquor on board.

I wince, sometimes, now, when I think of the care and cash I expended on the *Arethusa*'s refitting. I had grown so intimate with her, as a sailor must with a ship he knows and loves, that I could not imagine that we were not to go on together until the end came for one of us.

We put her into the Lunenburg Outfitting Company's dry dock. The men who worked on her were loud in their praise of my beautiful ship. For the first time in her seventeen years of life we recaulked her, we dropped down her rudder and inspected her pintails and repainted her. When she left drydock we installed a new fuel tank on her deck, for the earlier had been too heavy.

We jacked up her deck two inches, and I had the best mechanics in Lunenburg put a double diagonal bulkhead at the main beam, another forward, and another aft. These took all the sag and give out of the *Arethusa*'s top structure and made her as stiff as a new ship. I had always been fearful that the schooner's pig-iron ballast might shift in one of the storms she had fought, but with the bulkheads to hold it down, I knew that danger was eliminated. I recaulked her decks and had the waterways re-wedged.

I supervised and shared in all this labor, and the extra exertion, coming on top of a summer of hard work and nerve tension, knocked me over. The physician I called prescribed absolute rest for a few days. I crawled into my bunk to get it. No sick man ever had a more strenuous convalescence.

Rum-runners in the harbor, when they heard I was ill, appeared with gifts of refreshment. In a day or so my cabin looked like a liquor dealer's sample room, with apricot brandy, chartreuse, benedictine, champagne, whisky, stacked all about.

Riggers and carpenters were at work on deck, and visitors from Lunenburg came aboard to inspect the *Arethusa* daily. A day or so after I had taken to my bunk, and while I was still listless and weak, two buxom and jolly Nova Scotia girls peered down the hatch and asked if they might come down. They wandered about the cabin and made friends with my Newfoundland. Presently Captain Arey came aboard and suggested that we invite the pair to supper. I was able to take only a little milk, but we had a pleasant meal, and Arey and I spun yarns for our visitors' amusement until it was quite late. Presently, the captain and our guests went on deck, and I fell asleep. I imagined that he had escorted them home.

In the morning I woke suddenly and sat up. From one of the staterooms came giggling and feminine conversation. I yelled for Arey.

"Didn't you take those girls ashore?"

He looked at the ceiling with a cat-in-the-cream-jug expression.

"Well," he explained, "I was going to, and then—well, somehow I didn't, Bill."

"You get them off this ship right away, you old goat," I ordered.

"Sure I will. Right away," he promised, but the women took an interminable time dressing and before they appeared work had been resumed on the deck.

"Ashore, both of you," I told them when they emerged from the stateroom. The prettier of the pair, and they both were pretty enough, widened her eyes. "Oh," she exclaimed, "we couldn't go now, Captain Bill. What would our husbands say?"

"Once you get off my schooner, honey, I don't care what your husbands say," I told her.

"But we can't get off," she insisted. "Our husbands are working overhead now."

It would have saved me a peck of trouble if I'd yelled for their husbands right then, but they begged, and Arey argued, and I let them stay. They did help me in one way. Worry over the jam they and Arey had got me in kept me from thinking how sick I felt.

Lunenburg is only a small town, and two attractive young wives can't disappear from their homes there without resultant scandal. There was a good deal of talking as well as caulking on deck that morning, and it didn't cheer me overmuch when I heard a woman's voice, acid and triumphant, call from the dock:

"Well, they were seen goin' aboard that awful old rum-runner's schooner yesterday."

I ordered the girls to go back into the stateroom and stay there, and when they tried to argue, threatened to call their husbands. Toward noon my convalescence was helped along by a visit from the sheriff.

"Any girls down here?" he asked, looking around and laughing. I tried hard to laugh too.

"No. Send some down," I told him and offered him a drink. He took a big one and then went away with the bottle.

When dinner came I didn't want any food. Arey, who went around with a grin that I could have killed him for, served the girls in the stateroom at my order. There was a lot of giggling in there before I could get them to pipe down.

Old Captain Hurtel, who was assisting me in refitting my schooner, was the next caller. He was a dumpy, good-natured old sea rider and spoke the German-English that so many Lunenburgers use.

"You haff girls down here, eh, Bill?" he queried, and I confided the whole story.

"Captain," I concluded, "you've got to help me out of this. Tonight, bring your dory alongside the *Arethusa*. We'll put the girls aboard her, and you row them over to the other side of the harbor and set them ashore."

He promised, and later reappeared to tell me that his dory was already tied to the seaward side of the schooner, but when darkness fell and I had high hope of getting my visitors away, Hurtel came down again.

"Bill," he said, "I been thinking. Suppose someone sees me rowing these girls about the harbor. What will they say? I tell you. They will say, 'Captain Hurtel, he has been off with these women,' and I have a wife and daughters, and I am a deacon in the Methodist Church. Bill, I cannot do it. It is too big a risk."

I got him to promise to have an automobile on the dock at midnight, and he left. We pulled the curtains over the portholes, and all four had supper in my cabin. The girls then curled upon a settee to wait for Hurtel and his car, and I dropped to sleep in my bunk, with Old Faithful beside me. His leap and sudden barking woke me. Someone was pounding on my cabin door, and above the racket the Newfoundland was raising I heard a German voice calling:

"Open, I am der chief of police to search dis ship."

Arey, who had fallen asleep in his chair, was blinking, and the girls seemed frightened for the first time. I mumbled to him:

"Get them into the engine room."

There was a secret sliding panel between my cabin and the engines. While Arey was hurrying them through it, I called, to cover the noise.

"Captain, there are thieves on the schooner. Get your machine gun ready."

"No shoot, no shoot," an immensely concerned voice begged on the far side of the door. "I am a peace officer."

"Peace officer or not," I shouted, "you've no business to search my ship without a custom officer along."

"I have one mit," the chief announced, and another, English voice added:

"I represent His Majesty's Customs, Captain."

Old Faithful, at my command, jumped back upon the bunk. Arey returned from the engine room and slid the panel into place. I got up and opened the door.

A stout man, shaggy of hair and mustache entered. You could tell he was chief of police a half mile away by the enormous gold letters on the band of his cap and his five-inch star. He was dressed in blue, with brass buttons as large as silver dollars. A little man was the representative of His Majesty's Customs and immediately confiscated a bottle of Black & White to see if its contents were genuine.

The chief swelled out his chest and said, glaring at me: "I have orders to search dis ship for two vimmen."

"Help yourself," I told him, and he and his associate, who clung to the Black & White bottle, went through the staterooms and found nothing.

When they returned they began to apologize, and I prevailed upon His Majesty's Customs to let the chief have a drink too. There still seemed a chance of bluffing my way out of this mess, but the husband of one of our visitors came storming in from the deck.

"Go look in the engine room," he yelled. "I'll bet that's where he has hidden them."

He was big, and he was angry, and he shook his ugly caulker's fist under my nose. I had been through a good deal that day for a sick man, and I socked him in the jaw and kicked him up on deck. In the engine room, the girls began to laugh. They had no sense of propriety. The chief yelled for them to come out, and they obeyed.

"I haff," Old Brass Buttons said, fumbling in his jacket, "a varrant for you girls. It says dot you half assulted or deserted or someding. Vare is dot ting?"

He had had several shots of Black & White, and the customs authority had begun on a second bottle. Between times, he looked at the girls more in admiration than reproach. The chief found the document.

"Ach," he mourned, "now I haff not my glasses. You blease read him."

I read it aloud. The girls seemed to think it the best joke of the day.

"Now," said the chief and waggled a forefinger before his eyes that were beginning to cross, "de mayor, he tell me, eider I take you home or else I lock you up. Vich?"

I poured him another drink. He swallowed it and pulled out a red bandanna to wipe his eyes.

"Gertie," he mourned to one of the girls, "I see you grow up from so high. When I hear you are lost, I vorry. And now I must put you in der jail."

Gertie curled his mustaches for him. The other patted his cheeks and said: "Put the handcuffs on me." The chief beamed and took another drink.

"Bill," he said, "make dese liddle rasgals behave dereselfs." His Majesty's Customs was asleep at the post, one hand on the neck of the Black White bottle.

I was urging the girls to go ashore quietly when Gertie's husband came storming down the stairway again. He had been ashore and had drunk the level of his courage higher. He yelled at me, and I hit him again, so hard that after he had picked himself up, he went back on deck without further urging.

The chief of police was insulted and pounded on the table.

"Hah!" he snorted. "You strige a man in my presence. Dere will be trouble Monday morning, and I shall be der chief vitness."

"No," His Majesty's Customs announced, waking up, "I shall be the chief witness," and fell asleep again.

"Louis," I said to the chief, "I hate arguments. Let's forget." I had a wad of bills in my pocket, and I tossed it to him. It might have been $500, but it was only five tens. He snapped it up like a lawyer and counted it out carefully.

"Dis is too much," he protested, and gave a ten to each girl, and thrust another into the customs man's hand. It was almost daybreak of Sunday when I got that gang off my boat.

I went back to my bed. It had been no sort of a night for a man with a nervous breakdown. And my trouble was not over yet. Bill Acker, collector of the port of Halifax, called that afternoon with the doctor, who was his brother-in-law. While they were aboard, my ship chandler came down, stuttering with excitement. The husbands of our late guests, he said, had engaged an attorney and were going to sue me for abduction.

I got dressed.

"What's the idea?" Bill Acker asked.

"I'm going to get my money out of the bank and get my crew together and go to sea," I told him.

"Bill," he protested, "you can't get away without a clearance."

"Watch me," I told him.

"But if you do," he urged, "you can never come back here without paying a big fine."

"Collector," I said, "I'm never coming back here anyway. Not with two husbands after me."

The ship chandler intervened. He said he knew the lawyer. Maybe it could be fixed up. He took part of my roll and fixed it. There was no trouble Monday morning, but a day or so later, with my ship in perfect trim and a new crew aboard her, we stood out for St. Pierre.

There was a valentine waiting for me when I reached the island. Sturgeon had received a cable from the Halifax branch of the Royal Bank of Canada, reading, "Wire whereabouts Bill McCoy and *Tomoka*. He had replied at once, "Whereabouts unknown," and had asked who wanted to know. The reply read, "U.S. Department of Justice."

Since it was a year now since I had run foul of the law, I could only presume that this was what came of kidding cutter captains and calling a lot of attention to myself, with, perhaps, the Jersey mob also involved. Knowledge that the government was hunting me once more made me redouble my efforts to clean up while I still was free.

Through Folquet Frères, my old associates in St. Pierre, I chartered a brand-new fishing schooner, the *Vera Thornhill*. She sailed at once from Grand Bank for Miquelon, where we planned to load her with champagne.

St. Pierre was no longer the frugal little fishing village of my first landfall there. The liquor business, thanks to a change in the island's law, was now well under way and growing weekly. Everyone was prosperous, the harbor was packed with rum craft and the town noisy with rum-runners. My old friends, the Italians, had a three-masted schooner loading. They and numerous other sinful friends gave me a great welcome when I came ashore.

There was a hotel in town now, a three-story structure owned and operated by the local barber. Most of the rum-runners put up there. These men hailed not only from Canada and the United States, but from Europe as well. Furnishing America with liquor was an enterprise in which all the world was joining. There were Germans, Swedes, Italians, and a group of Frenchmen from Paris. These last had brought a big bark over from Europe, laden with vin-

Bill McCoy firing a Colt-Browning machine gun. To protect *Arethusa* and her cargo from hijackers, McCoy armed her crew with an array of weaponry sold surplus after the Armistice of 1918. (*Courtesy The Mariners' Museum, Newport News, VA.*)

Target practice was a popular way to spend down time, and day time—as most offloading occurred at night—on Rum Row. (*Courtesy The Mariners' Museum, Newport News, VA.*)

tage champagnes. They had not sailed her across, but had towed her behind a tug. The most self-important and boastful of this group was a young man, son of a former military governor of Paris, who had been an aviator during the war—and a most daring and skillful one, by his own testimony.

We veteran rum-runners had only our seagoing togs, but this former flier was dressed in the raiment of the boulevards. He had a watch on one wrist, a heavy gold bracelet on the other, and a voluble scorn for everything that was not wholly French. He particularly disparaged America's part in the war, and especially her prowess in the air, insisting that Frenchmen alone had the flair and coordination to make good aviators. In time, his continual patronage began to rasp our nerves a little.

I broke in upon his comments one day and challenged him to do a simple trick, which, I said, would prove whether his sense of balance and coordination was perfect. All the Americans in the hotel were in the plot. I got a silver dollar, and dared him to balance it on his forehead and then, with a forward movement of his head, make it fall into his hand, held rigid at his waist. He did it.

"Ah," he exclaimed, "what I tell you?"

"You moved your hand," I objected and we had a hot argument on that point which concluded when someone produced a tin funnel. I shoved that into the waistband of his breeches and handed him the coin again.

"Now," I said. "That funnel can't move. Let's see you drop the dollar into that."

When he threw his head back to place the dollar on his forehead, I poured a pitcher of ice water into the funnel. Everyone was much pleased except the young aviator, who later forgave me.

The *Vera Thornhill* reached St. Pierre just ahead of a hurricane. A cablegram from farther down the coast warned us of its approach, and we went frantically to work to prepare for it. The harbor in which we were trapped was no secure place to ride out a heavy wind, for the bottom was a solid rock ledge with little sediment thereon, and no matter how heavy your anchors, they would drag in a blow.

The trawler fleet came scuttling into port and at once preempted the only dock. Not only did they make fast to this, but they ran steel cables ashore and passed them around stone houses for additional security. There was a small pool in back of the pier, and into this we managed to cram the *Vera Thornhill*, while the *Arethusa*, through the influence of the Folquets, was permitted to make fast to the dock, outside the trawlers and despite their wild objections.

The gale broke next morning, from the southeast, a solid blast of wind that continued without intermission until noon, when it died away as suddenly as it had come, leaving several craft aground and one big French bark, deep laden with salt fish, away up on the beach. There was no feeling of relief when the gale ceased, but a scurrying about to make things more secure. The islanders knew it would be back again, and at two o'clock it returned, reinforced, out of the northwest.

Outside, everything became a gray, furious blur, and the sound of the wind rushing by drowned even shouted speech. The streets of St. Pierre were swept bare. No one could even stand up against that gale, and in almost every house women knelt and prayed for members of their family who were with the fishing fleet on the Grand Banks. Many of these never returned.

My schooners rode the hurricane without damage, and next day, which was calm, we began loading. Three thousand cases of champagne went into the *Vera Thornhill*, 5,000 of assorted whiskies into the *Arethusa*. We had a deckload, in addition—a dozen Newfoundland puppies, which I took south with me to save their lives.

St. Pierre is one of the few places where that grand old breed still is maintained. In the fall of each year the police of the island kill all surplus dogs. Food grows scarce on the islands in winter, and these great beasts, gentlest and most intelligent of animals under normal conditions, sometimes go mad with hunger and become a menace.

The pups were black little devils with mournful brown eyes, great paws, and curly tails. We made a big box for them and placed it on top of the deck house, where, we believed, they would be entirely safe. In Connecticut, New York, and New Jersey today, there are many Newfoundlands which my ships saved from the Miquelon fall massacres and later gave to bootleggers who begged for the pups.

The Newfoundland always has seemed to me the most nearly human of dogs. My own Old Faithful was as reliable and trustworthy as any man of my crew, and more intelligent than many of them. We went through a good many tense minutes together, and he never failed me. There was a Newfoundland bitch in St. Pierre who was the only dog I ever saw of equal brain power. She had good common sense and reasoning ability.

A child wandered out to the end of the St. Pierre dock, one day, and fell overboard. The dog saw her go and, as all Newfoundlands will, dived over after her and hauled her ashore. For a day the Newfoundland was the heroine of the town. They praised her and fed her, and she was human enough to resent it when, in a few days, her heroism was forgotten and she became again just a dog. So she waited until another youngster was playing on the pier, pushed this kid overboard and performed another thrilling rescue. Eventually they had to keep the dog tied, for she had become a professional lifesaver who pushed the unwary into the sea and then hauled them out.

I was eager to get back to the Row, and we rushed our loading as rapidly as possible. The *Vera Thornhill* was ready for sea on October 12th and started out twelve hours ahead of the *Arethusa* with my promise of a bonus of a hundred dollars to her captain if he beat us to New York. We sailed on the 13th, caught a howling nor'easter, and raced down the coast in a tumult of wind and spray, carrying full sail.

All went well except for the fact that on our first night out a big grayback caught us, breaking solid on our decks, but we saw its approach, and all leaped for the rigging. It smashed the box in which the puppies were caged, and above the crash of the water we could hear their yelping as they were floated across the deck.

I yelled, "Save the pups," and we all leaped into the waist-deep water and hauled them out. They stayed for the rest of the trip in a corner of my cabin, shepherded by Old Faithful, who taught them dog manners with snarls and prompting nips.

We did not glimpse the sun once on our trip to the Row. The sky was a gray mass of storm cloud and we went along by dead reckoning and frequent soundings. After five days, Arey and I calculated we must be off New York, but the weather had bewildered us further by growing foggy, and we could make no landfall. We were groping about and beginning to be worried when the schooner slid through acres of floating garbage. It was a foul sight but as comforting to a skipper as a glimpse of the Woolworth Building. This was where New York's refuse scows had dumped. We hove to for the night, certain now of our position, and reached the Row next morning, twenty-four hours ahead of the *Vera Thornhill*. The wind had been too strong for her, and she hove to in the lee of Nantucket until it abated.

Three days on the Row emptied both ships and disposed of all our pups. I sent the *Thornhill* back home and started the last voyage I was ever to make on my *Arethusa* with liquor.

Chapter XV

THE UNITED STATES GOVERNMENT ran down and captured me, at last, thanks, as I believe, to my enemies in the liquor trade. As a rum-runner I was too successful and, also, too noisy about my success. By making the cutters ridiculous, I had driven many captains who patrolled the Row into fury. As I have said, the reports they transmitted to Washington did my reputation no good there. The mob I was fighting blackened me additionally. Furthermore, I had been so active in the game that I was the best known of the rum-runners. Publicity does some occupations no good at all. All sorts of rumors floated about concerning me and my activities. They were lies, but the prohibition authorities never stopped to test them.

I was a pirate, the American drys insisted. My only association with pirates had been to save a group of them from drowning. I was a briber who corrupted government officials. I never paid an official a cent for protection or leniency of any sort, nor did I ever have a chance to. I was the most unscrupulous of the rum-runners and continually flouted American law, my enemies said.

The truth is that, except for my first rum running venture to St. Catherine's Sound, I had never landed a case of liquor in American territory. As the law read at the time, my subsequent career had been entirely legal. I had bought liquor legally in foreign possessions, had brought it no nearer the coast than the government permitted. Once I had sold it, also legally, it was none of my business or responsibility what became of it.

The government had captured three ships of mine—the *J.B. Young*, the *M.M. Gardner* and the *Henry L. Marshall*. It had been compelled to admit that it had no case against the first two and had returned them to me, intact. The *Marshall* was taken while she was under charter to a crook, who, in 1923, had begun a two-year term in Atlanta. If her skipper had followed my orders she would never have been captured, or if she had been, would have been released. It was the *Marshall*'s seizure that began my downfall.

I was a rum-runner. Certainly, I was. And probably, from a prohibitionist viewpoint, I was a sin-stained character. Morals, however, are a matter of personal opinion. Law is something else. I sold rum, but I drank water. Congressmen drink rum and vote for water. I go to jail, and my fellow sinners are privileged to put "The Honorable" in front of their names.

I was captured, as far as I have ever been able to determine, because I was a bad influence, because an influential mob hated me; because I was a thorn that bothered the prohibition enforcement organization, and, primarily, because the government had embarked on a noble experiment that made it necessary to enforce morals as well as law.

And even at that they had to make new law before they could bring me in. The State Department told the British Ambassador that I was a nuisance who should be abated, and Sir Auckland Geddes finally assured our officials that although mine was a British ship, England would make no protest if I were chased down and captured on the high seas. A lot of venerable and hallowed statutes were broken or ignored when they caught the *Arethusa*.

I sailed for Bermuda with as clear a conscience as a rum-runner could have. Winter was drawing near, and I wanted to do as much business as possible before it closed in. Bermuda was closer than Nassau, so I went there and loaded 4,500 cases of assorted Scotch. Residents of St. George told me that they had heard the government was determined to get me, but I laughed at them and said it couldn't. I knew my law—or thought I did.

I do not know whether any of the folk with whom I talked were spies. Subsequent events have made me believe my departure for the Row was wired at once to the prohibition authorities. We left Bermuda on November 13th the second month in succession we had started on that date. Twice in a row was to prove fatal.

We had a bad time beating across the Gulf Stream, with continual head winds and enormous seas, and reached Rum Row on November 17th, but the weather remained foul, and customers did not come out in any number until the 20th. On that one night, we sold out clear, except for 150 cases of Bacardi rum a dealer had induced me to include in the cargo. No one wanted this, and we hung on the Row another day in hope of getting rid of it.

While we were selling on the night of the 20th, Arey called from his lookout that the cutter *Seneca* was bearing down on us. I immediately got under way and went down the coast. She followed us a little distance, and then apparently lost us, for she turned back and resumed her patrol along the Row.

If we had sold our Bacardi we should have sailed the following morning, but we hung about, hoping to get rid of it. Bob Cameron, a Nassau friend, passed by in a launch looking for his schooner, which had vanished from the Row. He hailed me and said: "Bill, I'll have to eat pork for Thanksgiving if I don't find my ship."

"I've a hundred and fifty cases of Bacardi," I told him. "Take it on consignment, Bob, and you'll have turkey all right."

He agreed eagerly, but his launch was too small, and he went ashore for a larger boat. The day was murky and looked as though a fog were making. The wind was steady, and the sea reasonably calm. We lay waiting for Bob to return with his boat, when out of the mist loomed the white, high shape of the *Seneca* bearing down directly on us. I did not leave my position. My conscience was clear. I had no idea Britain was double-crossing me. When he came within hailing distance he called, "*Tomoka*, ahoy! I'm sending an officer to examine your papers."

Even then I was not worried. My papers were O.K., but in order that there might be no mistake, I told my mate, St. Clair Tanner, a keen young Nova Scotian and veteran of the war, to take the British flag aloft and lash it to the mainmast.

The *Seneca* lay close in between an ashy sky and a dark, slick sea, and put over a whaleboat into which an officer and a half dozen seamen tumbled. The wind switched around now and began to blow from the northwest. We started our engine and let her idle. I began to feel, as the whaleboat crawled toward us, that there was trouble ahead. I knew I was legally safe, for there were rum schooners and several British tramps anchored between us and the shore, and yet there was an ache in my bones that foreboded trouble.

The whaleboat floundered alongside, and Lieutenant Perkins came overside.

"Two on board is enough," I told him, but he turned to his crew and shouted:

"All aboard."

They swarmed up to the *Arethusa*'s deck, husky squareheads, each with a Colt on his thigh. I grinned at Perkins.

"Lieutenant," I told him, "you're going for a ride, then," and I yelled to Arey, "Full speed to sea, Captain!"

I had been boarded, illegally as I believed, and without permission.

I was willing to have Perkins inspect my papers. I'd be damned before I'd see him or anyone else pirate my craft.

The engine pounded. The *Arethusa* quivered as she took the thrust of the screw and turned her bows to the open main. There came a warning blast from the *Seneca*'s siren, but I only laughed. Though her guns were on us, she did not dare fire with her men aboard. She started in pursuit. That wheezy old tub, trying to catch my *Arethusa*!

Perkins was flabbergasted and then angry.

"Heave her to!" he yelled.

"Who are you to give orders on my ship?" I wanted to know.

"I'll damned soon show you," he roared, his face crimson, and snapped to his boatswain's mate, a big lad named Ryan, "Take that wheel!"

Arey and Tanner were at the helm. Both were big men too, and after one look at them the boatswain's mate decided he was deaf. The oil engine was pounding full blast, and our foresail, staysail, and jib were fairly lifting our bows clear, as the waddling old *Seneca*, her siren tooting bloody murder, dropped farther and farther astern.

"Just what did you want, Lieutenant?" I asked Perkins politely. I think he was worried. I know that, beneath my outside calm, I was angrier than I had ever been in my life. "I want to look at your papers," he said more mildly.

I invited him below, and he insisted on being accompanied by a bodyguard. After he had inspected them he pretended he found something wrong and requested me to return to Sandy Hook and have them examined.

"No," I replied. "Never. We're outward bound for Nassau, Lieutenant, and I hope you like your trip."

"You're Bill McCoy," he snarled.

"Never heard of him," I replied.

"Well," he insisted, "he's on this ship somewhere."

We returned to the deck. I called man after man aft and asked him gravely if he were Bill McCoy. Each replied with great solemnity that he'd never heard of anyone with that name. I thought Perkins was going to have a fit of apoplexy.

"I've stood enough kidding," he blurted at last, "and I'm going to take this ship in."

"Like hell," I told him. He yelled to his men, "Draw your guns!" and to Arey, "Get away from that helm!"

The boarding party faced my skipper with cocked automatics in their fists. Arey grinned at them and spat overside.

"Make a good job when you start," he invited and kept her head to sea.

I lost my temper then. For a moment I was red mad. I remember running forward and calling to my crew, who had retired to the forecastle. I remember that Frenchy Rivert, the cook, delayed, pleading, "Wait till I get my coat on," but that the others came storming up with guns in their hands. I led them aft. Across the cabin hatch we faced each other, revenue men on one side, rumrunners on the other, armed and scowling. Perkins was white now instead of flushed. He knew and I knew as my anger ebbed, that one false move would spell massacre.

"This is a British ship," I told him more quietly, "and you're seizing her on the high seas."

"Where's Bill McCoy?" he asked.

"I'm McCoy."

"I thought so. McCoy, you're making a big mistake."

"The only reason you're still here," I told him, "is that you're my countrymen. If you'd been anything but Americans, you would all be overside by now."

I pointed to the seas. They were getting up and beginning to come aboard. We were seventeen miles offshore, and the wind was making. The *Seneca* was only a blur of smoke astern.

"Suppose," Perkins suggested more quietly, "we keep our tempers and talk this thing over."

I agreed. He pointed out that if I resisted I would only drive myself deeper into trouble. If I fired on the boarding crew, the best I could expect was jail for life. If I carried them away, the entire navy would be warned by wireless to catch me.

"Be sensible," he urged. "If the government hasn't anything on you now, it will if you try to kidnap us. And we won't be kidnapped without a fight. Heave her to, McCoy. I'm advising you for your own good."

He was right. I was clear headed now. So we hauled down the jib and threw her into the wind and waited for the *Seneca* to catch up with us. She bore down, all hot and bothered. Perkins and his crew rowed back to her. I lay hove to, waiting for his next move.

The skipper of the *Seneca* could not have been too certain of the legality of his course even then, for there was a long wait while we rode the surges and heard the splutter of his wireless, talking with the shore. There was more trouble in store, that was evident. I called my crew together:

"Boys," I told them, "destroy every bit of paper you have with you except your Bibles. Arey, we'll clean out the cabin."

Every scrap of paper aft, except law book, Bible, clearance, and manifest went into the cabin stove and was burned. We dumped all arms overside too—machine guns, rifles, sawed-off shotguns, revolvers.

At last the *Seneca* hailed us again. She had orders from Washington to bring me in or destroy me.

"You will follow me into harbor," the captain hailed. "If you do not, I shall fire one shot across your bows and then proceed to sink you by gunfire. Understand?"

"Aye-aye," I replied, and turned to my men. Most of them were Canadian army veterans, and their flag still snapped at our masthead. I could see that their anger was mounting.

"Boys," I said, "I think he's bluffing. It's jail or open sea. It's up to you."

"Run for it," they decided.

"We'll wait our chance," I promised.

The *Seneca* had turned toward the harbor. We turned, too, and on the port tack, with engine running slowly and foresail and jumbo drawing, made as if to follow him. The cutter was bucking right into the teeth of the wind on a northwest course while we had to lay our course north-northeast. I was watching a big liner coming in from Europe. Her presence would give us our chance.

"Cap," I said to Arey at the wheel, "ease along on this tack. The *Seneca* is drawing away from us. When that steamer gets into line, let her go off and clap on sail. He won't dare shoot with that liner in range."

We waited, scarcely breathing, loosened the jib and mainsail. The *Seneca* was about a mile ahead of us now. I yelled:

"Let her go off and hoist the jib!"

Captain Arey spun the wheel. Around came the *Arethusa*. For an instant that seemed minutes long, she hung motionless. Then she caught the breeze. Her masts slanted, her lee bulwark went down into solid water, and she drove away, eager and swift, straight for the liner.

"For God's sake," I roared to the crew, "get the big rag on her! Set that mainsail. Fast."

Liberty seemed bright before us now. The cutter was astern, and with quickening speed we were leaving her as though she were a can buoy instead of a ship.

In the midst of the flurry of action on the *Arethusa*'s deck I found time to be proud of my schooner. She was winging it to freedom like a flushed wild goose, with wind-tauntened canvas and a line of foam under her forefoot. It was not the first such dash she had made. I knew that years before she had shown her heels to a Newfoundland revenue cutter when this had surprised her poaching. Like many another lovely lady, my *Arethusa* had a past.

We saw the *Seneca* put about. It was late afternoon now, and the flash of her bow gun was an orange streak in the gray. A shell struck up a fountain before my schooner's bow, and another, smaller, rose beyond as the projectile skipped before burying itself in the sea. My men had heard gunfire before. They had fought for the country that was turning them in. Now, they swore as they quickly led the halyards through the snatch blocks to the hoisting engine. Tanner, my mate, was on the main gaff. He was letting the lashings go and yelling curses at the cutter. There was another flash, a spout of water beyond us, and then the boom of the gun. Arey, at the wheel, solemnly chewed tobacco and held the flying *Arethusa* on her course.

In another moment we would have the mainsail set. Darkness was coming, too. Again the cutter fired, and again the shell roared over our heads and dived into the water. That had been closer. There was a fourth flash from the *Seneca*'s bow. Arey ducked but clung to the helm. The shell seemed to have missed him by not more than ten feet. It burst in the water, so close to our bulwarks that the schooner staggered and several of the crew were knocked from their feet. His next shot would come aboard, I knew. I sang out to Arey.

Obediently, he eased down his helm. We let the jib run down. There were tears in my eyes. We had taken our chance and just missed winning free. My *Arethusa* and I were caught at last.

We waited, rolling meekly in the swells until the *Seneca* came abeam of us once more. There was a good deal of confusion on her decks before she got two boats away. Twenty seamen, each armed with rifle and revolver, swarmed over our side to our forward deck. Their captain bawled from his bridge:

"I'm putting a boarding crew on you. If you molest them, I'll open fire."

I did not point out that he would kill his own men by so doing. I was too heartsick to talk back even to a cutter captain.

They got a hawser aboard the *Arethusa* at last, after a lot of maneuvering so stupid and clownish that my sea-bred Canadians guffawed. Then we started for the harbor, from seventeen miles offshore and in the teeth of a howling nor'wester. The revenue lads walked wide around me at first. Apparently they had been told I had hoofs and tail. They grew more friendly during our shoreward ride, and one, sidling up to me, said out of the corner of his mouth:

"Bill McCoy, they certainly want you bad. I heard the orders that came through by wireless from Washington. I'd slip into a dory, if I were you, and blow."

I thanked him but said that I thought I'd see it through this time, called my men aft, took them into my cabin, and paid them their salaries and bonuses. My big mate cried when I told them goodbye, and I had tears in my own eyes. They were a loyal, fine crew. I assured them the British Consul would look out for them, but I didn't know the British Consul.

There was $68,000 in my desk. My Newfoundland stood by while I packed it into a small bag. He stuck his cold nose into my hand, as if he understood. I had twenty $1,000 bills in my pocket besides.

As night came down, the *Seneca* transferred me and my crew to her deck, evidently fearing we would run away again. We could have done it too, for my men were on deck with two guards only, and the rest of the boarding party was in the forecastle. I thought of overpowering the guards and trapping the rest of them below, severing the hawser and running out to sea again. But I didn't. There was nowhere we could have gone. The seas are too well patrolled now for a play of that kind.

When we jumped from the *Arethusa*'s deck into the whaleboat the coxswain missed his footing went down between the boat and the schooner. I grabbed him and hauled him out. He wrung my hand.

The captain of the *Seneca*, a little dark man and newcomer on the Row, was dry, official, but most courteous. I was permitted to go to the officers' quarters and wash up. While there, a Negro servant told me that a rum-runner, whom I knew well, had dined aboard with the captain only a few nights before. I never learned why, or whether this had any bearing on my capture.

I gave the captain my bag of money, which he wrapped in red tape, sealed in the presence of the chief engineer, and stowed in the ship's safe. Thereafter the three of us chatted, without animus.

The U.S. Coast Guard cutter *Manhattan* was the most despised cutter on Rum Row.

Bill McCoy commissioned marine artist Charles Robert Patterson to paint a canvas of *Tomoka/Arethusa* being fired upon by the Coast Guard Cutter *Seneca*. Today, the whereabouts of this painting is unknown.

The Cutter *Seneca* was the Coast Guard's lead cutter operating on Rum Row off New York and New Jersey. Her crew captured both the *Henry L. Marshall* and *Tomoka/Arethusa*. (*U.S. Coast Guard Photograph*)

The officers and crew of the Coast Guard Cutter *Seneca* taken just weeks after the capture of *Tomoka /Arethusa*. (*U.S. Coast Guard Photograph*)

I told the captain how close I had come to kidnapping his boarding party that morning.

"You'd never have got away with it," he snapped "I'd have had a dozen destroyers after you inside an hour."

I asked permission to send a wireless to my lawyers. He answered that Washington had given him strict instructions not to permit me to communicate with the shore. So presently I excused myself and went on deck. Astern I could see the red and green lights on the hawser-bound *Arethusa*. They made me heartsick.

A seaman with a rifle followed me around. The gun wasn't loaded, though. I asked him, and he told me. Then he handed me the rifle, and I threw the breechblock back and made sure.

I wrote out a message to my lawyers and walked into the wireless house. Evidently Sparks hadn't heard about the orders from Washington, for he sent it and another besides to my brother Ben. The coxswain I had pulled out of the sea came in and volunteered to take any other messages ashore for me. I offered both these lads money, but they wouldn't take it.

I had a pleasant chat with the lieutenant who had been at the range finder that afternoon. He said that he had taken off his shiny shoulder straps before going up the mast because it was feared I would pick him off with long-range rifles. He explained that in the confusion when we started out to sea again, some butter-fingered seaman had dropped an automatic rifle, which went off. Its bullet had gouged a splinter out of the deck, and they had thought for a minute that we were firing at them.

"I never was gladder, Bill," he said, "than when you surrendered. It's one thing to shoot at a target or a derelict. It's another to fire at an unarmed vessel with your countrymen aboard."

They were genial, courteous hosts, these cutter men. I could see they were surprised to find me a normal human being instead of a rum-soaked pirate.

The captain of the cutter took me into the chart room and pointed out the spot where he said he had seized me, claiming it was only six and a half miles from shore. I consented that and pointed out, in addition, that he hadn't made a seizure there, but that I had. He didn't laugh very heartily at that crack.

It was midnight when we arrived off Staten Island. A harbor cutter took the *Tomoka* in tow, and we went aboard her. In her smoking room, forward of the lower deck, I was introduced to a group of Treasury special agents. They were a hard-looking crowd too in their seagoing clothes. I squared myself for some form of the third degree, and from the appearance of these citizens I did not expect any simple version of it.

One of them, a giant who looked vaguely familiar, asked: "Do you know Pete Sullivan?"

I said, " No." I had determined to know absolutely nothing about anything until I had seen my lawyer. My questioner grinned.

"You've got a short memory," he said. " Didn't you stand by Pete in Nassau a year ago when the gang was set to rub him out? Sure you know him. And you ought to know me. I've chased you enough. I'm McAdam."

The others were grinning at me too. He introduced me to Lynch, Cortelyou, Simpson, and several others. You would have thought I was the best pal they had instead of a caught rum-runner. McAdam said:

"Pete couldn't get down tonight but he told us to give you the best in ship. You'll get it, Bill."

We had landed at the Battery. They docked the *Arethusa* carefully at a barge office slip. Lynch said, "Better take that flag down her mast, Bill. The British Consul's office is right across the park, and it might make him feel badly." Arey went aloft and unlashed the flag. It never flew over *Arethusa* again while I owned her.

My captain, my crew, and I were taken to the barge office and held there for arraignment on Monday morning. Washington had ordered that I be kept in a room with two guards over me, Arey in another with two more, and my crew in a third with a guard for every man. I wonder that they didn't call out the militia too. I had brought my bag of cash off *Seneca* and turned it over to Lynch. He posted two guards over that also.

My lawyers, summoned by wireless, finally ran the gauntlet of guards and got in to see me. From then on, until after I had served my sentence, I was being guided by one attorney or another. There is no easier way to spend money, but I know of many pleasanter.

CHAPTER XVI

THIS IS A YARN OF RUM RUNNING, not of my experiences as a meal ticket for lawyers. I spent more than enough time and money in that role, too, but it would make dreary reading, and I have the average sucker's wish to forget my suckerdom as quickly as possible.

We were arraigned Monday morning. My crew were held in $5,000 bail each; I, in $15,000. At the hearing my men demanded their rights as Britishers and the protection of the British Consul, who was in court but took no part whatever in the proceedings. It was arranged that they be permitted, while out on bail furnished by me, to live aboard the *Arethusa* until it was decided what should be done with her.

After I was released on bail, Lynch and McAdam took me down to see Pete. He was a different-looking customer from the shabby and harried little man I had first seen in the lobby of the Lucerne Hotel. He was spruce, immaculate, and official, but I got real comfort out of the grip of his hand and his voice when he said: "Bill, I'm with you all the way, and that goes."

Pete took me to Washington. Rumors of all sorts grew out of that trip, but it was merely a social jaunt to meet the dry officials I had been troubling for years.

"Come on, Bill," Sullivan said. "I want to introduce the boss rum-runner to the people who have been chasing him."

I had a chat with Judge Moss, then assistant secretary of the treasury and in charge of the revenue cutters. I yarned to him of my rum running adventures, and he congratulated me on surrendering.

"I'm not a prohibitionist, Bill," he said, "but the law has got to be enforced. I ordered the cutters to capture or sink you."

We called on Mrs. Mabel Walker Willebrandt, who at that time had full charge of prohibition enforcement. Again, we chatted of the sea and my adventures. Neither Judge Moss nor Mrs. Willebrandt even suggested that I give them any information whatever. They were square, straight people and assumed that I was too.

In spite of our pleasant acquaintance, Mrs. Willebrandt, when she found an indictment that she could make stick, landed on me hard and put me in jail. I hold no grudge against her for that. It was part of the game, and I had a lot of fun in jail. I feel more bitter toward those who grabbed hold of that purely social visit to Washington and spread the rumor I had gone there to squeal.

When Major Walton Green, chief investigator for prohibition under General Lincoln C. Andrews, wrote a magazine article on the liquor question, he spread that false rumor farther.

In his article, Major Green said:

> "I remember the incident of Bill McCoy. Now Bill, be it said, was a pet bootlegger of Mrs. Willebrandt's. For convenience, she kept him in jail at Trenton, New Jersey. Also she kept him in a communicative and stoolish frame of mind with half a dozen other indictments dangling over his head. Whenever she needed underworld dope she'd dicker with Bill and, so to speak, trade him an indictment *in passe* for his information. It was a splendid arrangement—and a perfectly orthodox police method.
>
> "Now it happened that Bruce Bielaski in New York also ran across the trail of Big Bill and also wanted some dope. So he took a half day off and hied him to Trenton. He did not bother to telephone for an appointment because jail is a place where you may commonly expect to find your man in when you call. But Bielaski should have telephoned. For when he presented his card and begged for a short conference if Mr. McCoy was not too busy, he was informed that Mr. McCoy was out to lunch and that the time of his return was a trifle uncertain as he had said something about getting a haircut and doing a couple of errands. But that if Mr. Bielaski cared to wait, Mr. McCoy would surely be back in the evening, as he made it a point always to sleep in jail."

The Bielaski incident is approximately correct, except for the fact that it took place in New Brunswick, before I was transferred to Trenton. Major Green's charge of a working agreement between Mrs. Willebrandt and me was on a par with most of the rumors afloat about me—entirely false. The photostatic copy of Mrs. Willebrandt's comment on Major Green's accusation is reproduced in this yarn.

I returned to New York from Washington. Thereafter followed

LAW OFFICES
WILLEBRANDT & HOROWITZ
INVESTMENT BUILDING
WASHINGTON, D. C.

UNION BANK BUILDING
LOS ANGELES, CALIFORNIA

January 14, 1930

Captain Bill McCoy
Royal Palm Dock
Miami, Florida

Dear Sir:

You never gave me information and insofar as Major Green's statements, to the effect that you worked with me and got any consideration from me as a result, are concerned he speaks without knowledge of the facts and therefore inaccurately. At all times I prosecuted your case as vigorously as I was able to through the United States Attorney's office. You are at liberty to use this statement as you see fit.

Very truly yours,

Mabel Walker Willebrandt

(Mabel Walker Willebrandt)

MWW:B

Letter from Mabel Walker Willebrandt to Bill McCoy. At the time it was written in January 1930, Willebrandt was in private practice and McCoy was wintering in Miami aboard one of his yachts.

Many federal and state officials believed that Rum Row was only a myth. In April 1923 the Coast Guard sent a group of them, along with reporters, on board the cutter *Manhattan*, to witness the rum fleet first-hand. (*U.S. Coast Guard Photograph)*

Mabel Walker Willebrandt and Congressman I.M. Foster (R-Ohio) standing behind President Calvin Coolidge, circa. 1924. Willebrandt was a California lawyer, who in 1922, at age 32, was appointed an assistant attorney general by President Harding, heading the division in the Justice Department responsible for prohibition, prisons and taxes. She served until 1929. (*Library of Congress Photograph)*

weeks of legal maneuvering. The government had me but did not know what to do with me, it seemed, for, despite the indictments, they were reluctant to bring my case to trial. They desperately tried to unearth evidence proving that I had landed liquor, and failed. I admitted freely enough that I had sold it on the high seas, for I knew no law could touch me for that.

One of the many rumors that helped blacken me in official eyes alleged that I had my schooner full of narcotics. Agents went down to her and almost took her apart searching for them. They even unloaded my shotgun shells, thinking they might be charged with drugs.

The revenue cutter seaman who told me when he boarded the *Arethusa*, "They want you bad in Washington, Bill," had said a whole bookful. They did want me. They had finally got me. They weren't going to let me go again. Neither were the lawyers I hired, while my money held out. I was caught in the legal mill, and, when the authorities wish, that can grind more slowly than the machinery of the gods. On every hand I met with delay. Britain and the United States, having combined to capture me, were making certain now that I stayed ashore.

I went to Halifax to get certain charter and incorporation papers my attorneys there were holding for me. These gentlemen had drawn them up, and, I presumed, would be willing to endorse their legality. They turned over the documents, but when I asked them to join in my defense they washed their hands of me and declined flatly.

I ran into Bill Duff in Halifax. He was a big bear of a man and the boss of the county from which most of my crew hailed. When I told him of the seizure and of the homesick Nova Scotians kept practically prisoner on my *Arethusa*, Bill roared like a walrus. He came down to New York, had a stormy scene with the British Consul there—and my crew remained just where they were. Bill went back to Canada insisting he would take up this outrage with the Premier. Nothing came of it.

I appeared at innumerable hearings. I talked myself hoarse to federal attorneys in New York and New Jersey. The more candid admitted that the indictments against me were not strong enough to go to trial with, but none of them were dismissed. I was marooned in New York in a Sargasso Sea of legal quibbling.

Bootlegger friends brought me rumors of the antagonism against me in Washington. They insisted the rum mob had turned me in and was now pulling every available wire to keep me ashore. That may have had no more truth behind it than most of the stories that floated about in trade circles. At all events, I was held in New York, under indictment, from November, 1923, to March, 1925, before I finally got action.

The endless luffs, jibbings, backings, and fillings of that legal ordeal would make sorry reading and is not the sort of memory that even I cherish. Let's skip over it rapidly.

At length even the Treasury agents sympathized with me, and it was through the intervention of Pete Sullivan, staunchest of friends, that I at last, even partially, broke the deadlock.

He dropped in one evening at the apartment I had rented just off Broadway. I had decided by then that I would be in New York a long time and might as well be comfortable.

"Bill," he told me in his abrupt way, "I think your lawyers are gypping you. You aren't getting a square deal. Why not come down to the office and talk things over with Esterbrook, my chief?"

With Pete, I went down and saw Esterbrook, laying every one of my cards face up before him. He was a hard, brisk citizen, and he heard me through with gradually narrowing eyes. When I had finished, he banged the table.

"The worst crook that comes into this office," he told me, "is entitled to a square deal. And you're not a crook. You're not getting one. Change your lawyers, McCoy."

I think of Esterbrook and his squareness when I hear bootleggers peddling dirt about the crookedness of government officials. No one was ever chased harder than I was by Treasury agents. No one was ever treated with more scrupulous fairness. From Esterbrook down to the youngest agent, I knew them all. They were my official enemies, but it made an American rum-runner prouder of his country to have officials of this type fighting him.

Coast Guards, Treasury and Department of Justice men, and I played the game against each other, but without a single dirty trick or an under-the-belt blow. If they could have caught me breaking a law they would have arrested me without qualm. Socially, many of them were—and still are—my best friends.

New York bootleggers could not understand this. New York bootleggers have minds of that sort. They peddled rumors that I was bribing Treasury agents. I might as well have tried to pirate a dreadnought, but Washington seemed to swallow that yarn whole and set a Department of Justice man after me to catch me red-handed.

He was of the same breed of which the government should be proud. He investigated me thoroughly and, reporting to the authorities, absolutely cleared me of charge.

The 75-foot Coast Guard speedboats for use on the Row were coming out fast now. I visited Twentieth Century Shipyard, where several of them were building, at the invitation of Nicholson, its owner, and an old friend. There I ran across the boatswain that had boarded my *Arethusa*, a keen youngster named Ryan.

We had a pleasant party together, swapping yarns, and by the time it had ended he was somewhat down at the head from the Scotch he had drunk. I took him to my flat to sleep it off. I heard a few days later that I was now under suspicion of having corrupted the revenue service. I did not see Ryan again. I heard from him, or someone who said it was he by telephone.

"Bill," the voice said, and it sounded amazingly clear for a long distance call, "I'm Ryan, phoning from Baltimore. I'm in a jam. Can you wire me a hundred dollars right away?"

I grinned as I replied, "I'm sorry, Ryan, but you're in the government service. I'd like to help you, but if I sent you money, it would lay me open to a charge of corrupting an official."

Then I hung up. I never heard anything more of that bribery charge.

The new lawyer I retained, Carl Whitney, was a live wire. In a few weeks he had had my crew released, with the charges against them dismissed, and had arranged that both the *Arethusa* and the *Marshall* were to be sold at auction. I bought them in, the *Arethusa* for $7,500 and the *Marshall* for $3,000. I sold the latter to a friend in Gloucester, and she returned to her former occupation of fisherman.

I anchored the *M.M. Gardner* twelve miles off Jones's Inlet, Long Island, as a station ship. She was literally a floating liquor warehouse, and I supplied her from ships chartered for me by friends in the north and later by the *Arethusa* as well. The *Mary Hurtel* and the *Ethlyn*, both big schooners from Nova Scotia, plied to and from Halifax and kept the *Gardner* well laden.

Business done at such long range meant that much cash would pile up aboard the *Gardner* and that pirates, once they found the ship was stationary, would rob my customers on the way out or else attack the schooner herself. In addition, the revenue-cutter men were beginning to seize cash found on rum buyers and compel them to report at the barge office next day to get it back. Finally, the task of going out, getting the proceeds of sales from the *Gardner*, and bringing it back to shore was not only troublesome for me but dangerous as well.

I invented, to solve this difficulty, the "dollar-bill" scheme which came into general use on the Row. I would get a package of one dollar bills and give my supercargo on the station ship the serial numbers of these. Buyers who wished to get liquor from the *Gardner* purchased these bills from me. Each dollar of which my supercargo had record was good for fifty cases of Scotch. Before my customer had got his liquor I had payment therefor safely in the bank.

Pious Halifax, which in 1922 had considered a rum schooner too low and despicable a craft to permit in her harbor, had now embarked on the rum trade herself, with a whoop and a yell. Scotch was cheapest there—$12 a case and no export duty—and her wharves, which had refused to receive my *Arethusa* two years before, were groaning under liquor cases and jammed with liquor craft.

Halifax, however, still insisted on the proprieties being observed. Officials cleared my schooners for a certain Banana republic. My captain would then take the papers across to the republic's consul who, for a consideration, would stamp them. Before my craft sailed from Nova Scotia their skippers had in their pockets proof that they already had discharged their cargoes in Central America. When the schooners returned to Halifax after a voyage to Jones's Inlet and back, their masters would be solemnly congratulated on the record runs they had made to and from the Gulf of Mexico.

To avoid all difficulties, my ships carried five manifests—for 1,000, 2,000, 3,000, 4,000, and 5,000 cases. No matter how nearly empty they were when examined, they always had the proper manifest for an alibi.

The early months of 1924 saw the Rum Row I had founded in its heyday with swift decline just ahead. Liquor was cheap and plentiful. Besides Halifax and its Scotch, St. Pierre was selling champagne at $12 a case, and Bermuda, Canadian Club, imperial quarts, at $15 a case. Nassau was still the chief supplier of rye and Bourbon at somewhat higher prices.

Life on the Row was running at a faster tempo, with all activities intensified. There were more shore boats, more revenue cutters, more vigilance, more prohibition enforcement men, more pirates, more and bigger rum ships, larger and more competition-eliminating combinations.

A new ruling had been issued by the government concerning territorial waters. It was necessary now for rum ships to lie, not seven miles, but "an hour's steaming distance from shore." The line, accordingly, had moved out farther from the beach, but some of them, though they thought they were safe, still lay too close.

In one instance at least, bootleggers who had grown enraged over a combination in restraint of trade allied with the prohibition authorities to bring about the seizure of the *Bernard M.*, a black tramp from England with 15,000 cases of Canadian Club aboard.

The distillers of Canadian Club had planned to sell on the Row without competition. They had arranged that independent rum-runners could not buy this whisky in Canada but were forced to purchase it at Bermuda or Nassau where they would be compelled to pay duty. The distillers then loaded the *Bernard M.* with their wares and sent her over to undersell rival vendors.

It was a canny plan, but it was not successful. Runners and prohibition agents combined. A couple of the former got aboard the fastest sea skiff in the trade, went out to the *Bernard M.*, whose captain believed she was a safe distance from the beach and bought twenty-five cases of Canadian Club. Then they turned the skiff's nose for the shore and opened her up wide. They proved that the English tramp was only forty minutes "sailing distance from shore," and the next day the *Bernard M.* was towed in.

Rum mobs were no longer working in harmony. The 75-foot and 36-foot cutters were coming into commission fast. Pirates swarmed along the Row, and crooks in many instances no longer were selling straight liquor but hootch of their own concoction which was made aboard ship. That summer a cutter overhauled a lighter going out to these floating hootch factories. She was laden with bottles, corks, and labels. The Row rapidly was passing its peak and starting downhill.

During those months in New York I averted one piracy and found myself embroiled, entirely innocently, in another, and the largest ever committed on the Row.

My chartered schooner *Mary Hurtel* was on the Row with 3,000 cases of champagne from St. Pierre under command of old Captain Hurtel, the Methodist Deacon from Lunenberg. One evening I began to worry about her and him. I had no reason for my anxiety, but it began and increased, for no more apparent cause than a tooth starts aching. At last I could stand it no longer and telephoned Sammy Randell, a bootlegger who owned a fast powerboat. This was the same Sammy who hailed the *Gresham* by mistake for a rum-runner and then did a hippodrome race about her under fire with his clutch jammed. It was the same boat too, but she ran straight that night, though Sammy's luck as far as cutters were concerned was still bad. We almost rammed one that was slipping along the Row without lights, but ducked away into the darkness before she could fire.

It was a bitter night, with a storm making. We could not find the *Mary Hurtel*, and my feeling that something was wrong solidified into certainty. It began to snow, and we turned reluctantly for shore. On our way back, by sheer good fortune, we ran across my schooner.

There were two big motorcraft alongside her. I recognized them both. They were pirate boats. Sammy and I slipped over the *Hurtel*'s rail without being challenged. Once on her deck, I saw why. Her crew was bunched forward, with several men shepherding them and in the glow from the open forecastle hatch I could see the glitter of firearms.

I dived down into her cabin, so suddenly that both its occupants jumped. There on a stool, with his mild old face red and determined sat Captain Hurtel, a white canvas sack crammed with cash between his knees and a submachine gun across his lap. The light of a swaying oil lamp played down on him. He looked like a militant Santa Claus.

In the corner stood an elephant of a man, his hands in his pockets, and I saw as the radiance from the swinging lamp touched him for an instant that the cloth of each pocket was stretched by the muzzle of a gat. Poor old Hurtel was doing his best to protect my cash. He did not know that before he could have raised the gun that rested on his trembling knees, at least two bullets would have hit him.

The man in the corner wheeled on me with a snarl, and I knew him. It was Big Eddie, a kingpin in the old Nassau gangdom, and always a square shooter with me. He recognized Sammy, but continued to glare at me.

"Ed," I told him, "you'll have to lay off. This is my schooner."

"And who are you?" he growled, watching both Hurtel and me like a cat.

"Bill McCoy," I said. "Is your memory short as that?"

I was in a city dress, with a stiff collar. The tan had faded out, and I had grown soft and fat. He glared at me a moment and then grinned, took his hands from his pockets, and held one of them out to me.

"My mistake, Bill," he acknowledged. "I didn't make you for a minute. You came just in time. I'll call off the boys."

We sent them on their way with a half dozen cases of Lawson's Liqueur Scotch as a good-will gift. Pirates never troubled the *Hurtel* again.

I don't know whether Big Eddie was in the Row's greatest piracy. I know he did not plan that coup, for the man who engineered it died.

A syndicate in France chartered the steamer *Mulhouse*, loaded her with 33,000 cases of Scotch, champagne, and liqueurs, and sent her to Rum Row. They also sent representatives to New York who opened an office in the old Netherland Hotel and prepared to sell her cargo. A New York mob, directed by an experienced pirate, mobilized twenty-one "go-through men" and went out in sea skiffs from Sheepshead Bay to an empty schooner that was waiting for them offshore.

She was a big black Lunenberger, and they laid her alongside the *Mulhouse* as handsomely as ever Harry Morgan sailed his craft. Twenty-one thugs swarmed over the steamer's rail and, with a .45 in either fist, took the vessel without a shot being fired. The French crew were terrified out of their wits and were captured. Eight thousand cases were placed as payment for the ride aboard the Lunenberger, and her captain was told to spread word along the Row that the *Mulhouse* was selling out at $10 a case.

In three days and nights, while members of the mob kept the French syndicate's shore representatives amused along Broadway, their companions cleaned out the *Mulhouse*. Thereafter her captain proceeded to Halifax and cabled to her owners that he had been pirated. That was in 1924. In 1930, the highest French court decided that the *Mulhouse* had been on legitimate business when captured and ordered the insurance companies to pay her charterers.

I knew the man who planned and executed that piracy. He was one of the many rum-runners who resented European interference in the trade. He told me, shortly before the taking of the *Mulhouse*, that if English and French did not stop sending steamers across and underselling the rest of the Row, something would happen.

"'American rum running by Americans,' Bill," he insisted. "That's our motto."

He never was arrested for his crime. He never was seen again. I was told later that he quarreled with two of his lieutenants on the way back to shore and that they settled the argument by killing him and throwing his body overboard.

When the piracy was reported, I at once was suspected. It was popular rumor along Broadway and in the side-street speakeasies that I had planned and executed the entire thing. For once I had a complete alibi, for on the night the *Mulhouse* was taken I had dined with Sullivan and some other Treasury agents and we had spent the entire evening together. The testimony of these men stopped the investigation which Washington started. In anything that happened, from a taxi collision to an earthquake, Washington immediately saw the hand of Bill McCoy.

The agents' testimony did not avert other trouble, however. A woman called to see me at my apartment one evening. She was tall and black gowned, and her eyes were as hard and bright as the big diamond on one hand. She spoke with a French accent, did not introduce herself, but asked if I were Bill McCoy. I admitted it and watched her carefully, for she was trembling and white of face, and I expected her, any moment, to pull a gun.

"Do you know So-and-so, and So-and-so, and So-and-so?" she asked, rattling off a list of names that represented almost everyone of note among New York's racketeers. It was about as tough a roster as she could have recited.

"Most of them," I replied. I thought she was going to jump at me like a cat.

"Ah," she exclaimed, "zose men and you 'ave stolen my 'usband's weesky from ze *Mul'ouse*. At ten tomorrow I shall be 'ere wis two men to get it back. You will 'ave money 'ere, or we shall keel you."

She left without another word. This was cheerful news. I called up Sullivan and told him of my interview. There were two agents in my flat all next morning, but she did not reappear. At ten she telephoned, said she was ill, and asked me to come to her address at once. I declined with thanks and never heard from her again.

Some weeks later I got a letter from Paris, signed by most of the members of the syndicate, warning me that if I did not return the proceeds of the *Mulhouse* piracy by a certain date I should be killed immediately. There had been considerable delay before I got the letter, and, as the date set for my execution was three weeks past when I opened the warning, I worried over it very little.

I was sick of New York. I was homesick for the sea. Broadway life was sour in my mouth. The gang that handled liquor was too fast for me.

Sullivan could see my sea-fever mounting. He had been placed in charge of the Marine Customs Patrol and occasionally took me on blue-water jaunts.

While the *Arethusa* was still under seizure he and his partner McAdam, Arey, and I, put out from Freeport on a fast sea skiff and searched Rum Row for a criminal the government believed was hiding aboard one of the ships there. This was in March, 1924. There was murk on the horizon, and the sea had an oily, ominous look. Four miles from shore the cutter *Gresham* hove out of the mist, and, at my suggestion, Sullivan headed for her to explain his business. I had been shot at too much to care for a repetition.

I waited in the skiff. Captain Covell accompanied Pete back to the rail, and I heard him say: "Mr. Sullivan, any assistance I can render, just call on me." Pete thanked him, and the captain called after him that the barometer was falling rapidly and there was dirty weather coming. Sullivan only laughed and we got under way.

We headed again for the Row, and, looking back, I saw the *Gresham* following us. Pete swore when I called his attention to her.

"How am I going to find a crook with that chump right on our tail?" he grumbled, but a half hour later we all were grateful for Covell's interest. Our engine coughed and gave up the ghost and, as if that had been a signal, the wind started to sing out of the northwest. While we worked over the engine, seas tumbled our skiff about with increasing roughness. It grew so cold, our hands were numb. I knew the signs, and Pete didn't. He insisted we were going on to the Row. I signaled the *Gresham*.

Sullivan introduced McAdam and Arey correctly when we had climbed the cutter's high side and were welcomed by Covell, but at my whispered request he presented me as "Mr. Smith." The captain, after turning his craft shoreward, led the way to his cabin, and we sat there and chatted of the Row and its residents. Pete asked Covell if he knew Bill McCoy.

"Yes," said Covell. "He's a man of about Mr. Smith's build, I should say. Not a bad scout, either. I've always felt he is not as black as he is painted." I kept a straight face in spite of Pete's grin.

A whaleboat towed our skiff to shore at Freeport. Two hours after we had been helplessly adrift on the ocean in a gale, I was back in my apartment.

Freeport in those last days of Rum Row, was a sleepy little

town by day, but immensely busy after nightfall, and Otto St. George's place at the head of the harbor was headquarters for bootleggers and customs agents alike. At one end of the cozy restaurant was an old-fashioned mahogany bar with beer on tap, Canadian ale, and all varieties of wine and liquor the Row could boast.

Late in the afternoon, agents and rum-runners, the lions and the lambs, would rest their stomachs against Otto's mahogany and enjoy a brief millennium while standing each other drinks. Business conversation was taboo at these peaceful gatherings. When darkness fell, they would break up. Rum-runners in sea boots and fleece-lined coats would leave the smoky redolent atmosphere of Otto's to board their skiffs and put out to the Row. The enforcement men would depart too, to catch their former drinking mates on their return—or to look the other way when they came back.

When Bill Fort of the *Chicago Daily News*, received permission from Assistant Secretary of the Treasury Moss to visit Rum Row, he declined the cutter Judge Moss offered him and asked that he be conducted by a rum-runner who knew the ropes. Moss assigned me as his guide, and Bill Williams, a big Treasury agent, was detailed to accompany us.

We got a launch at Freeport, and the three Bills—Fort, Williams, and McCoy—headed for the Row. We ended our tour on the *Newton Bay*. This was a steamer that had served as one of the British antisubmarine "mystery ships" during the war, and I had purchased her through friends and had sent her to Rum Row with 16,000 cases of assorted liquors aboard.

We spent the night on her, and Fort got a close-up view of Row procedure in business hours. Williams and I went to bed at last but the newspaperman did not shut an eye all night. He stayed on deck watching boats come alongside, load, and vanish. Now and then he would duck back into the cabin, have another drink of Scotch, and wake Williams and me to assure us he was having the time of his life.

The *Newton Bay* was emptied of her cargo before morning, and since the boat that was to have returned for us did not appear and none of us wanted to steam to Halifax, we jumped aboard a liquor-laden shore boat and rode her back to Freeport. The wind freshened on the way in, and we all got soaked from flying spray, but Fort, still fortified by Scotch, insisted that he had lived all his life for just this one twenty-four hours.

Arey, skipper of the *Tomoka/Arethusa*.

McAdam and Cortelyou, two of the Treasury Agents who pursued Bill McCoy

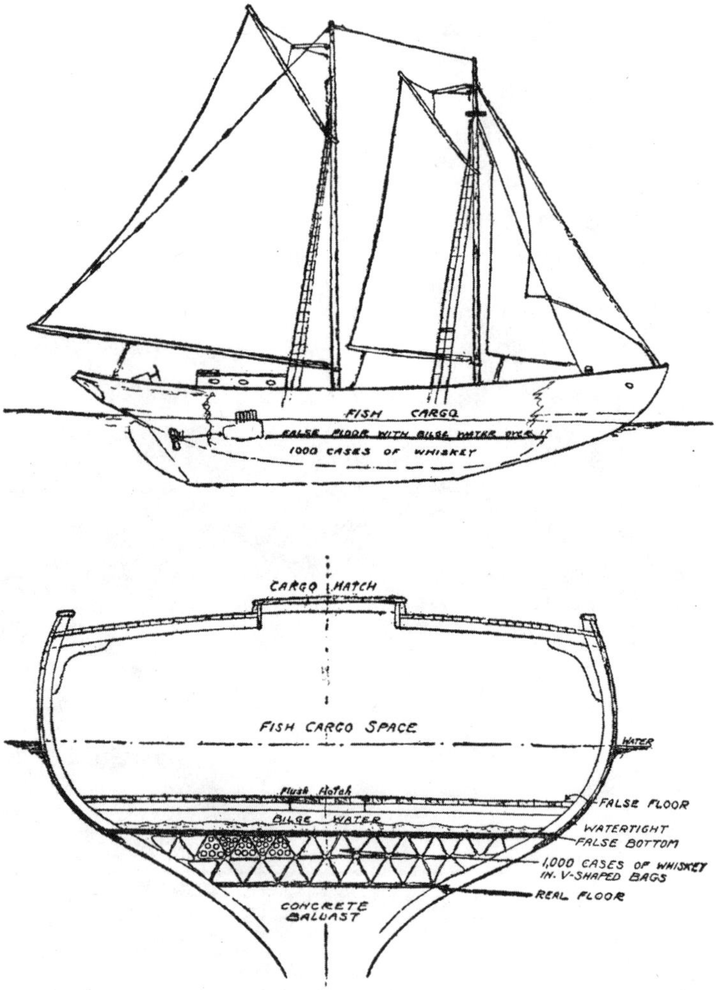

An outwardly innocent fishing schooner "trapped" for liquor smuggling.

Our liquor-laden craft had just got inside the inlet when a launch full of officers bore down upon us, rifles in hand. I had known them all at Otto's bar, and I hailed them. They did not answer but sheered away. Fort gaped at me, started to say something, and then shut his mouth with it unuttered. We had a big fish dinner before Otto's fireplace and then returned to New York.

Fort's description of Rum Row was published in the *Daily News* in due course. He thought he was doing me a favor by the amount of space he gave me. One of the headlines read:

"Bill McCoy, Notorious Rum-Runner, Well Liked in Washington Though Often Indicted." Which did not help me much.

I had been indicted all over again the previous June. Six counts had been returned against me, based on a "confession" by the *Marshall*'s charterer, who was doing time in Atlanta. It was on this indictment that I finally was sentenced. There was no trial. I merely appeared and pleaded guilty.

In the same month the indictment was returned, I said farewell to my *Arethusa*. While she was refitting I had placed her under French registry and had changed her name from *Tomoka* to *Marie Celeste*. Arey, who still captained her, was listed on her papers as "Captain Trigoli." He had appeared before the French Consul, who looked at him and demanded, "Parlez-vous français?"

"Oui," said Arey, which was all the French he knew. The Consul appeared entirely satisfied that he and my captain were countrymen.

With Arey and two sailors aboard, the *Arethusa* sailed for St. Pierre. In my old friend Fred's rum boat, the craft that landed the first load of liquor I ever brought to New York, I rode down to see my schooner leave. My friends in the government service had warned me that it would be fatal to my ship and me if we were to go to sea together now. It would only mean another capture, a fresh indictment.

So I told her good-bye at New York's threshold. I took her down the bay myself. Foresail, jumbo, and jib drawing, she and I walked Ambrose Channel together for the last time. Off Rockaway, she lifted her bow to the first long Atlantic swell. You could feel the eagerness and delight run through her. She was back where she belonged.

I took her along till we were well clear of the land. Then I turned over the helm to Arey and dropped into Fred's shore boat. I watched her leave us. Sea-hungry and beautiful, she heeled and fled, her canvas and fresh-painted hull bright against the blue of sky and water, the rake of her masts lovelier than any song. I watched her over the horizon before Fred took me back to New York. I never saw her again.

For a time, she carried liquor for me from St. Pierre to my station ship off Jones's Inlet. When I went to jail and the increasing vigilance of the government had smashed Rum Row, she was sold to a Frenchman and became the sealer *Mignonette*, the fourth name she had carried on her stern. I always think of her as *Arethusa*. She was caught in the ice and lost with all hands in 1930. I am glad that my last memory of her is the lift of her counter to the sea and the foam under her forefoot and the blithe slant of her masts as she left me.

Chapter XVII

IN MARCH, 1925, JUDGE LYNCH, in the federal court of Newark, New Jersey, sentenced me. I had pleaded guilty to the indictment with the understanding that the case would be dismissed with a fine. At the last minute I learned that the Washington authorities were implacable and demanded that I get a prison sentence. I had the opportunity to change my plea, but Sullivan urged me to take my medicine. "They've got you, Bill," he said. "The only way to get out of this jam is to face it and get it off your chest."

But before Judge Lynch sentenced me, Pete asked the court's permission to speak. He told what I had done for him in Nassau. His Irish tongue made the story of his rescue sound like the charge of the Light Brigade. When he had concluded, I braced myself for at least two years in Atlanta. That was the average dose of punishment they were administering to rum-runners. I was sentenced to nine months in Essex County Jail, thanks to Pete.

The warden was McGuiness; the principal keeper, Reilly; the doctor was Murphy; the sheriff, O'Connell. This was not a bad spot for a man named McCoy. McGuiness was a former sailor. The jail was full of convicted rum-runners and bootleggers. I had a fine time. I had so good a time, in fact, that Mrs. Willebrandt decided I had better be removed to another jail.

I was taken to New Brunswick. The prison was full, and more rum-runners and bootleggers were coming in every day. Those of us who could afford it took lodgings at an apartment hotel near by.

"I want you to understand," the warden would tell us, "that this is a God-fearing jail. At nine o'clock in the evening I lock up. If you hyenas aren't in by then, you'll have to stay out all night."

At the Walker-Shade prize fight, I had the tough luck to sit right in front of a couple of moralists in ringside seats. The roar they raised afterward brought about a shake-up in the jail, and I was transferred to Trenton. There I completed my term. I came out Christmas Eve.

Ben was waiting with my car. We went south, happy as a couple of kids, and were back in Florida long before New Year's Day.

And there I still am, back where I started. If I have not made a fortune out of rum running, I am at least better off than many of my former playmates. Some of them are flat broke. One, a big shot in the trade, is doing two years in Atlanta after paying more than $50,000 to a lawyer who guaranteed for that amount to keep his client out of prison.

If I can't point to a big bank balance as wages for the sin of selling the best of liquor to customers on the high seas, I have had a lot of fun. The rum running game as I played it was hard, swift sport. I got a big kick out of it, and a lot of memories that will stick longer than cash would, anyway. There were crooks in the trade, but there were keen, speed-loving adventurers too. They gave me memories, and they gave me friends that I shall always keep. There are men I know I could turn to in trouble now, for the sake of the recollections we share.

There are the Smith brothers—"Smith" is not their actual surname, by the way—two Jersey lads, all nerve and muscle, whom I helped out of a jam. They ran rum in from the Row for years and never were caught.

In 1923 a gang of Wop gunmen were getting fat by a modified hijacking racket. These thugs patrolled the beach about Atlantic Highlands and extorted a fee of $1 a case from every shore boat that landed a load, except that of the Smith brothers.

The Smiths refused to pay and responded to threats by buckling on Colt .38's and inviting the Wops to strut their stuff. One night the gang did just that. At 3 A.M. while the brothers were bound for Newark with their truck in which were 100 cases of rye, a railroad-crossing gate was dropped in front of them without warning, and there was a crackle of gunfire from the other side of the tracks. The Smiths switched off their lights and jumped from their truck. Ralph spun and fell with a bullet through his shoulder but he and his brother had jerked their guns free as they leaped, and, lying in the ditch, they returned the gang's shots.

There was a moment of furious hammering, and then the mob fled, leaving one of its number dead. The Smiths clambered back into their truck, returned to their sea skiff, and ran her out to where the *Arethusa* lay. I dressed Ralph's wound and bandaged it. Then we talked things over. For all their nerve, the dead Wop worried them.

"All right," I told them at last. "If you lads say 'run for it,' we'll run. Pick whatever land you want to go to, and I'll take you there. If I were you I'd go back. You've licked that mob, and you can beat the rap."

At length, they took my advice and returned to face the music. They had no difficulty in clearing themselves. The Smiths have told me since that they'd go a long way for me. I believe them.

There was another Jersey lad too, a greenhorn at the game, who came out one night in a sea skiff to buy from me. He was so obviously nervous and new to the racket that I talked to him. He confided that the police of a certain town had framed him and then had given him the choice of coming through with several thousand dollars or taking a long prison term. I gave him a lift that enabled him to buy his way out of the jam he was in. He has been straight as a die ever since. I can count on that boy too.

A smoky sou'wester was blowing across the Row. Visibility was low. The air was filled with a gray murk. Through this half fog we on the *Arethusa* heard the uneven coughing of a crippled motor, and a sea skiff came limping out of the haze from seaward and dodged behind us like an exhausted rabbit. The skiff owner, white of face and desperate, called out to me that he had loaded at a rum ship lying farther offshore and was being chased by a cutter.

I yelled to my crew. The sea skiff's whisky came over our side. We hooked on the dory tackles, heaved, swung her upon our deck. In a minute, we had her covered over with a sail so that she looked like part of our deckload. A minute later the cutter *Seneca* came out of the murk. She was steaming fast on the course the fugitive had taken and paid no heed to us or the innocent-looking, canvas-covered mound on our deck.

There was adventure in the old game, and friendships based on incidents like these are long of life. The men who chased and finally caught me were adventurers and sportsmen too. I have no sore or sour spot in my memory of them, and many of them today are my pals. I went to jail, where a lot of better men than I have spent time, and I enjoyed every month of my nine months' sentence. I've had fun out of my life, and if there's anyone walking who thinks he's had more, I'll match experiences with him.

My chief regret, as I look back, is that I permitted the *Arethusa* to be sold. I miss her still, but a ship is only a ship, after all, and when our Florida property sells, a new ship will come in for me.

She will be a larger *Arethusa*. I shall fit her for a long voyage, get together a crowd I already have selected and who say they are ready to share the expense, and I'll make the South Seas yet. We'll stop at Pitcairn Island, too, and call on its "king," another Bill McCoy and a descendant of the mutineers who took the ship *Bounty*, filled her with Polynesian girls, and landed at Pitcairn to start a country of their own.

Bill's ancestors had better luck with their South Sea scheme than I have had, so far, but I must have some mighty interesting cousins among the islanders of Pitcairn.

I'll make the South Seas yet. Meanwhile, I'm getting fun out of my life ashore. Life is always interesting as long as you keep wondering what tomorrow will bring. There is only one thing it can't bring me: that is another whirl at rum running. I am out of that game for good. This is not repentance. If the racket today promised half the fun I've had out of it in the past, I'd jump into it tomorrow. But the game has altered. The Row has gone, and the old fashioned rum-runner and his fast schooner are now as much of the past as the clipper ships and their skippers.

Times and methods change. Modern efficiency does away with individual enterprise and the spirit of adventure. Big business wants safety and results, and present-day rum running is big business.

It still goes on. Officials may say that their five-ply sea blockade has wiped out the trade, but I know they are wrong, and they must, too. Their cutters and speedboats, their agents and spies have not decreased sea-borne liquor traffic. In spite of them all, liquor continues to stream in, but it comes through safer, better concealed, more thoroughly charted channels than in the old days. It never has been stopped, despite the hundreds of millions the government is spending and for which taxpayers are paying. It never will be.

The men on shore and sea who have been mobilized to keep liquor out are neither crooks nor inefficients. There are crooks among the dry forces, of course, but there are crooks among teachers and Sunday-school superintendents and even among politicians, for that matter, and probably just as many.

Corruption is not the cause of the continuing liquor flood. The influx of rum from the sea is a matter of brains and organization, not graft. From the beginning it has been a race of wits in which the rum-runner always has been one jump ahead of an enforcement official. And he is still ahead.

The battle between the liquor smuggler and the government is as endless as the strife between guns and armor plate. As soon as a heavier, more resistant steel is evolved, someone invents a cannon that can crack it. As soon as a liquor-proof defense is set up, rum-runners work out an offensive that can beat it.

The racket in my day was no more like the present game than the guns my father fired at blockade runners out of Nassau resemble the quick firers that stopped his son on the runaway *Arethusa*.

And the game the runner plays ten years from now will be craftier, better organized, more successful than even the present racket. Rum abhors a vacuum, and you can change it no more than you can alter nature herself.

There still is plenty of liquor. Rum-runners have no difficulty whatever in getting it.

When the Volstead Act became law, American distilleries shut down. There would be, the drys proclaimed, no more rye or Bourbon in the world. That was about as true as most of the predictions of prohibitionists. What happened?

Canadian distillers immediately went to Kentucky, which had just been robbed of one of its three greatest boasts—its liquor. The Dominion men bought several distilleries, lock, stock, and barrel, and transported them to Montreal and Toronto, setting them up there and employing the original Kentucky operators to run them.

Today, they are still running, full blast, and are producing on British soil the whiskies that once were American monopolies. The liquor is aged five years in the wood, then bottled, and—a new wrinkle— sealed thereafter in an airtight tin container. This prevents disaster in case of breakage caused, let us say by an automobile bouncing over a rough road or even a rum craft reeling through a storm.

Much of this whisky is shipped in bond to the French islands that nestle close to Newfoundland's bleak shore. In warehouses at St. Pierre, more than 750,000 cases of various liquors are stored. More keeps pouring in, and more keeps going out too, for the export duty is only 10 francs, about 35 cents a case. Here is the stock list with prices per case from which rum-runners can choose:

SCOTCH

Walker Black Label	$22.50
Dewar's Ne Plus Ultra	$21.50
Buchanan's	$20.00
Haig Pinch	$19.00
King William	$16.50
Old Parr	$16.00
Black and White	$13.00
Green Stripe	$13.00
Dewar's White Label	$13.00
Haig Gold Label	$13.00
King George Gold Label	$13.00
Walker Red Label	$13.00
White Horse	$13.00
Sandy McDonald	$12.00
Bullock & Lade Thistle	$12.00
Peter Dawson	$10.00
Bullock & Lade Gold Label	$10.00
Rob Boy	$10.00
Old Mull	$ 9.50
Munroe Square Bottle	$ 9.50
Huntly's Blend	$ 9.50
Strathdon	$ 8.00
Claymore	$ 8.00
Ambassador (24 pts.)	$ 8.50

GIN

Gordon Dry—Frosted bottle	$ 6.50
Burke's Dry	$ 6.00
De Kuyper's Holland	$ 5.25
Booth's High and Dry	$ 6.50
Gordon's Old Tom—Frosted bottle	$ 6.00

LIQUEURS

Benedictine	$14.00
Cointreau	$12.00
Marie Brizard & Rogers	$ 8.00

BOURBON AND RYE

Golden Wedding	$13.00
Golden Wedding (pts.)	$14.00
Lindsay (qts.)	$14.00
Lincoln Inn	$13.00
Lincoln Inn (pts.)	$14.00
Indian Hill	$13.00
Indian Hill (pts.)	$14.00
Old Granddad	$14.00
Gooderman & Wortz	$13.00

Gooderman&Wortz (pts.) $14.00
Seagram $12.50
Seagram (pts.) $13.50
Old Calvert $13.00
Kegs (Imperial gal.) ....$ 6.00
Old Worthy ....$ 6.50
Gold Thimble ....$ 6.50
High Card ....$ 6.50
High Card (24 pts.) ....$ 7.50
Old Times ....$ 6.50

BRANDY

XXX Henneseys $14.50
XXX Martell $14.50
Piriott Casteleon $11.00

CHAMPAGNE

V. V. E. Cliquot Yellow Label $22.00
Heidsick Dry Monopole $15.00
Chas. Heidsick, 1920 ....$16.00
Pommery, 1920 ....$20.00
Sparkling Red Burgundy $12.00

RUM

Charleston ....$ 6.50
Rum in kegs (gal.) ....$ 2.00

ALCOHOL AND MALT

Alcohol and Malt in 12 gal. steel drums
(gal.) ....$ 1.00
Red Hand Brand (cases of 2 and 3) ....$ 6.00
Sheriff's Original Malt, Stevort Malt, 50
Kegs and over (imperial gal.) ....$ 3.75
Under 50 kegs ....$ 4.00

WINES

Port and sherry $10.00
Oloroso sherry $15.00

In March, 1930, 110,000 cases of this liquor were landed in the vicinity of New York City from St. Pierre alone. The brands were chiefly Knickerbocker and Log Cabin ryes. That, remember, was just the metropolitan district's supply. Only a congress of rum-runners could estimate the amount landed all along the Atlantic seaboard, but rum running is one of the few modern big business enterprises that doesn't go in for trade conventions. As this is written, the dry forces are complaining to the French government about the rum running trade of St. Pierre, which I started. I don't believe anything short of a war can stop it.

St. Pierre, also remember, is only one of the sources of supply. Bermuda warehouses are full of Scotch and rye. Nassau, that little old independent, stand-pat island, has just completed the biggest liquor exporting season in its history. America may be as dry as the prohibitionists say, but the rest of the world is wetter than ever.

There the liquor is, but there, too, is the five-ply sea patrol that, officials allege, blockades the Eastern seaboard to the rum-runner. How can booze get through that formidable ocean barricade?

In two ways: By smuggling; by blockade running. The first method belongs to the individual rum-runner; the second to the highly organized mobs that have most of the trade. Let's look first at the smuggler.

He is not an out-and-out rum-runner. He is usually the owner of a small trading or fishing craft, but whatever profit he makes from his obvious lawful enterprise is small compared to his gain from bringing in liquor in his "trapped" ship.

A "trapped" craft is one that has been altered so that rum may be carried in concealment. One method is to trap the bulkheads. These are the walls in a ship that run crosswise to her length. The smuggler builds his bulkheads double with a cargo space between and into this space he loads cases of liquor. He can, of course, bring in only a few hundred cases on a ship that has capacity for several thousand, but these few hundreds are profitable.

Other smugglers, generally fishermen, trap the bottoms of their schooners. Below deck, there is a cargo space, below that a watertight floor awash with bilge water, below that, a further secret cargo space in which a thousand cases of liquor can be stored.

At least one of these craft has been captured. She was sailing meekly and openly into New York by daylight when a revenue cutter bore down upon her. The boarding officer was so sure of himself that the smuggling skipper knew someone had squealed. He waited resignedly while his unbidden guests cleared the fish out of the schooner's hold, a long and slimy job, and tore up planks that revealed the bilge beneath.

"Now are you satisfied?" the smuggler demanded.

"Not yet," the officer answered, produced a long auger and thrust it down through the bilge water to bore at what was apparently the schooner's bottom.

"Want to sink us?" the outraged schooner captain screeched.

It appeared that the officer did, but when the auger at length broke through, the sea did not spout in through the hole. The bilge water ran out!

The smuggler stumbles now and then, but not even the augmented Coast Guard has time and men enough to make a thorough inspecting of each small craft that sails into New York harbor. Attempts they have made to do this have only bred trouble. Fishermen squall to their congressmen if they are delayed on the way to market by cutter men who insist on measuring their bulkheads, shifting their cargoes, and boring holes in the bottom of their schooners.

So smuggling goes on, and liquor flows in upon thirsting America by way of "trapped" ships.

Yet only a small fraction of the nation's yearly rum ration is smuggled in. Most of it is run through the quintuple blockade by the big business organizations that now dominate the liquor trade. I am told that there are several mobs that together control some 90 percent of the rum running business.

Consolidation was under way and the individual rum-runner was beginning to feel the pressure before Rum Row finally was broken up. As I have told already, one mob tried to force me to ally myself with it.

When the Row finally starved to death because of the excessive attention of revenue cutters, the flow of liquor into America was abated only temporarily and today it comes in more plentifully than ever before. Before the last of the individual rum-runners was chased away from the coast, the mobs had seen the change in strategy and had reorganized themselves to meet it.

It is the old story of the big gun and the armor plate. By the time a new system has been evolved to check the influx of booze, the runners have evolved a newer system to beat it.

From the beginning, the rum-runner has out thought and outmaneuvered the dry navy and army. In the battle of wits he has always been ahead. In equipment he also has remained in front.

Despite the destroyers and the regular cutters, the 75-footers and the 36-footers, and the harbor craft of the five-ply patrol; despite the increased size and renewed vigilance of the prohibition forces and their transfer from one government department to another, liquor continues to abhor a vacuum.

It was the small government craft that starved out Rum Row, but by the time that vanished the rum running combines had evolved boats that could beat the 75-footers and 36-footers at their own game. That was simplicity itself. There never is any secrecy about the government's plans. Bids on new boats it desires to add to its dry navy are announced publicly together with the specifications therefor.

The rum mobs get these specifications, take them to a naval architect, and say, "Here, draw me up something that will be able to run circles around this tub." And the newest offensive of the government has been stopped before it even got under way.

At first, modern rum-runners placed their chief reliance upon speed. The three swiftest craft ever to snake five hundred cases of whisky away from under the nose of a cutter were built in a New York shipyard from designs prepared by a young Southerner who had been in the trade himself.

These boats were 65 feet long, 15 feet wide and drew $4\frac{1}{2}$ feet of water. They were triple screwed and engined with three Liberty motors of 450 horse power each which were fed from a 1,000-gallon gasoline tank. Long and low and unbelievably fast, they were literally young destroyers in everything but offensive armament.

The engine-room hatch was of sloping, bullet-proof steel. Armor plate surrounded the engine room. The pilot house was steel, also, with bullet-proof glass. Their capacity was 500 cases.

Under normal conditions, these boats slid along swiftly enough with only two engines working, but the third always was kept primed for the approach of danger. Under only two thirds power they could jog along at 20 knots. Nothing the Coast Guard had could catch them from behind. The only peril lay in two of the 75-footers trapping them from in front.

One night during the late days of the Row, I saw one of these craft, the *Dick*, almost caught in this fashion. She was heading shoreward, laden, when two 75-footers which had lain in wait for her converged on her bows and opened fire.

Machine guns yammered, and tracer bullets smeared chalk lines against the blackness. As the cutters closed in, the *Dick*'s skipper threw his third engine into action. The roar of the motors almost drowned out the tumult of firing. The *Dick* surged forward as though she were going to take the air. Foam boiled at her stern, and she shot away into the darkness so fast that her attackers found themselves shooting only at empty sea.

Of the craft that outwitted the government armada during the last days of Rum Row the most successful were the "fresh fish" boats. Two of these were built in utter secrecy in an old shed on Long Island. Their success and efficiency is attested by the fact that the government never found out anything about them.

These boats were 60 feet long by 12 wide and equipped with two Liberty motors which gave them a speed of 35 knots empty and 25 laden. Their novelty and the secret of their great success lay in the fact that their holds were divided by watertight bulk heads into five compartments, each with a capacity of seventy-five cases and each having a trapdoor in its bottom. Hence the "fresh fish" nickname. If they had gone out after fish instead of liquor, they could have brought their catches still alive to market.

If a cutter pursued one of these craft and showed signs of overtaking her, the rum-runner in the steel-sheathed pilot house pulled a lever, and seventy-five cases of whisky dropped out of one of the hold compartments and sank, lightening the fugitive and giving her increased speed. Another lever would drop another seventy-five cases and so on until the boat was empty. Thereafter, if overhauled, her captor had no evidence whatever on which to hold her. They were simply innocent fishermen being abused all over again by the Coast Guard. They always had fishing gear and bait aboard to carry out the illusion.

I don't know what became of these craft. It may be they are still running.

Speed in the up-to-date rum-runner is not the prime requisite. The craft that keep America wet today depend on their silence and low visibility and the organization ashore with which they are in constant communication.

Instead of the fishing schooners, the rusty tramps and all the varieties of mongrel craft that hung on the Row in the old days, the modern rum-runners own as fine a fleet of vessels as the ocean ever bore. They are 150 feet long with a minimum of freeboard to cut down the chance of being seen, and their capacity is 8,000 cases. Their draft is light, so that they may enter shoal inlets and creeks, but they are seagoing vessels, nevertheless, and it is on them that most of America's liquor is carried. Their cost is $100,000 per craft.

Their Diesel engines give them only a maximum of 16 knots, but these have Maxim silencers over their exhausts and run with absolute silence. Every ship has a short-wave wireless apparatus and is in constant communication with a mob headquarters somewhere on the coast which is similarly equipped. It is against the law, of course, to operate an unlicensed radio station, but when you're breaking one law regularly, smashing another makes small difference.

These craft load at St. Pierre, or Nassau or Bermuda. Quarters for the crew are small, but pay is high, and there is no trouble getting men to handle these modern blockade runners. The low visibility of the boats and the size of the ocean are the chief factors in their favor. There is nothing to proclaim their presence, no smoke smudge on the horizon, no glint of sails over the ocean's edge. Long, low, and gray, the modern rum-runner is twin to the long, low, gray seas on the Atlantic, and it takes a keen eye to tell them apart.

A hundred miles or so offshore, the runner heaves to beyond the outer beat of the five-ply patrol and talks to mob headquarters by wireless. One such headquarters, with radio station, machine guns, and secret stairways was captured, it may be recalled, on the Jersey coast a year or so ago. None of the mob was caught, however. There are other headquarters and several more mobs.

Far offshore, then, the runner's wireless sputters directions: where the "drop"—the landing—is to be, what course to take, what time to be there.

In darkness, with all lights out, with engines running noiselessly, with no talking above a whisper permitted on board, the modern rum-runner comes shoreward. There is no sound and little visible to tell the patrols he is sneaking through them. If sighted and fired on, there is armor plate over the craft's vitals, and her 16-knot speed lets her show her heels to anything prohibition's navy possesses. If things go wrong on shore, she can be reached by wireless and turned back.

When she reaches her "drop," usually about a mile off some lonely beach, there is a swarm of small boats waiting to transship her cargo. These load and scatter, carrying from 50 to 400 cases with them to places already selected for landing. It is these shoreboats, not the modern rum-runners themselves, that are caught now and then by the Coast Guards.

Several might be captured from one unloading, and still the mob would come out better than even. Rye which costs $18 a case off the coast sells for $50 a case on the beach and $100 a case or better in New York. There is a good margin for profit.

This is written in midsummer. For the moment, the cutters seem to have the upper hand. They have caught several shore boats. They have compelled some of the rum-runners themselves to go back to St. Pierre with their cargoes intact because of interference with the landing facilities. Old hands in the game say this is to be expected. Summer is the worst time for modern rum running. When the nights are so short, it is hard for a craft to dash in and out again under cover of darkness. If she starts from a hundred miles offshore, she needs six hours to get in, an hour to discharge and six hours to get out again. There is complete darkness of only six hours during midsummer. When the days begin to get shorter and nights correspondingly longer, the odds will not be on the side of the government.

But suppose the cutters finally beat the present-day rum-runner, what then? The mobs already are looking forward to the time when their present craft will be obsolete. When that happens they will try some other scheme or pull out and quit, as all the old crowd of the Rum Row days have done. If they quit, new mobs with newer equipment will take their places. If the dry navy becomes so active that the surface of the sea is no longer safe, the rum-runners will go underneath it.

That is no idle prediction. I happen to know that rum-runners already are talking about the possible construction of submersible craft, merchant type submarines of high surface speed that, if too hard pressed, can make their getaway under water. I have actually seen tentative plans for the construction of such ships. If the Germans and their *Deutschland* merchant submarine could dodge the entire British navy in 1915, the far more modern craft that rum-runners may employ should have no difficulty with the vessels of the Coast Guard.

So the battle goes on and will continue for as long as prohibition endures. Neither side will win completely, but the rum-runner will keep one jump ahead of his pursuers most of the time, and hundreds more millions of taxpayers' cash will be spent trying to catch him.

It is my game no longer. I can sit in Florida and watch it go on with only an outsider's interest. Since I don't drink, myself, it means little to me now which side wins.

My crowd has left the racket, squeezed out by big business. They and I belonged to the time before modern efficiency took hold, when the old era of sail came back into the world for a little while, and racing schooners were talked of and praised; when every man took his own risks and played his own game. It was a cleaner game than they play today. It was more of a sport than a business.

Year by year the racket grows bigger and more complicated. Year by year the government's efforts fail to stop rum running. They have transferred prohibition enforcement from the Treasury Department to the Department of Justice. If that does not kill the trade, there is only one further step to take: the United States navy will have to be called in to protect America from rum-runners. Before that happens, Bill McCoy's earnest hope is that he will be hull down on his way to the South Seas.

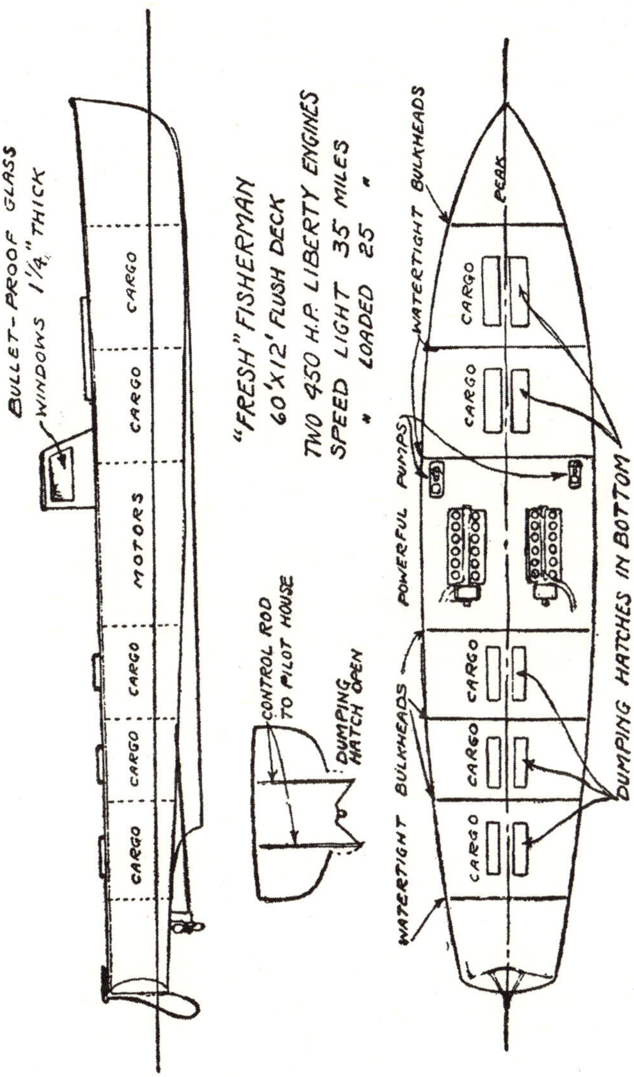

Plan of the "Fresh Fish" boats that the government never caught.

PUBLISHER'S AFTERWORD

THE U.S. GOVERNMENT'S FILES on Bill McCoy's rum running history are, today, scattered through several record groups at the National Archives in Washington, D.C. and New York City. Included are indictments; interviews with crewmembers; U.S. Coast Guard cutter logs and cruise summaries; intelligence reports from Nassau and Halifax; U.S. Customs arrival and departure sightings from Rum Row; inter-department correspondence; and reams of legal proceedings.

These extensive files support McCoy's account as told in *The Real McCoy*. Rather than embellishing his tale, as one is often apt to do in recounting it, they reveal that McCoy instead downplayed many incidents. The records indicate that he omitted episodes and altered names, perhaps due to the fact that, when the book was first published, Prohibition had not yet run its full course.

This history, described by Frederic F. Van de Water in his Foreword as "pardonably acid and prejudiced," tells only part of the story of William F. McCoy.

Add to this newspaper accounts, from major dailies to small-town weeklies, from Canada to Massachusetts, New York to Florida. Magazine articles by writers who met McCoy reveal further details of his character and his actions. Local lore all along the Atlantic coast includes sightings and meetings of the legendary Bill McCoy. There are books penned by fellow rum-runners; interviews and articles of and by McCoy long after this book was first published; and then there are McCoy's personal effects, correspondence and photo albums which he donated to museums.

All the evidence supports the fact that Bill McCoy's tale is nothing short of being much like the man himself: the genuine article—"the real McCoy."

William Frederick McCoy was born in Syracuse, New York, in 1877, in to an old-line American family. His father, William B.

McCoy, was a Civil War veteran, having served in the Union Navy, even for a time prisoner of war in a Confederate prison. Bill's family had roots in upstate New York, and his great-great-grandfather fought, and was killed, in the American Revolution.

Bill was the middle of three children. His older brother, Benjamin, was five years older, and their sister, Violet, was seven years younger.

After attending the Pennsylvania Nautical School on board the USS *Saratoga*, Bill McCoy went on to serve as a mate and quartermaster aboard various steam vessels, including the Tampa-Havana liner SS *Olivette*. In February 1898 the *Olivette* made newspaper headlines when she arrived at Key West with the news, and survivors, of the USS *Maine*, which had exploded in Havana Harbor.

Around 1898, the McCoy family made their way to Holly Hill, a small town just north of Daytona, Florida. By this time Ben had become a professional yacht skipper and the family decided to go into the boatbuilding business. With help from their father, Bill and Ben started McCoy Brothers, builders and charterers of fine motor yachts. During the early 1900s the McCoy boys also dabbled in motor cars in Daytona as beach racing grew popular, but soon concentrated their efforts on the water.

After Mr. McCoy passed away in 1912, Bill and Ben continued their popular boatbuilding business and spent parts of the next few years operating yachts for well-heeled clients. Ben skippered a commuter yacht on Long Island Sound, and Bill made summer runs on a large power yacht from New York to Bar Harbor Maine.

McCoy Brothers specialized in building large, shallow-draft power yachts. Some doubled as freight and excursion vessels. Around 1918 they launched the McCoy Brothers' Everglades Line, with service from West Palm Beach to Fort Meyers, across Lake Okeechobee. By 1920 this service could not compete with buses and the new highways opening up across Florida, and the brothers were forced to fold the operation. That same year Bill and Ben's mother died. Then Bill's 21-year-old wife, Maude, with whom he had eloped, left him to return to her family.

With their ties to Daytona gone, Ben, 48 and Bill, 43, looked for a new occupation. Prohibition had become effective in the United States on January 16, 1920, and one result was the development of a new industry known as rum running, the smuggling of liquor from adjacent countries or nearby islands. With a solution to their money problems lying some hundred miles to the east in the

Bahamas, Bill and Ben sold the assets of the Everglades Line and went north to Gloucester, Massachusetts, where they purchased the schooner *Henry L. Marshall.* The brothers decided that Bill would handle the operations at sea and Ben would coordinate things on land.

Bill McCoy's time in the rum running business was only four years, as outlined in this book, but he had a profound impact on the trade. Both a pioneer and an innovator, Bill was an experienced mariner and knew the maritime laws. By establishing his company in Halifax, Nova Scotia and documenting his schooner under the British flag, Bill knew he would be beyond U.S. jurisdiction as long as he remained on the high seas. Thus he founded Rum Row. His opening St. Pierre to the liquor trade was brilliant as that port would go on to surpass the Bahamas in the number of cases of liquor shipped to America.

Bill McCoy's capture in November 1923 was compelled by his own success. He was, after all, a U.S. citizen openly engaged in violating the laws of his country. As the one Coast Guardsman intimated to him upon his capture, they wanted him bad in Washington.

According to government records, McCoy's smuggling actions were closely monitored for the three months leading up to his arrest. McCoy's undoing may have ultimately stemmed from his firing upon crewmen from the Coast Guard cutter *Manhattan.* As McCoy describes, this event occurred on August 23, 1923, and, according to official U.S. Coast Guard correspondence, raised the stakes.

It was decided in Washington that capturing McCoy would achieve many goals. The legend of "the real McCoy" was becoming well known. Even the White House had good reason to see his capture. McCoy, and the notoriety he was receiving, was making a mockery of the Coolidge administration's efforts to enforce the 18th Amendment.

The U.S. Department of Justice was eager to test the legality of a seizure outside the three-mile territorial limit. Bill and Ben McCoy were both under indictment in New Jersey for conspiracy to violate the National Prohibition Act relating to the seizure of the *Henry L. Marshall.* The *Marshall* was captured by the Coast Guard nine miles off Atlantic City, New Jersey. They needed Bill McCoy for the *Marshall* case to go to trial.

Further, the Department of Justice wanted to resolve the stalled negotiations between the Department of State and the British government regarding an international treaty to combat smuggling. Capturing McCoy aboard his British-flagged schooner in international waters would force the issue.

Finally, the leadership of the U.S. Coast Guard was eager to forge a new identity. The service had been cobbled together in 1915 from the Life-Saving and Revenue Cutter Service and, after spending the years 1917 to 1919 as part of the U.S. Navy, was redefining its law enforcement footing. Capturing McCoy would send a signal to the service and to smugglers that the tide was about to change.

A Department of Justice memorandum dated November 15, 1923, ordered the U.S. Coast Guard to seize McCoy's schooner *Tomoka* if within 12 miles of shore, and arrest Bill McCoy.

Ben McCoy had already sought legal counsel stemming from the *Henry L. Marshall* case and had turned himself in to the authorities. He had posted bail and his hearing was repeatedly postponed by his lawyer, a common practice as the courts were overwhelmed. The case against Ben was not as strong as that against Bill.

The legality of the method by which Bill McCoy was eventually captured—the treaty with Britain was not yet in place—had little bearing on the legal proceedings against him. The British government objected to the seizure of *Tomoka/Arethusa* prima facie, in that she was a British-flagged vessel in international waters. Protests waned, however, when details of *Tomoka/Arethusa* and McCoy became apparent.

At the time the regular sentence for conspiracy to violate the National Prohibition Act was two years at the federal penitentiary in Atlanta. It is likely that McCoy would have lost the trial, especially with the testimony of John. G. Crosland, a former fish wholesaler from Miami who used his own fishing fleet to run liquor and who had had many dealings with McCoy. The *Henry L. Marshall* was under charter to Crosland—or, as McCoy describes him, the "Georgian"—when she was captured in 1921. Crosland was eager to testify against McCoy to have his sentence commuted.

Before Bill McCoy was finally brought to trial, his defense had been strung along by an scurrilous lawyer named Thomas Felder. The well-connected Felder, and his associates, mulcted McCoy—and other trusting bootleggers—out of thousands of dollars with promises that they could get cases dismissed. At the time Felder was under investigation by the Department of Justice for his practices. McCoy changed lawyers at the urging of a U.S. Customs official and his case was expedited. Soon after McCoy served his time, Thomas Felder was found guilty of conspiracy to defraud and was disbarred. Felder died of chronic alcoholism in March 1926.

Bill's guilty plea avoided a drawn out trial and was made in exchange for the dropping of charges against his brother Benjamin. Further, he received leniency at his sentencing for assisting U.S. Customs in combating alien and dope smuggling. McCoy, though a smuggler, despised trafficking in humans or drugs.

Peter Sullivan, the customs agent whose life Bill had saved in Nassau a few years before, was by this time the head of the service's New York marine enforcement unit. His impassioned plea at Bill's sentencing also contributed to McCoy's light sentence and his confinement in a New Jersey jail rather than the Atlanta Penitentiary.

McCoy's beloved *Arethusa*, which sailed away from New York under the name *Marie Celeste*, returned to Rum Row as the French-flagged *Mistinguette*. She supplied liquor to McCoy's vessels lying off Rum Row. Sold by McCoy just before he went to jail, she continued rum running and was captured by the Coast Guard in 1927.

In the mid-1930s, Bill learned of the true fate of *Tomoka/Arethusa*. When McCoy related this story to Frederic Van de Water, he believed she, as *Mignonette*, was caught in the ice and lost with all hands in 1930. However, McCoy later learned that the *Saucy Arethusa*, as she was then known, was in the legitimate fish trade and forced aground off Sambro Ledge, Nova Scotia, in September 1929. Bill made two failed trips find the wreckage. After being contacted by a local fisherman, he made a third trip. It was then he cut out the main beam, complete with her registry tonnage carved in, and collected other pieces, including a knee.

Adding to the McCoy legend, in 1944 Robert L. Ripley of "Believe it or Not" acknowledged Bill as the inspiration for the phrase "The Real McCoy," meaning the genuine article. The syndicated cartoon, then at the height of its popularity, appeared in over 300 newspapers around the world, was translated into 17 different languages and had a readership of over 80 million people.

In the mid-1940s, the McCoy brothers purchased the old motor yacht *Taormina* and turned her into a retirement home of sorts, mooring her in Gloucester, Massachusetts. Among the individuals who visited them there was Gertrude "Cleo" Lythgoe. Following her memorable trip to Rum Row with Bill in August 1923, Gertrude had become a celebrity. Newspapers touted her as the "Queen of

Rum Row." In 1964 she penned her own autobiography, *The Bahama Queen,* in which she detailed, among other things, her time in Nassau and her trip to Rum Row with Bill McCoy.

In 1945 Bill McCoy designed and built *Blue Lagoon*, a 48-foot power yacht, which he lived aboard in Stuart, Florida. On December 30, 1948, at the age of 71, Bill McCoy died on board his yacht of a heart attack after experiencing complications from food poisoning. He was cremated and his ashes were scattered off the mouth of the Halifax River near Holly Hill. Benjamin McCoy died November 9, 1960, in DeLand, Florida.

Frederic F. Van de Water

It may be surprising that William McCoy, a raconteur of note and a man given to expressing himself in visual arts and craft, should have had someone else tell his story. Though told in the first person, *The Real McCoy* was the effort of the veteran professional writer Frederic F. Van de Water. Van de Water had already written a series of articles for the *Saturday Evening Post* and *Colliers* magazine that mentioned McCoy. *The Real McCoy*, published by Doubleday Doran in 1931, emerged from meetings and many conversations between McCoy and Van de Water. Although these accounts "left a hack writer dazed and a little dizzy," Van de Water himself was no wild-eyed cub reporter, but a veteran New York newspaperman and already author of ten books. Although Van de Water refers to himself as a "hack," McCoy had found a writer who was far better than that. It is tempting to undervalue the workman who sets down the tale of the colorful subject. In the present case, Van de Water turns out to be an interesting man on his own hook.

Frederic Franklyn Van de Water was born on September 30, 1890, in Pompton, New Jersey, of Dutch stock. He honed his natural tendencies at Columbia School of Journalism, from which he was graduated in 1914. He first tried his hand professionally as a reporter for the *New York American* (1915-1922). Working at the *New York Tribune* broadened his range as he ascended the ranks, going from reporter to special writer, to night city editor, columnist, and literary and theatrical critic. In 1921, Van de Water published his first book, *Grey Riders*, an expanded newspaper topic and a history of the New York State Police, for which he was given the rank of honorary sergeant. In 1922 he left the *Tribune* to freelance. By now he composed in all genres, including verse, except plays.

In 1934, Van de Water and his wife Eleanor "left Manhattan with brief and non-recurrent regret" and moved to a hillside farm in Vermont. By 1952, the man who called himself a "hack" in the McCoy book had officially become a man of letters, receiving a Doctor of Humane Letters from Middlebury College.

In all, Frederic Van de Water was the author of 36 published books (see page vii), among them the first debunking biography of another American larger-than-life hero, General George Armstrong Custer. Published in 1934, *Glory Hunter: A Life of General Custer*, is today seen as a groundbreaking book in American culture.

Frederic Van de Water lived to the age of 77, dying "after a long illness" on September 16, 1968, in Brattleboro Hospital, just downriver from his Vermont farm. His wife died the next day.

Additional Sources

Like many an adventurer before and after him, William McCoy, in his retirement, was persuaded to compose his memoirs. He was possibly urged to tell his story by others and, as it seemed at the time, it was "the thing to do."

Mabel Walker Willebrandt, the assistant U.S. Attorney General charged with enforcing Prohibition from 1922 to 1929, and an acquaintance of McCoy, penned her memoirs, *The Inside of Prohibition*, in 1929.

Scotsman Alastair Moray had his *The Diary of a Rum-Runner* published in Britain in 1929 and in the United States the following year. Moray, a supercargo aboard a large Scottish schooner, told of his eleven months on Rum Row, starting in September 1923.

Eric Sherbrooke Walker, using the pen name James Barbican, was another Scotsman who spent time on Rum Row in 1923. His *The Confessions of a Rum-Runner* was released in Britain in 1927 and received write-ups in many newspapers. The *New York Times* used the review to call Prohibition a "Huge Farce." Walker later used his rum running profits to open the Treetops Hotel in Aberdare National Park in Kenya, Africa. Treetops—literally built into the tops of trees—is best known for being the place where Princess Elizabeth spent the night of February 5, 1952. During the night her father, George VI, died and the princess became Queen Elizabeth II of the United Kingdom. It was said she went up a princess and came down a queen.

Bill McCoy's account, as told to Frederic Van de Water, did not receive the attention it deserved. Perhaps it was due to the timing. By 1931 America was tiring of Prohibition, and the nation was in the grips of the Depression. A copy of *The Real McCoy* sold for $2.50, not an insignificant sum. Today, an original copy of the book is considered "scarce."

The most intimate picture of Bill McCoy and his time on Rum Row was painted by Gertrude "Cleo" Lythgoe in her 1964 self-published autobiography *The Bahama Queen*. More scarce than *The Real McCoy*, this book has also been republished.

Ellery Thompson, a fishing captain from Stonington, Connecticut, who achieved national attention when Joseph Mitchell wrote about him in the *New Yorker* magazine, wrote of his meeting with McCoy in his 1950 book *Draggerman's Haul*. Thompson was the young boatman who carried McCoy from New London, Connecticut, out to his schooner, as described in Chapter IV.

Robert Carse, a well-known maritime writer of the mid-20th century, focused about a third of his 1959 book, *Rum Row,* on Bill McCoy. While much of Carse's information parallels Frederic Van de Water's book, from some events described it is clear Carse either spoke with McCoy or gleaned additional information from his colleague Van de Water.

Harold Waters's book, *Smugglers of Spirits: Prohibition and the Coast Guard Patrol,* is the sole personal account from the Coast Guard enforcement perspective. Waters's book, published in 1971, is filled with colorful descriptions of Rum Row and includes pages on Bill McCoy.

Everett S. Allen's *The Black Ships*, first published in 1965, is a detailed account of liquor smuggling in and around New York and New England. Allen, a reporter for the New Bedford *Standard-Times,* drew from interviews with rum-runners, government reports, and his own boyhood memories. Allen acknowledges the help of Frederic Van de Water in the sections regarding Bill McCoy.

William McCoy also holds a prominent position in Malcolm Willoughby's 1964 book, *Rum War at Sea*, considered the official U.S. Coast Guard account of the service's actions in enforcing Prohibition.

The forthcoming *The Actual McCoy* by Stephen Jones, scheduled for publication in Fall 2007, pulls from the above accounts and primary sources to provide the most complete picture of the life and times of William F. McCoy. Readers of *The Real McCoy* with artifacts, memories or stories from or about Bill McCoy, are requested to contact the publisher. See page iv for contact information.

In the 1930s Bill McCoy travelled to Nova Scotia to find the remains of his schooner *Tomoka/Arethusa*. He would bring many pieces back home to Florida, later donating a knee to The Mariners' Museum. (*Courtesy of The Mariners' Museum, Newport News, VA.*)

Nova Scotia fisherman Joe Flemming knew the site of *Tomoka/Arethusa*'s wreckage. He is shown holding the main beam indicating the vessel's registered tonnage. McCoy is wearing the white shirt and tie. (*Courtesy Maritime History Archive, Memorial University of Newfoundland*)